THE DECLINE OF
AMERICAN GENTILITY

Stow Persons is Professor of History at
the University of Iowa.

Library of Congress Cataloging in Publication Data

Persons, Stow, 1913–
    The decline of American gentility. New york + London,
Columbia University Press, 1973.
    Bibliography: p. 325   336 p.
    1. United States—Civilization—19th century.
    2. American literature—19th century—History and
criticism. I. Title.
E169.1.P476   917.3'03   73-534
    ISBN 0-231-03015-0

E
169.1
P476

THE DECLINE OF
AMERICAN GENTILITY

• STOW PERSONS •

COLUMBIA UNIVERSITY PRESS

NEW YORK & LONDON   1973

PREFACE

DURING THE COURSE of the nineteenth century the theory and practice of gentility in America underwent a continuous process of diffusion and attenuation, so that after the First World War it served no useful purpose to make the older distinction between gentlemen and common men. The principal object of this book is to explore the reasons for the final disappearance of a social type that had flourished throughout the Western world for three centuries or more.

By the time of American colonial settlement, the gentleman had achieved a well-defined status among the privileged classes of Britain and the continental European countries. Everywhere, he combined a measure of author-

59549

ity and prestige with a prescribed code of manners and style of living that distinguished him from less favored social types. In the rapidly growing colonial societies of British North America, a gentry class modeled explicitly on the British gentry formed the apex of the social structure. Composed of merchants, planters, professional men, and civil servants, the colonial gentry well-nigh monopolized both the tangible powers of the community and its formal intellectual and cultural life. But the colonial gentry had scarcely attained maturity as a class before the political and social changes initiated by the Revolution and culminating in Jacksonian democracy destroyed its class character and substituted for it a number of functional elites, one of which I have designated the new gentry elite. The first four chapters of this book describe the characteristics of the nineteenth-century gentry, with particular emphasis on their response to the democratic mass society. The remaining chapters consider selected aspects of gentry decline.

The frame of reference in which these essays are cast represents my own understanding of the nature of a mass society. During the nineteenth century, the general availability of the norms of gentility to anyone who cared to pattern himself upon them was explicable only within the context of a mass society in which class lines disintegrated and functional leadership elites became increasingly distinct from each other. Under these circumstances, gentility furnished a mantle of respectability readily available to a wide variety of creative people uncertain of their roles in a fluid democratic society. During the course of the century, as gentry spokesmen themselves became increasingly conscious of their isolation and vulnerability, they began to develop in mass theory a rationalization of their own predicament.

The assumption that the mass society destroyed gentility is supported by the account of the history of mass theory in chapter VII. The gentry scholars who pioneered in the development of mass concepts clearly revealed their sense of vulnerability and alienation from the mass of the population whose characteristics they described. Within the space of a generation, from the qualified complacency of Henry Adams in the 1880s to the utter despair of Barrett Wendell in the 1910s, the change of mood signified the deepening conviction that the mass despised the values and style of gentility. The academic sociologists who since the 1930s have refined the concept of mass as an aspect of collective behavior have quite properly cast their findings in the neutral hues of professional social science, although their implicit ideological commitments have been clarified by Leon Bramson in his *The Political Context of Sociology* (1961). But the continuing cries of anguish from the cultural critics suggest a far more ominous situation than is indicated in the academic literature. Concepts of mass behavior may now be absorbed as a minor category in the total corpus of sociological theory; but in the real world of cultural conflict the status of the high culture of which the gentry were always the patrons and practitioners has been found by many observers to be precarious in the extreme. The successor to the nineteenth-century gentleman is the alienated intellectual.

While preparing this book I was privileged to receive a research fellowship from the National Endowment for the Humanities, which permitted me to explore the treasures and enjoy the amenities of the Henry E. Huntington Library. The University of Iowa generously provided a research professorship and clerical assistance. Of the many individuals who have helped me in various ways I should acknowledge particularly the aid of Andrew Franklin and Jonathan Kolb.

CONTENTS

THE DECLINE OF
AMERICAN GENTILITY

· I ·

DEMOCRACY
AND GENTILITY

IN THE COURSE OF HER TRAVELS in the United States in 1834
and 1835 Harriet Martineau noted frequent encounters
with ladies and gentlemen. These gentry folk constituted
for her a social category of fundamental importance. They
were people of cultivated manners and refined speech, dis-
playing cultural interests and living with style and dignity. She carefully distinguished the gentry from the
social-economic elite, those who composed "the first rank
in society" and who were to be found at fashionable watering places. She was properly contemptuous of these
"aristocrats" who lived for grandeur and show, and whose
affectations were depressing. More importantly, their anti-

republican prejudices seemed scandalous in a democratic republic. The gentry, on the other hand, showed a spirit that was thoroughly democratic and rational. They pursued honorable and useful careers without ostentation. Much of the burden of sustaining cultural life in the nineteenth century rested on their shoulders.[1]

The gentry, then, consisted of men and women who subscribed to a distinct code of values, and who modeled their lives in accordance with the traditions of gentility, modified by American circumstances. Their position was not a birthright, either in theory or in practice. Anyone could assume gentry status by conforming to the standards of gentility; newcomers were constantly being recruited. It was commonly acknowledged, however, that membership in a gentry family conveyed great advantages. The elder Oliver Wendell Holmes, who applied to the gentry of New England his well-known designation "Brahmin caste," even went so far as to say that the gentry of that region were a distinctly recognizable physiological type. But this was a permissible literary conceit which the facts of New England cultural history confirmed only in part. Nor were the gentry necessarily people of wealth. Some eminent representatives had little or no money. All that survived of the older association of gentility with economic power was a style of living which was difficult to maintain without at least a modest income. Many members of the gentry were professional people: doctors, lawyers, the educated clergy, college professors, artists, writers, editors, and publishers. Also included were a substantial number of businessmen bankers, and merchants.

James Fenimore Cooper, a prominent spokesman for
the gentry interest, sought to clarify the ambiguities of
the American situation for the benefit of European readers. He explained that because Americans were in more
comfortable circumstances, wealth did not have the importance it had in less favored lands. Money here could not
buy preferment in church or state. After a rich man had
educated his children, given them good manners, and
entertained his friends, his money was of no further value
to him. For these reasons Cooper persuaded himself that
money was less important to the American gentleman than
good breeding and high character—although he felt obliged to admit that when money was added to merit, more
could be done than merit could do by itself.[2] In the same
vein, when Jefferson spoke of a natural aristocracy of virtue and talent, as opposed to an artificial aristocracy of
wealth and birth, he was defining his own conception of
a gentry elite.

"What fact more conspicuous in modern history," Emerson asked, "than the creation of the gentleman?" The
word rattled in his ear like a flourish of trumpets. The
gentry were a self-constituted aristocracy of the best, mo-
nopolizing virtue, beauty, and power. "The gentleman is
a man of truth, lord of his own actions, and expressing that
lordship in his behavior, not in any manner dependent
and servile either on persons or opinions or possessions."
The American gentleman did not hold himself aloof from
the crowd, but in accordance with the spirit of the times
displayed an easy affinity for all classes of men. The gentleman, in short, personified the great Emersonian principles of individualism and self-reliance.[3]

THE EMERGING MASS

In the half-century between the American Revolution and the Jackson era a major social transformation had occurred. The old colonial gentry class had been destroyed and its powers dispersed among several struggling elites. Never again would American society be dominated, as it had been in colonial times, by a powerful and self-assured ruling class. Historians have debated whether the American Revolution, conceived narrowly as the war of independence, was indeed a social revolution. But in a broader context, the destruction of gentry leadership and the emergence of a mass society in which powers were dispersed to a degree hitherto unknown constituted perhaps the greatest social transformation in American history.

The form and course of development of the new society were indicated by characteristics already well established in the eighteenth century. The widespread distribution of property ownership was confirmed and extended through rapid westward expansion.[4] The republican ideology of liberty and natural rights paved the way for the democratization of political institutions and social attitudes. At the same time, there occurred the rapid growth, in both relative and absolute numbers, of what has usually been called the middle class, but might be more precisely designated the newly emergent mass.

Foreign observers of the American scene in the 1830s were all impressed by the equality of social conditions which Tocqueville fixed upon as the salient feature of the new society. The French engineer, Michael Chevalier, noted with surprise that the living conditions of the richest merchant and the average mechanic or farmer were not essentially different. Both had similar houses with carpeted rooms; both slept in real beds, and ate the same number of meals of nearly the same food. The differences were those of degree, not of kind. Harriet Martineau observed that there was no class of truly impoverished. She saw no beggars, and even the swineherds wore spectacles. She attributed the political conservatism of Americans to their dedication to law and order, arising out of a universal interest in property. The poor were relatively content, while the rich seemed to have diminished in stature.[5]

The democratic equalitarianism of the mass society fostered a pervasive materialism which furnished the incentives for rapid industrialization. With the disappearance of hereditary privilege and the ever-widening diffusion of knowledge came a universal ambition for personal advancement, even if aspirations were often modest.[6] Cooper believed that the "natural" rank order in which the individuals of a free society disposed themselves according to merit and achievement was certainly superior to the artificial social distinctions of traditional societies, although it could not be denied that many people displayed envy and malice toward those more fortunate than themselves.[7]

Although modern discussions of the mass society often presuppose mass inertia, social mobility was in fact a central feature of its historical development. Mobility, however, took many forms, to which the rags-to-riches myth provides at best an unreliable guide. Tocqueville was probably right in surmising that for most Americans a modest improvement in economic status was sufficient to satisfy the universal craving for success. On the other hand, none of the many nineteenth-century elites were wholly self-perpetuating, and many of them sustained themselves by continuous recruitment from below. To rise from the mass to elite status spelled success by any criterion, a success limited only by the measure of prestige attached to the elite in question. The rewards which American society bestowed upon the able and ambitious were unprecedented.

Upward mobility as an aspiration reflected in the large nineteenth-century library of success literature has received more attention from historians than has the data on mobility as a historic fact. Stephen Thernstrom's study of Newburyport indicates that in at least one community modest advances in economic status occurred in sufficient numbers over a thirty-year period to lend some measure of credence to the myth of upward mobility.[8]

Votaries of the success cult extolled upward social mobility as the crowning glory of American life. This was understandably the mass point of view, referring almost exclusively to economic success. The gentry attitude, however, was more complex and qualified. Much of the success literature of the nineteenth century had a strongly moralistic ring, and much of it indeed was written by clergymen. Under these auspices success, ostensibly the end and object of self-discipline, was in fact the by-product of it. The gentry could readily sing the praises of the disciplined self-made man because his mastery of the social and moral

qualities that assured his success readily accommodated
him to gentry values. Robert C. Winthrop, nineteenth-
century descendant of Massachusetts' founding father,
found exhortations to achievement addressed to young men
to be admirable occasions for preaching "diligence, economy, and virtue." [9] So long as success could be equated with
self-discipline and restraint the gentry could safely bestow
their blessings on the self-made man. This task was the
more congenial because prior to the Civil War the avenues
of advancement to the social-economic elite and to the
gentry elite roughly paralleled each other, leading to
destinations of comparable prestige. Both groups frequently originated in humble rural circumstances and culminated in success in the city.[10] Both emphasized the importance of sound home training, in which the elevating
and purifying influence of the mother was duly acknowledged. The disciplining of character which was the happy
outcome of such influences was more valuable than worldly
success, which in any event would be achieved only by a
relatively small number of exceptionally able or fortunate people.

The gospel of success through self-mastery was the more
appropriate because of the vulnerability of elites to mass
pressure. It was well enough for the democratic revolution to have swept away privilege; but democracy was
jeopardizing the very notion of superiority as well. Without the external support of class or institution, those who
were possessed by a vision of excellence must learn to rely
on their own inner resources. Tocqueville judged harshly
when he attributed the absence of great writers or distin-

guished political leaders in America to the tyrannical coercion of public opinion exercised by the democratic mass: "In that immense crowd which throngs the avenues to power in the United States I found very few men who displayed any of that manly candor and that masculine independence of opinion which frequently distinguished the Americans in former times, and which constitutes the leading feature in distinguished characters, wheresoever they may be found." Belligerent affirmations of mass equality scarcely concealed the underlying realization of inferiority or the determination to expropriate the visible symbols if not the substance of superiority.[11]

The absence of effective leadership was an aspect of the mass society which required for its comprehension a more elaborate conceptual apparatus than Tocqueville or any of his contemporaries possessed.[12] Leadership functions were no longer exercised by a single social class but by a number of separate functional elites.[13] There were as many elites as there were organized social interests, some of them overlapping in membership, others wholly distinct. Two of these elites derived directly from fragments of the old colonial gentry class: the social-economic elite, and a new gentry elite. Others, such as the journalistic, religious, and entertainment elites, were composed largely of newcomers who gained elite status through their own achievements. All the elites existed in a relationship of satellite dependency upon the mass, being highly vulnerable to mass pressures.

Tocqueville noted the private, club-like character of the elites. Publicly, Americans all stood on a common footing,

acknowledging no distinctions or precedence. But those of
similar occupations, education, and interests tended to
draw apart in order to satisfy their social needs in coteries
of congenial and like-minded individuals. Social life thus
acquired an element of exclusiveness which furnished an
ironic commentary on the indiscriminate gregariousness of
democratic expectations.[14] Tocqueville concluded, perhaps
too hastily, that Americans were generally content with
exclusiveness in private so long as equality prevailed in
public. In fact, there was much evidence to suggest a pervasive suspicion that private association was at least potentially subversive of equalitarianism.

The social-economic elite, composed of wealthy business
and financial leaders who had organized themselves socially as fashionable society, were a very different group
in the 1830s from the flamboyant, self-assured plutocracy
they were to become by the end of the century. In various ways their social life and attitudes revealed a defensiveness resulting from the hostility and suspicion of the
democratic mass. Concentrated in the large cities of the
Eastern seaboard, and constantly subjected to the im-
portunate assaults of the newly rich, the social-economic
elite could only retreat behind barricades of social exclusiveness and complain peevishly of the times. The coun-
terfeit quality of their pretensions to gentility was nowhere
more glaringly apparent than in their ineffectual efforts
to convert wealth into hereditary distinction. Wealth
stubbornly refused to yield to other social values; as Francis Grund put it: "the whole composition of our society
is arithmetical, each gentleman ranking according to the

numerical index of his property." Since only a quarter
of American wealth was believed to be inherited, the
remainder exerted irresistible inflationary pressures on
the exclusive ranks of fashion.[15]

The social insecurity of the economic elite of the Jackson era was reflected in their snobbishness and timidity.
Conventions were strictly observed because no one dared
to defy them. One must know only the right people, live
in the right place, and do the right things. Harriet Martineau noted how fears of vulgarity, responsibility, and
singularity all made for conformity. Among such people
the expression of antidemocratic prejudices was commonplace. When Cooper returned to the United States in
1833 after several years' sojourn in Europe, he noted
with dismay the prevalence of such sentiments in the
fashionable circles of New York. Francis Grund reported
conversations with those who hoped for the establishment
of an aristocracy comparable to Britain's, and Miss Martineau encountered resentment against universal suffrage
together with zeal for monarchy.[16]

It was clear that the rich had yet to master the strategies
of power available to wealth in a democratic society. As
late as 1852, George Templeton Strong was complaining
that property was denied its proper influence because men
of wealth refused to use their power. Tocqueville had
earlier remarked that the universal struggle for wealth
had developed habits of prudence and restraint which had
the effect of narrowing the outlook and circumscribing the
powers of the successful. They had achieved potential

power without learning how to use it. "A man cannot enlarge his mind as he would his house." [17]

TOCQUEVILLE AND
MIDDLE-CLASS DOMINANCE

Tocqueville's analysis of the emerging mass society is
worth closer inspection because of his heavy reliance upon
the observations and opinions of many leading members
of the American gentry to whom he presented his letters
of introduction and whose comments on American conditions he faithfully recorded in the notebooks and other
records of his visit. Although he had come to America
for an official investigation of prison management, he
already had in mind a comprehensive study of social conditions and had been preparing himself by reading and
by soliciting letters of introduction. Because he was in
the country for only nine months (May 1831 to February
1832), he had to make every moment count in seeking
out and questioning the wisest and most knowledgeable
men of the day. His aristocratic background and bureau-
cratic connections gave him a ready entré into American
gentry and official circles, and it was from this perspective
that he viewed American society. In Boston he found an
extensive overlapping of gentry and social-economic elites,
but for the most part his hosts comprised the local gentry
elites of the various communities he visited. Seeing little
of either great wealth or deep poverty, he was free to
focus his attention on the characteristics of the mass as

seen from the gentry point of view. He found that the
two post-Revolutionary countries, France and the United
States, had much in common, and that the American gentry were preoccupied with many of the same questions
that troubled. Frenchmen of his own class and expectations.[18]

Tocqueville knew that equality before the law was the
central feature of American democracy, and he proposed
to seek out its implications in social institutions and social
psychology. He was particularly impressed by the fact that
literacy, the precondition for legal equality, was so widespread. Everywhere he went, even on the most remote
frontiers of Michigan, he found literate, well-informed
citizens bound together by an effective communications
network of roads and newspapers. Everyone he met agreed
on the value of public education, especially important in
newer states where voting rights were unrestricted. Few
feared the consequences of a mere smattering of learning,
perhaps because of the general confidence in the restraining influence of religion. Because there were no class
barriers to restrain the able and energetic, Americans had
no need to fear the consequences of educating people beyond their social standing of the moment. Near the end
of his tour, following a conversation in Washington with
Joel R. Poinsett, Tocqueville noted that "the American
people taken in the mass is not only the most enlightened
in the world, but—what I put much higher than that
advantage—is the one whose practical political education
is the most advanced." [19]

Another feature of the democratic mass society was the

central role played by public opinion. Tocqueville had brought with him a deep conviction that the uninhibited expression of public opinion might have a disruptive effect on the governmental process, although when he voiced this fear to Charles Jared Ingersoll in Philadelphia the latter had assured him that public discussion of issues was a salutary form of persuasion. Nevertheless, Tocqueville was more inclined toward the view of the Baltimore physician Richard Spring Strout, who observed that "public opinion does with us what the Inquisition could never do"; and when he wrote his book the Frenchman concluded that "whenever social conditions are equal, public opinion presses with enormous weight upon the mind of each individual." [20]

The function of forming and articulating opinion was chiefly that of the newspaper press. Tocqueville attributed the superficiality of American journalism of that day to a variety of local influences that inhibited the development of an effective press. Too many papers of small circulation and meager resources served to cancel out each other's potential influence. Too much space was allocated to advertising and trivia. Because the limited opportunities and rewards discouraged men of ability, most journalists were of humble origin, uneducated, and vulgar. They made blatant, coarse appeals to the passions of their readers, ignoring principle and dealing largely with personalities. But the fundamental reason for superficial journalism was the absence of great issues, "the germs of revolution." Americans had had their revolution and were now engaged in the work of stabilizing the newly emergent democratic mass society.[21] Under these circumstances, the effect of public opinion was the conservative one of regulating and restraining a mobile and individualistic population.

Since neither Tocqueville nor his American gentry informants were as yet prepared to give up their social class terminology, they regularly referred to the mass of the population as the middle class. Writing to his mother of his first impressions on landing in New York, the Frenchman reported that "the whole society seems to have melted into a middle class." He found neither the refinement of the European high classes nor the boorishness of the lower classes. This first impression was repeatedly confirmed by both his own observations and the opinions of his American acquaintances. Mayor Benjamin W. Richards of Philadelphia remarked to him that the United States represented the victory and rule of the middle classes. The social-economic elite might isolate themselves in contemptuous disdain from the mass; but the latter would defiantly thumb their noses at the rich, while electing their own kind to office. In New York, John Livingston confirmed this statement, qualifying it only with the opinion that leadership by the rich and well educated could be accepted if they would deal with the mass on terms of social equality—at least in public. The historian Jared Sparks expressed the equivocal view that while the majority was generally right, it was sometimes difficult to detect it.[22]

The ambivalent attitudes of the American gentry toward the democratic trends of their own society con-

formed with Tocqueville's apprehensions over the future
of French democracy. Roberts Vaux of Philadelphia expressed open disapproval of universal suffrage because it
put governing power in the hands of "the most excitable
and worst informed classes of society," against whom the
superior classes had no guarantees.[23] It did not escape
the Frenchman that such complaints were invariably
couched in social and cultural rather than in economic
or material terms. The American gentry might complain
about the "frenzy" or ignorance of the mass, its blunders
and passions, but they were not in fact being dispossessed.
James Carroll of Baltimore pointed out that the disad-
vantages of democracy should not be exaggerated. Class
conflict was abated precisely because of universal suffrage.
The upper classes might complain of the bad manners of
the mass, but the complaints were muffled by the general
prosperity. Tocqueville was obliged to concede that although lacking in manners, education, and stability the
mass had the intelligence necessary to govern.[24]

Although in the form first stated the thesis of middle-
class dominance was placed in a social context—refinement and ill-breeding—it could also be examined in the
more familiar economic terms. Revolutionary movements,
Tocqueville observed, were almost always caused by economic inequality. Either the poor plundered the rich or
the rich enslaved the poor. But where everyone owned
property peace was more likely to prevail. In America
there were to be sure some very rich and others very poor.
The latter, however, far from constituting the vast majority, as they did in aristocratic countries, were small in

number and not bound by law to hereditary poverty. The rich were similarly few and powerless. Between the two extremes stood the mass of the population, possessed of enough property to be conservative and law abiding, ambitious but not revolutionary.

As an afterthought the Frenchman hazarded the guess that if a revolution were ever to occur again in America it would come from the Negroes. His American acquaintances were generally agreed that slavery had bequeathed to the future an insoluble race problem. They anticipated that the slaves would eventually be freed, but that the races would not be able to coexist peaceably in freedom. He recorded no dissent from the conviction that either of two drastic solutions would prevail: colonial segregation, either external or internal; or the destruction of the Negroes. It was perhaps an indication of the apparent remoteness of the issue that responsible American leaders could contemplate such a catastrophic outcome with apparent equanimity.[25]

In fixing upon equality rather than liberty as the operative ideal of American democracy, Tocqueville was attempting to characterize the prevailing temper and expectations of the mass society.[26] Equality defined the personal relations between individuals—no man need defer to another. It had immediate appeal for all those who were sensitive to any pretensions of superiority among their fellows. Liberty, on the other hand, pertained to opportunity; it was mere freedom to act, conferring no benefit in itself. One must capitalize on one's opportunities in order to realize its advantages. Liberty consequently appealed to the able and energetic minority who constituted the elites, while equality was more attractive to the mass.

The subtle tension between liberty and equality suggested to Tocqueville a refocusing of social analysis which was to have far-reaching consequences in intellectual history. He noted that in aristocratic societies historians had customarily taken for granted the self-determined power of leaders, and their narratives had appropriately recounted the deeds of great men. In the mass society, on the other hand, they now saw that society was dominated by great impersonal forces to which individuals had no choice but to bow.[27] Democratic social conditions thus created an intellectual environment in which science would flourish, both physical science and, especially, social science. For science deals with aggregates of phenomena, the behavior of which is indicated by statistical probabilities. In American social science the earliest attempts to interpret social problems in terms of mass phenomena occurred in the generation following Tocqueville. These attempts took the form of naturalistic determinism, in which individuals were found to struggle powerlessly in the grip of great social forces. Later, however, it became increasingly apparent that if science dealt with the behavior of aggregates it was not addressing itself directly to the behavior of individuals within the aggregate, which remained indeterminate. But whatever the outcome, it was clear that Tocqueville had initiated an intellectual revolution.

Although the concept of social mass readily associated

itself in Tocqueville's mind with that of inertia, he successfully resisted any inclination he may have had to make
a vulgar application of the idea of inertia to the individual
Americans who constituted the democratic mass. On the
contrary, he was deeply impressed by the social mobility
to be seen on every hand. His observations on this subject
were undoubtedly influenced by conversations in Philadelphia with Pierre Duponceau, a Frenchman who had
come to America during the Revolution and had subse-
quently distinguished himself as an international lawyer
and ethnologist. Duponceau remarked that because the
road to riches was open to all, there was a universal restlessness of spirit and greed for wealth. Because everyone
wanted to get ahead, and believed that he had the qualities requisite for success, there was continuous activity,
intrigue, and competition.[28] Tocqueville's task was to indicate how such mobility accommodated itself to the mass
context. He noted the pervasive materialism that underlay
the universal ambition for wealth and prestige. Social
equality fostered a love of well-being and a rising standard
of living. Everywhere men were being disciplined by the
principle of "interest" into habits of regularity, temperance, and foresight. And yet, although everything seemed
in flux, nothing changed very much. The Puritan ethic
did not produce great acts of self-denial or of virtue. Without lofty ambitions people generally coveted small objects
within reach; their status expectations were modest. For
these reasons mobility was not in fact as divisive a force
as one might have expected.[29]

The consequence of mobility in a mass society was a

new phenomenon to which Tocqueville attached the term "individualism." His Scottish translator, Henry Reeve, observed that this transliteration from the French would be unfamiliar to American readers. But the concept, if not the term itself, had been suggested by President Josiah Quincy of Harvard, who remarked that men born in freedom were accustomed to take the initiative in a variety of matters, such as schools, hospitals, and roads, that were usually left to the state under more paternalistic circumstances. The development of strong individuality resulted from minimal government. Admittedly, however, this was desirable only where the citizens had the knowledge to see clearly what was needed and the self-control to achieve it. Caught up in the hopeful spirit of his host, the visitor noted in good Jeffersonian style: "The most important care of a good government should be to get people used little by little to managing without it." [30] But when he finally cast his mature deliberations in published form several years later, Tocqueville shifted the context of individualism from the public to the private sphere. "Individualism" now denoted that which disposed a man to form a private circle of family and friends and to leave society to itself. Such an act of withdrawal enlarged the sphere of the private at the expense of the public and undermined the virtues of public life. It tempted a man to forget his responsibilities to both his ancestors and his descendants. It was individualism that gave the mass man his atomistic social quality.[31]

The principal problem facing any European observer of American life in the early nineteenth century was the

difficulty of describing the social class structure of the
United States, given the notions of class that he brought
with him. There were social distinctions, certainly, but
they were not those with which Europeans were familiar.
In Europe, industrial and political revolutions were occurring within the structure of traditionally established
social classes. In America, everyone agreed that the nascent
colonial gentry class had been swept away by the Revolution, and that there were no social barriers to contain
the rapid industrial development. Shortly after his arrival
in New York, Tocqueville learned from John Livingston
that the distinguished gentry families of the pre-Revolu-
tionary period had been destroyed by new laws of inheritance that prevented the transmission of landed estates.
Money was now said to change hands so rapidly that most
prominent families "disappeared" after the second or third
generation without building up durable estates. A "mon-
eyed aristocracy" certainly existed, but it was as weak as
it was pretentious. Several months later, in Baltimore,
Tocqueville met the venerable Charles Carroll of Carroll-
ton, the last surviving signer of the Declaration of Independence, and "the exact counterpart of a European
gentleman." He recognized in Carroll an extinct breed.
The locus of power now centered in the mass, in men
of "middling abilities." Society was less brilliant but more
prosperous.[32]

It was as apparent to Tocqueville as to everyone else
that "the first of all distinctions in America is money."
But money was a fluid commodity that flowed from hand
to hand without creating permanent distinctions. Ameri-

cans were also prepared to recognize distinguished ancestry, professional services, or talent without according
to any of these the privilege of restricted marriage, which
from the traditional point of view was the touchstone of
stable class identification. His earlier distinction between
public and private provided Tocqueville with the clue
to the nature of American social discriminations. John
Quincy Adams, whom he met in Boston at a dinner given
by Alexander Everett, informed Tocqueville that full
equality before the law did not prevent the formation of
class differences. But Adams was referring to personal or
private distinctions scarcely noticeable to the casual observer impressed with the equalitarianism of public manners. An aristocratic Frenchman had to be impressed by
servants called "help" who found tipping humiliating,
and who considered themselves their employers' social
equals.[33] The social distinctions that did undeniably
emerge out of this indiscriminate welter had a peculiarly
private and elusive character that would scarcely impinge
on the consciousness unless one realized that certain doors
were not opening to him.

> The people of the same professions, the same ideas, the
> same education choose each other by a sort of instinct and
> gather together, exclusive from the rest. The difference
> [from the European situation] is that no arbitrary and
> inflexible rule presides at this arrangement. Thus it
> shocks no one; it is final for nobody, and no one can be
> wounded. In this way, less in America than anywhere
> else do you see the ardent desire of one class to partake
> not only of the political rights but of the pleasures of

others. That's what distinguishes American society favorably from ours. And unfavorably.[34]

In order to discover how traditional, publicly recognized classes had been transformed into privately maintained coteries Tocqueville was forced back to the foundations of class in distinctive styles of family life. He knew that the classes of Europe were sustained by corresponding patterns of family life, and he was prepared to acknowledge that changes in family behavior could signal changes in the class structure. He was not surprised to discover that in America the Roman or aristocratic type of family no longer existed (if indeed it ever had existed here). In that type of family the authority of the father, reinforced both by law and aristocratic expectations, was absolute. Under democratic conditions, without the support of an aristocratic class, the father could not sustain an autocratic role even if he wanted to. The idea of the father as an authoritative person had gradually given way to more intimate, affectionate, and informal familial relationships. Freed from the restraints of class expectations the family became a wholly private institution in which a wide variety of relationships reflected the accidents of individual temperaments. Only during the earliest years of childhood did the parent exercise anything like absolute authority. Tocqueville noted the absence of adolescence in America, the boy passing quickly to the freedom of manhood. No struggle was involved in the emancipation of the son from parental control because society sanctioned it and all parties accepted it as inevitable.[35]

The mobility of the mass society was greatly facilitated by the nuclear family of parents and dependent children. One of the ultimate sources of social mobility lay in the children of such a family, who had been reared in the expectation that they would in time depart from the home of their parents to establish their own homes. Convention decreed that parents should make every effort to provide their children with better opportunities than they themselves had enjoyed. Successful upward mobility necessarily occurred at the expense of family solidarity and continuity. The same was true of downward mobility; everyone knew local gossip about "black sheep" or "degenerate" individuals who had sunk to a lower status than that of their parents. In either case, the bonds between generations were loosened, and men lost touch with the ideas and traditions of their forebears.[36]

The function of the nuclear family in preparing its children for independent social careers was suggested appropriately enough in their designation as "offspring." The social values with which it equipped them were designed to facilitate their adaptation to whatever circumstances they might confront. Adaptability was at a premium. When in his later years a successful person had occasion to set down autobiographical recollections of his childhood family experiences, he often did so in the tranquil perspective of social distance. The process of detachment from the parental family and the establishment of his own family in a higher social stratum—since "success" was the usual incentive for the recording of such reminiscences—provided the broad framework for the familiar American autobiography as a form of success literature.

Although Tocqueville did not amplify the modern distinction between mass culture and folk culture, such a distinction was at least suggested in his comments on the significance of individualism. He knew that folk culture was tradition-oriented, conservative, and solidaristic, in the sense that the folk voluntarily submitted themselves to the dictates of the whole society in its customs, rituals, prejudices, and convictions. Mass culture, on the other hand, was relatively self-conscious, synthetic, and rationalistic. Its precondition was the ethos of individualism. Tocqueville found that the American had come to locate the standard of judgment in himself alone. He believed that everything was comprehensible; and he denied whatever he could not understand. All of this made for extreme psychological independence.

Paradoxically enough, democratic individualism went hand in hand with a striking uniformity of manners and outlook. Wherever he went, Tocqueville found the same ways of acting, thinking, and feeling. There was no significant difference between the New Yorker and the frontiersman of Michigan. Such uniformity was the consequence in part of greater spatial mobility; but primarily it was the result of the fact that distinctive conceptions of caste, family, and profession were being washed away. John H. B. Latrobe of Baltimore had told Tocqueville that the New Englanders with their restless, driving energy were gradually making over the whole country in their own image. Later, in writing his book, Tocqueville generalized this conception of the Yankee as the distinctive American type. By stripping off their social accretions Americans were approximating the basic constitution of man, "which is everywhere the same." [37] Here was at least part of the answer to the questions Tocqueville had posed for himself at the outset: "Why, when civilization spreads, do the outstanding men grow fewer? Why, when there are no longer any lower classes, are there no superior classes? Why, when the knowledge of government reaches the masses, are great geniuses missing from the direction of society?" [38] Americans were answering these questions by honing down each individual to the quintessential man.

The last question led to the problem of leadership in a mass society. Tocqueville knew that in the absence of a ruling class leadership must be furnished by functional elites, but he was less concerned with analyzing the character and relationships of elites than with the coercive controls over them exercised by the mass. The vulnerability of elites to the pressures exerted by public opinion was most apparent in the political sphere, but the effects were felt in the cultural world as well. There were no great writers in America because the necessary atmosphere of intellectual freedom did not exist. There were no anti-religious or pornographic books because the pressure of opinion from a decent and orderly public suppressed them. The same pressure presumably functioned to suppress all kinds of thinking that might be at odds with prevailing opinion. "The majority lives in the perpetual practice of self-applause," and no writer however distinguished could "escape from the tribute of adulation to his fellow-citizens." Exaggerated though these judgments may have been, one can detect in them the jingoism of Young America, as well as echoes of the conflict over literary nationalism raging in the magazines of Tocqueville's day.

Making a distinction between the public and private spheres of life helped the American gentry to preserve their optimism in the face of sordid political realities. Everywhere he went, Tocqueville was told of the vulgarity of public officials and of the exclusion of the gentry from public office. In Cincinnati, for instance, the rising young abolitionist lawyer Salmon P. Chase remarked that universal suffrage resulted in the election of unworthy candidates who triumphed by means of flattery and fraternizing with the mob. And yet, paradoxically, Chase believed that the influence of the abler men prevailed in the end. The latter opinion was supported by the celebrated physician, Dr. Daniel Drake. The Reverend Louis Dwight of Boston believed that the success of republican government depended on the stability, piety, and enlightenment of the people, who would somehow survive the dizzy gyrations of public life. A Massachusetts legislator, Francis C. Gray, explained the paradox at least in part by pointing out that the practice of judicial review put great power in the hands of the courts, which thus exerted a stabilizing influence. Albert Gallatin confirmed the judgment that the judiciary was the principal stabilizing force in the American system. In the face of these uncertainties the Frenchman could only conclude that universal suffrage was viable only where public issues were of secondary importance, and where enlightened self-government was understood in the private rather than the public sense.[39]

In the 1830s infant industries had not yet spawned the large fortunes that would support the flamboyant fashionable elite of a later era. Doubtless for this reason, Tocqueville had surprisingly little to say about the social and political functions of wealth in a mass society. The universal concern with money and commercial values meant that the rich would become the principal elite in the eyes of the mass. His theory insisted that the rich no less than other elites should be subject to mass pressures, and there was little as yet in the contemporary scene to suggest otherwise. Wealth did indeed create a privileged class, but the consequences were not presumed to be fatal so long as the money changed hands rapidly and everyone believed that he had a fair chance to obtain some of it. Tocqueville clung to the traditional assumption that without restricted marriage, social classes in the strict sense could not crystallize. He did predict that the rapidly growing class of manufacturers would eventually result in a new aristocracy. But constantly fluctuating personnel and the absence of any common class bonds or sense of social responsibility would render it the most confined and least dangerous aristocracy that could be imagined. He also assumed that after securing their fortunes these new aristocrats would emulate the older commercial leaders of the seaboard in pursuing pleasures of the intellect by patronizing the gentry. In this, of course, he was to prove to be largely mistaken.[40]

In the final analysis, Tocqueville's conception of the

democratic mass society rested on an archaic psychological theory of the universal natural man. According to this theory, the distinctive social institutions of any nation or region stamped the citizens with the traits by which they were commonly identified. Should these institutions be stripped away, as Tocqueville believed they had been in America, the individual would emerge in his universal form as the natural man. It was doubtless indicative of his loyalties and affiliations that Tocqueville's vision of the natural man in the primitive democratic state should not have been a particularly attractive or flattering one. A universal "restlessness of heart" was found to be the consequence of equal opportunities for advancement. Envy, a distinctively democratic sentiment, took a thousand different forms. Because of their lack of respect for competence and authority Americans displayed "a consummate mixture of ignorance and presumption" in the conduct of their affairs. Although great progress had admittedly been made in correcting or offsetting these natural defects, the future of the democratic mass society remained clouded with uncertainties.[41] A sense of the momentousness of these uncertainties and of the social conditions which generated them were to constitute Tocqueville's heritage to American social thought. It is only proper to add, however, that whereas twentieth-century commentators on the mass society were often to regard mass characteristics as symptoms of social pathology, Tocqueville usually believed them to be normal and inevitable expressions of a democratic and equalitarian society.

· II ·

AN AMERICAN THEORY
OF MANNERS

IN ITS EARLIEST USAGES in West European languages, the
word "gentleman" signified a privileged social status. But
the component ideas of gentility were much older than
the gentleman as a social type, going back through the
Renaissance courtier and the medieval knight to the stoic
philosopher of antiquity. These elements of gentility
formed a curious compound of opposites: gentleness and
valor, honor and self-effacement, tact and allegiance to
principle, agreeableness and pride. In Britain at least,
according to the historian Wingfield-Stratford, the gentleman existed before these qualities had come to be associated with him—the first identifiable English gentleman

having been a ruffian.[1] By the time America was settled
however, the gentleman had become firmly identified with
the qualities of gentility, the interplay between the social
and moral dimensions being the intriguing thing about
him.

Another meaning of the word was indicated by Samuel
Johnson in the eighteenth century when he defined a
gentleman as one distinguished by birth from the vulgar.
In this sense mankind was divided into two classes, gentle
and simple, and the finer things of life were presumed to
be the proper possession of the former. But that gentle
birth in itself was not sufficient was already apparent in
the fact that it had been felt necessary to elaborate the
standards of gentlemanly behavior in great detail and
to set them forth in countless handbooks on gentility. To
be born a gentleman entailed an obligation to act like
one, and doubtless for this reason gentility never became
a wholly distinctive class status in English-speaking lands.
Its distinctions were always blurred by its identification
with the prescribed personal qualities. Before the ideal
gentleman could be fully conceptualized by Emerson, he
had to be emancipated from the confines of privileged
blood lines.

In the meanwhile, the gentleman reached his full development as a social type, both in England and in America. Of the two branches in the eighteenth century the
American gentry were by far the more impressive, doubtless because they exercised a near monopoly of power and
were not overshadowed by an aristocracy. In all the colonies, the basis of their power was wealth, whether in

land or obtained through mercantile enterprise. Everywhere they allied themselves with professional men and civil servants, and accepted educated persons on terms of equality. Within each colony the tendency of the gentry to intermarry resulted naturally in a growing sense of the value of heredity and family ties; yet everyone knew that new men were constantly pushing up into the class and marrying their children into established gentry families.

The colonial American gentry modeled themselves on the English gentry, carefully imitating their manners and style of living, and frequently seeking further reassurance by establishing family derivation, however dubious, from British landed families. On both sides of the Atlantic a shelf full of manuals on gentility was available to the gentleman and his family. Some of these manuals were translations from the French, but others were prepared by English authors and presumed to be adapted to English requirements. Louis B. Wright's study of the Virginia gentry showed that copies of these handbooks were commonly found in gentry libraries.[2] One of the earliest was Thomas Peacham's *The Compleat Gentleman* of 1622. Peacham mixed his instructions on manners and deportment with a strong moral emphasis on duties and a temperate control of the passions. The complete gentleman envisioned by Peacham was an all-around man in the best Renaissance style. He developed and preserved his body with sports and physical culture. His public responsibilities were acknowledged by military service. Improvement of the mind was insured by a continuing regimen of study and travel. The gentleman was expected to master Latin grammar and to write a decent English style. He should appreciate art and music if he did not dabble in them himself.[3]

The manuals of Peacham, Brathwaite, Allestree, and Halifax circulated widely in the colonies, and were frequently reprinted. So was Chesterfield's celebrated *Letters,* with thirty-one reprintings in the last quarter of the eighteenth century. But Chesterfield was too opportunistic for American tastes, and the decadence of his morals resulted in extensive expurgation of American editions. Local writers began to publish works of the genre, and at the age of fifteen young George Washington compiled for his own use a set of 110 rules of behavior, ranging from such practical admonitions as "spit not in the fire" to the exalted injunction, "labor to keep alive in your Breast that little spark of Celestial Fire called Conscience." [4]

Beyond these adornments of their class the old eighteenth-century gentry also commonly possessed the skills associated with their practical activities. Knowledge of the law was essential to an English landed gentry who dominated local government; and it was equally essential to an American gentry with extensive commercial, landholding, and speculative interests. Medical knowledge was also frequently possessed by gentlemen, especially in rural regions where professionally trained physicians were virtually unknown. Finally, library inventories reveal large numbers of religious works both theological and devotional. If the gentry were not always men of deep personal piety, they at least appreciated the public functions of religion and gave it their formal support.

The celebrated diary of William Byrd II (1674–1744) provides an intimate glimpse of the life of the plantation gentry of Virginia at the beginning of the eighteenth century. Byrd inherited a large estate and increased it by land speculation and real estate promotion. He was a surveyor, merchant, miller, and mineral prospector. He had a lifelong career in Virginia politics, serving in the House of Burgesses and the Governor's Council, as Collector General of Royal Revenues, and as Colonial Agent in London. His duties as militia officer and vestryman were taken for granted. In spite of all these activities Byrd found time to pursue the cultural interests prescribed by the gentry code. He had been educated in England, where he had studied law and joined the Royal Society. Throughout his life he continued to read—or at least study—Hebrew, Greek, Latin, French, Italian, and Dutch. His library was one of the best in America.

Byrd's manner of living showed how closely the colonial gentry modeled themselves on their English counterparts. Although much of the day was devoted to the management of affairs, there was a constant stream of visitors at Westover, and much conviviality. Manners were, by later nineteenth-century gentry standards, coarse in the extreme. Byrd did not scruple to converse in Latin with a clergyman in the presence of other guests who did not understand the tongue, and when his wife reproved him they quarreled and the clergyman flounced off to bed. Guests sometimes swore in company; and on one occasion the master of Westover, seeing from a second story window a Negro maid pass beneath, emptied a pitcher of water over her. A similar crudeness was characteristic of the English landed gentry. It was to be the urban influence which would give the nineteenth-century gentleman his refinement and polish.

In the northern colonies, commerce rather than agriculture was the principal economic foundation of the gentry, and a larger professional element gave the class greater diversity. Centered around such families as Beekman, de Peyster, Livingston, Jay, and de Lancey, the New York gentry of the mid-eighteenth century were typical of the class found in the seaboard towns. They educated their children in private schools and at King's College, expecting them to have at least a nodding acquaintance with the classics, mathematics, and the modern languages. Fencing and painting were considered appropriate embellishments, while the presence of British officers and civil servants helped to keep the provincial gentry abreast of the latest fashions of the metropolis. Booksellers offered, in addition to the usual religious works, the current novels of Richardson and Fielding and the *Gentleman's Magazine* and *Lady's Magazine*. In these various sources a rich fund of material illustrative of gentility was available.[5]

George Washington's code of gentility reflected both the peculiar obligations of social class standards and the universal values which were ultimately to emancipate gentility from its class confines. Moncure Conway believed that the code had been dictated by Washington's tutor, the Reverend James Marye, a native Frenchman who was presumably using an English version of a seventeenth-century French Jesuit manual of civility.[6] In any event, the code was clearly intended for the use of a gentry class and not for common men. The bulk of its maxims dealt with the proper behavior among gentlemen. Although Conway noted that snobbery and social discriminations in Washington's version were less pronounced than in some of its prototypes, the fact remained that considerable attention was paid to the subtle distinctions of behavior toward unequals which it was the gentleman's responsibility to perpetuate. Why remove one's hat for superiors if one did not remain covered before inferiors? "Let your discourse with men of business be short and comprehensive." The adroit management of these distinctions required of the gentleman a delicate and perceptive awareness of mutual prerogatives and expectations. He should be neither too slow nor too hasty in insisting upon the proper marks of respect. "[It is absurd to] act ye same with a Clown and a Prince." [7]

Nevertheless, it remained a fact that in gentlemanly behavior invidious distinctions were often mitigated by the dictates of decency and kindliness. All good conduct was gentlemanly; all bad conduct ill-bred. The gentleman's function was not so much to insist upon social distinctions as to humanize them, alleviating the harshness of rank by a gracious deference on the one hand and a kindly condescension on the other. Thus in a sense he transcended the prevailing distinctions of rank, and unknowingly became a powerful force for destroying them. It was appropriate that from the sixteenth century onward many of the writers on gentility should have been clergymen, a class which stood apart from the secular social scale and enjoyed at least a tenuous status as universal arbiter on social as well as spiritual matters. These clerical writers made the gentlemen their secular allies by endowing gentility with the cluster of values which permitted it to bring moral standards into social relations.

In the end, the gentleman proved to be an incommensurable element in the status system. His principles, purged of their exclusiveness and broadened by a comprehensive goodwill to embrace all men, became a universal standard applicable to all. The final chapter of the gentleman's saga found him the apologist for the democratic way of life. Freed from awkward compromises with prescriptive rank he could apply the principles of gentility in appropriately universal terms to the relationships of social equals. The unexpected frustrations and painful rejections which he encountered in this enterprise constitute a major theme in the history of American gentility.

"MORALS IN BLOOM"

The democratization of culture in the nineteenth century precipitated a controversy over the meaning and function of manners. Gentility had always been symbolized by distinctive manners, the perpetuation of which was an important part of gentlemanly training. One of the symptoms of the decay of gentility during the course of the nineteenth century was to be the gradual erosion of gentlemanly manners, which coincided with a continuing debate over their value.

Two theories of manners emerged from the discussion. One might be called the common or utilitarian view. Manners were said to be the overt forms of social intercourse. Because they were conventionalized, they eased and facilitated personal relations. Yet, the conviction persisted that manners were but the superficial embroidery upon an underlying reality, and that this was especially so with respect to gentry manners, which were often regarded as florid or ridiculously out of touch with the spirit of the times. Gentry manners were associated in the popular mind with privileged status in a traditionally stratified society. They tended to perpetuate subservience and were thus incompatible with the equalitarianism of democracy.

The gentry themselves espoused a more comprehensive organic theory of manners. How could inner reality express itself except in outward form? Manners were indeed the outer forms of inner reality, and in them the tone and spirit of social relations were fully revealed. The American gentry especially emphasized the close identification of manners with morals. "Manners are only morals in bloom." Manners, said Catharine M. Sedgwick, were the expression of the dispositions and affections, the outward signs of the true qualities of mind and heart. They were mirrors that truly reflected the soul.[8] Emerson emphasized the spontaneity of manners as "the happy ways of doing things; each once a stroke of genius or of love,— now repeated and hardened into usage." [9] Good manners compelled acceptance because they were displayed by people of virtue and power. Charles Butler put the difference between the two schools in terms of Swift's distinction between good manners and good breeding. The former were approved forms of behavior; the latter comprised a much broader and subtler range of acquirements based on knowledge, reflection, and wide experience. Everyone could be expected to have some manners; but good breeding was much more difficult to come by, and would always be confined to a select few.[10]

The high seriousness with which the American gentry faced their social and cultural responsibilities was reflected in the range of qualities which seemed most pertinent to their conceptions of gentility. Apart from his manners, the gentleman, according to Edward Everett, was a person of character, integrity, and intelligence. The historian Richard Hildreth distinguished such "lesser morals" as good manners and politeness from the greater virtues of wisdom, justice, and benevolence. Charles Butler found in the simple mandate of politeness a whole world of obligations. Politeness, he said, is the art of pleasing, and in order to please one must be virtuous, wise, and well mannered. Thus a necessary ingredient of politeness proved to be "knowledge of mankind, of governments, of history, of public characters, and of the springs which put the great and the little actions of the world in motion." It was no wonder that many Americans shrank from assuming the arduous burdens of gentility.[11]

The democratization of culture had a profound effect upon gentility and its theory of manners. As Theodore

Sedgwick observed, in a free and equal country manners were bound to reflect the character of the institutions; and the detachment of gentility from privilege made it possible to purify and refine those manners. Manners in the context of a democratic social philosophy originate in mutual kindliness and good will among social equals.[12] By emphasizing the finest values in the tradition of gentility, the latter-day gentleman would achieve the highest perfection of the type.

Democratization made possible the perennial nineteenth-century distinction between "fine" and "fashionable" manners. Fine manners, said Caroline Kirkland, express love, simplicity, and truthfulness. They reflect appreciation and consideration for the feelings of others, regardless of status. Fashionable manners, on the other hand, are based on mere convention. We obsequiously imitate those we presume to be our superiors in rank or prestige, and such deference is often compatible with a revolting coarseness. N. P. Willis declared that what was needed was "a distinctively American school of good manners," without useless etiquette and superfluous graces but with every usage designed to promote goodwill and sensibility.[13]

One of the most eloquent exponents of this new American school was Catharine M. Sedgwick, a tireless critic of manners whose novels and didactic essays were all designed to disseminate democratic gentility. She would in fact push diffusion of good manners to the point where the terms "gentleman" and "lady" would be abandoned, and only well-bred men and women would remain. No

other country, she believed, offered so bright a prospect
of achieving a national standard of behavior based on
manliness, frankness, and self-respect. Intelligent and literate American farmers and mechanics whose sons enjoyed unlimited opportunities for success felt themselves
in no way inferior to professors, and distinctly superior to
the idle rich. Such men could not be provoked to either
rudeness or servility. Equal rights and opportunities for
advancement served to "restrain the temper" and promote mutual kindliness and forebearance. The mingling
of all classes was favorable to the dissemination of fine
manners in that it facilitated opportunities for direct observation of good models. From Hallam's definition of
gentility—ceremonious politeness, spontaneous modesty,
self-denial, and respect for others—Miss Sedgwick need
strike out only the ceremonious politeness in order to
demonstrate that it was not necessary to live in the fashionable world in order to learn good manners. Their essentials could be found in the farm house as well as the
city drawing room. "I have never seen better models of
manners, . . ." she reported, "than in the home of a New
England farmer, where the parents, respected and self-
respecting, were fountains of kindness to their household;
where the children blended in their manners to their
parents filial reverence with social equality; where the
strong bond of love between brothers and sisters was
manifest in reciprocal devotion graced with courtesy, and
where the guest was received with a manner that no code
nor instructor could have produced, because it expressed

conscious dignity, independence, and painstaking benevolence." [14]

The complete accommodation of gentility to democratic and Protestant America required in addition only a demonstration of the religious foundation of manners. Miss Sedgwick found this basis in the Biblical precept: "Honor all men." Reverence for humanity was in the last analysis the product of piety. Religion inspired that delicate regard for the rights and feelings of others from which all good manners arose. Active kindliness, as distinct from ceremonious politeness, was the direct product of religious benevolence.[15]

However, Catharine Sedgwick's celebration of the spontaneous good manners of the New England farmer presupposed a degree of social stability and contentment which was often lacking in American life. In urban and commercial contexts, especially, gentility was often called upon to perform quite different functions. The object of many writers on gentility, whether implicitly or explicitly stated, was to discipline and control the potential anarchy of a highly mobile and fluid society through the imposition of manners upon conduct which would otherwise be unrestrained. Gentry manners were well suited to play this role because of the traditional emphasis on independent, self-respecting integrity. The gentleman as individualist was well qualified to flourish in the bustling commercial world. He knew how to soften the contours of his aggressiveness with manners designed to ease the friction of personal relations; and in this respect, the bourgeois gentleman was ideally suited to the world of nineteenth-century American capitalism. The difference between the huckster and the broker was, in part, simply a difference in manners. But to the degree to which gentry manners were made to perform such prudential functions, they were inevitably reduced to bare essentials, and the etiquette books revealed all too clearly how much was lost when principle was reduced to prudence.

The democratic accommodation of gentility to conditions of civil and social equality, although cheerfully accepted by gentry spokesmen, nevertheless confronted them with a distressing consequence. A society of free individuals each pursuing his own objectives would inevitably result in wide differences of status and prestige. The gentry accepted such differences as necessary and proper, and generally took it for granted as a practical matter that their own status should command respect. But they were disturbed to note how frequently their fellow citizens in rejecting distinctions of birth, wealth, or position went on to reject all kinds of distinction involving subordination. Catharine Beecher observed that children were often regarded the equals of their parents, pupils of their teachers, servants of employers, and subjects of magistrates. What was needed was a code of manners expressive of necessary social distinctions. The fact that in a democracy women were free to choose the husbands they would obey, or laborers the employers whose orders they executed, did not obviate appropriate marks of subordination. Miss Beecher was hopeful that the Golden Rule furnished the principles of mutual respect and consideration which would mitigate the rigors of these inevitable distinctions.[16]

The strain of sober earnestness that ran through the theory and practice of gentility in America reflected the peculiar vulnerability of traditional forms in a society rapidly divesting itself of the restraints of class and community. In order to preserve his integrity the gentleman subscribed to the maxim that familiarity bred contempt. He scrupulously preserved a dignified distance between himself and others, including his peers and close associates. Charles Butler admonished him always to be restrained in his modes of address, never eager, loud or boisterous. Noisy mirth was a symptom of vulgarity. "The vulgar often laugh, but never smile; whereas well-bred people often smile, but seldom laugh." Passion was always to be subdued; and even wit was to be managed with care. Mimicry, satire, irony were all to be avoided.[17]

The distinction between "fashion" and true gentility regularly made by writers on manners always disparaged fashion. Emerson followed this practice in his comments on the origin of gentry manners, which are the spontaneous forms of social intercourse among gentlemen. Through usage they acquire a sense of propriety and thus become the badges of social distinction displayed by the fashionable. Fashionable society might be said to be the hard shell secreted by the living organism of the gentry. The ranks of fashion were constantly being filled from the gentry; fashion was "virtue gone to seed"; "a kind of posthumous honor." In terminology reminiscent of Jefferson's, Emerson observed that those who constituted the natural aristocracy (gentry) were not to be found within the actual aristocracy (social-economic elite) but only on its edge, "as the chemical energy of the spectrum is found to be greatest just outside of the spectrum." [18]

The New York journalist and essayist Nathaniel Parker Willis furnished a more circumstantial account of the distinction and its consequences. Willis lamented that New York could not boast of the kind of cultivated society found in the major capitals of Europe. "What we want is what they have in Paris—a society separate from fashion—the admission to which would be a compliment to the quality of a man—which would give its entertainments with humbler surroundings, but with wit, sparkle and zest." If the rich and the gentry could be brought together, Willis believed that New York would be found to have enough beautiful and accomplished women, dramatists, musicians, poets, and cultivated foreigners to combine with the better men among the merchants and brokers to form a society equal in brilliance to the best Europe could offer. Unfortunately, the "Pocket Aristocracy" was too insecure and fearful of the "aristocracy of the Brain" to be willing to risk the presence of outsiders in its exclusive circles. Willis was realistic enough to know that money must take the initiative if the two groups were to be brought together, and he knew that the likelihood was remote. He could only complain that what had been done elsewhere could also be done in New York.[19]

Wherever the social-economic elite and the gentry elite did come together, they constituted an overlapping sector composed of individuals who enjoyed status in both groups. Such favored folk always remained relatively

small in number, and their influence in American cultural history was never as great as their connections would
lead one to expect. Edith Wharton was one of these, and
in her autobiography she related how oppressive her exclusively fashionable connections had become to her before she broke away and established contacts in the world
of the gentry. She had been born in 1862, in an old New
York mercantile family. Although there were many in
her circle of acquaintances with genuine intellectual interests, they feared and avoided creative people. Irving,
Halleck, and Longfellow were among the few who were
conceded to have remained uncontaminated by their
literary activities. The major New York writers of the
mid-nineteenth century, including Poe and Melville (in
spite of the latter's Van Rensselaer connections) were unknown to the city's social-economic elite. It was characteristic of provincial societies, Mrs. Wharton concluded,
that the scholars, artists, and writers should obstinately
shut themselves away from fashionable people; while the
latter did not know how to make the necessary advances
to the creative people. Only in sophisticated societies did
the intellectuals "recognize the uses of the frivolous," and
did the frivolous know how to make their houses attractive to their betters. In the largest sense, the fault lay
with the American mass, which required the isolation of
the social-economic elite.[20]

Intermarriage of individuals from the two elites frequently enlarged the overlapping sector. Julia Ward of
the New York economic elite married Dr. Samuel Gridley
Howe of Boston, a zealous reformer and educator of the

blind. The Wards had gentry contacts, enjoyed the society of literary people, and approved the marriage of Julia's sister to the sculptor Thomas Crawford. Nevertheless, when she moved to Boston with her husband in 1844, Julia gravitated naturally from New York's "four hundred" to Boston's "forty," as she later put it. Her society friends disapproved of her interest in the radical Unitarian, Theodore Parker, and the "transcendental people." Julia herself at first found the language of the transcendentalists unintelligible. Soon she came to know personally the far more obnoxious abolitionists, including William Lloyd Garrison, whom she had always regarded as a coarse demagogue. To her surprise she found that Garrison, who had successfully assimilated the norms of gentility, was a saint rather than an ogre.[21]

The distinctions between these various groups were most readily observed in the larger cities of the seaboard. In smaller towns and in the West generally economic elite and gentry elite tended to be closely allied or even indistinguishable as separate groups. The well-to-do rarely sustained a style of living beyond the means of professionals, while the small numbers of both groups tended to draw them together. Merchants, doctors, and lawyers formed a single society in most western towns.

Oliver Wendell Holmes coined the phrase, "the Brahmin caste of New England," precisely for the purpose of distinguishing between the social-economic elite and gentry of that region.[22] Holmes himself belonged to the overlapping group in Boston. His father, Abiel Holmes, was a native of Connecticut who had attended Yale, married President Stiles' daughter, and had come to Cambridge as pastor of the First Congregational Society. Here he married again, this time a daughter of Oliver Wendell, who was described by his grandson as "a man of some property and high social connections." Wendell money made possible the younger Holmes's medical education in Paris and assured him an impeccable social position.

When Holmes spoke of the aristocracy, he meant the rich, "the untitled nobility which has the dollar for its armorial bearing." Some of these people were well bred and others merely purse-proud and assuming. But in any case, the distinctive feature of the class was its instability, money not being a durable basis for privilege without some special means of preserving it. In the absence of any such means the composition of the American aristocracy was always changing. The gentry of New England, on the other hand, had displayed such durability through successive generations as to have become an inbred caste, the Brahmin caste, with a characteristic physiognomy readily apparent to the appreciative observer. It was an earnest, studious caste, tending to produce scholars and clergymen in successive generations, as witness the Edwardses, Chauncys, and Ellerys. Holmes readily acknowledged that a constant stream of newcomers was working its way into the caste. Likely young chaps from the "ports" to the Northeast, Portsmouth, Newburyport, and Portland, came to the Boston metropolis to establish themselves in gentry ranks and realize their cultural ambitions. Or they came, like Holmes's father, from Connecticut, the land of steady habits. Actually, the gentry never remotely approached the condition of a closed caste.

Holmes also recognized the fact that the Brahmin gentry often merged with commercial or political families through intermarriage. In such cases the scholar's working books would be rebound in handsome calf, and his study would become a stately library. But the status of gentry individuals in the overlapping group was precarious, for it depended on money or social acceptance, the loss of either of which spelled social oblivion.[23]

Characteristic tensions within the overlapping group were revealed in the careers of two Boston gentlemen. The historian George Bancroft, son of a prominent Unitarian clergyman, graduated from Harvard in 1817, where he had been a favorite of Andrews Norton, Edward Everett, and President Kirkland. These sponsors raised a fund among wealthy Bostonians to send the young scholar to Europe in Everett's footsteps for clerical training. But Bancroft strayed from the narrow paths of theology and became infected by the heady romanticism of Hegel and Schleiermacher. When he returned to Boston in 1822 he was not only uncertain about a career in the ministry, but even worse, he had acquired flamboyant manners and an interest in writing verse. His patrons were estranged and quietly closed their doors to him, in striking contrast to their treatment of George Ticknor, who was careful not to defy local conventions. Bancroft veered off toward his subsequent career as teacher, Democratic politician, and historian, eventually settling in more congenial surroundings in New York. While his gentry associations always remained firm, he never regained his status in the overlapping group.[24]

Charles Sumner suffered a similar fate at the hands of

the social-economic elite who dictated the terms on which the overlapping group in Boston was to be constituted. Sumner was also the beneficiary of a European tour, in 1837, from which he returned in triumph to be welcomed in the homes of the rich and influential. Within a few years, however, the influence of Channing's humanitarian idealism led him into various reform causes, beginning with education and progressing through prison reform and the peace movement to antislavery. While it was generally felt to be permissible to interest oneself in good causes, a gentleman was also supposed to use restraint and good taste. Sumner was aggressive and censorious, and did not hesitate to criticize Webster and Robert C. Winthrop, whom he felt to be too timid and conservative. As a result he, like Bancroft, was excluded from the overlapping group and forced to fall back upon Longfellow, Prescott, Howe, and other gentry associates, who stood by him.[25]

The usual gentry condescension and disapproval of the social-economic elite reflected the ambiguities and uncertainties of their relationship. George William Curtis, for many years the "Easy Chair" editor of *Harper's Magazine,* published in 1853 a volume of essays, *The Potiphar Papers,* in which he satirized fashionable society from the gentry point of view. Curtis observed that although both groups professed allegiance to the traditions of gentility, the gentry understood the finer elements, and added democratic sympathies appropriate to nineteenth-century American culture. "Society," on the other hand, fastened upon the superficial aspects of gentility: correct manners, fashion, and snobbishness. Each group prized association with its own kind; the gentry for the stimulus of conversation, the social elite for emulative and invidious displays of fashion. Each acknowledged the obligations of service, which the gentry discharged by promoting good causes and speaking out on public issues, while the social elite restricted itself to fastidious dispensation of charity. Both groups were in a sense oriented toward Europe: the gentry for important cultural reasons, and the social elite because of its admiration for European aristocratic society. In short, fashionable society was a caricature of the gentry.[26]

The disintegration of the old colonial gentry class and the subsequent distribution of its functions among the nineteenth-century elites had the effect of leaving the social-economic elite with the niceties of manners and the gentry with the moral code. The latter had the substance of gentility, the former only the forms. Charles Butler attributed the falseness of fashionable manners to idleness made possible by wealth, which in the end was the corrupting influence. When she visited Saratoga Springs, Catharine Sedgwick noted with an accusing eye the variety of colors and complexions of the fancy belles assembled there. Her observation suggested a generalization shared by all those whose notions of status rested on nonmonetary values: "Wealth, you know, is the grand leveling principle." [27]

· III ·

THE NATURAL
GENTLEMAN

THE MASS SOCIETY that emerged in America at the beginning of the nineteenth century had little in common with
the propertyless rabble postulated by Gustave LeBon
and other early theorists of the mass society. The traditional classical and aristocratic fear of democratic mobs
had little relevance to what was occurring in America.[1]
Mass, as the term is used here, is at once a cultural and
a social concept. Literacy and the primacy of the printed
word suggest a cultural dimension; while active citizenship and property-holding indicate the characteristic self-
sufficiency and social mobility of the mass.

Literacy in Western culture had traditionally been restricted to the ruling classes and to the professionals, clerks, and tradesmen who served them. Both in England and in America the earliest detectable symptoms of an emerging mass society were to be found in the eighteenth century in the widening circles of literacy. Franklin believed that owing to their widespread reading habits, the common American tradesman and farmer were as intelligent as the gentlemen of other countries. Certainly the bulk of printed material circulating in the later colonial era was substantial in content. Lawbooks and histories were often the book-dealer's best sellers. Economic problems and political restraints may have inhibited the development of printing in the colonies, but they were offset in part by the ready availability of English imprints. On the eve of the Revolution, there were more than 60 subscription libraries in the colonies, the most famous of which was the Library Company of Philadelphia. Institutions of this kind perpetuated the serious tone of the old colonial gentry culture.

The abolition of colonial restrictions upon printing which came with the Revolution made its own revolutionary impact on literate culture. Because of the difficulty of publishing newspapers, the principal vehicle for revolutionary propaganda had been the pamphlet. A flexible and effective means of disseminating ideas, pamphleteering had commanded the best colonial talent. Some 1,500 pamphlets had been published in the decade prior to the Declaration of Independence. As soon as political controls over the press were swept away in the Revolution, newspaper journalism developed rapidly. Some 450 newspapers were established between 1783 and 1800, nearly half of which survived the period. During the first third of the nineteenth century the number increased to 1,200, including some 65 dailies. This was the largest number in any nation. The newspaper reading habit, upon which so many foreign visitors commented, was now firmly established. Prior to the 1830s, papers had been designed primarily for business and professional readers. But with the appearance of the "penny-press" in that decade, mass circulation was achieved. Between 1828 and 1860 the total number of papers and periodicals increased from 852 to 4,051, with a combined annual circulation in the latter year of nearly a billion copies. This vast sea of printed matter furnished an environment of ideas in which the mass society flourished.[2]

The growth of the press and the spread of the reading habit went hand in hand. Where every man was free to go as far as his ability, energy, and luck would take him there was much mobility. As soon as hereditary prerogatives ceased it became apparent, as Tocqueville observed, that the chief cause of human differences lay in the mind. Whatever improved the mind was of great value, and the importance of literacy as the key to self-improvement was universally apparent.[3] The spread of literacy was an integral aspect of the growth of the mass society, and resulted in a growing demand for public education. The states which first implemented public educational systems were those in which the press and other indices of literacy were most firmly established. Literacy preceded and paved the way for mass education. Had Tocqueville

looked more closely he might well have noted many quali-
fications to his comprehensive generalization. There was
in fact much resistance to the social and economic costs
of public education, voiced principally at the far ends
of the economic scale.[4] It was the gentry who pressed
educational programs upon an often reluctant public.

The influential role of the press in forming public
opinion in a mass society was recognized from the outset.
Harriet Martineau was concerned lest the worship of public opinion—"the established religion of the United
States"—would destroy true freedom by undermining reliance on truth and justice.[5] Tocqueville attributed the
poor quality of American journalism to the absence of
great issues, "the germs of revolution." America had had
her revolution and was engaged in consolidation and
growth. Moreover, the large number of newspapers, their
small individual circulation, and their meager resources
all made for superficial journalism. Most journalists of
this period were men of humble origin and vulgar tastes,
who could only indulge in personalities and make coarse
appeals to prejudice. It was undeniable that the press
debased the tone of public life.[6] Frances Trollope's American sojourn had been uninsulated by gentry associations,
and her judgments were correspondingly harsh. She concluded that because everyone read "periodical trash" and
no one read anything else, even the best writers had become infected by their forced identification with journalism. Cooper's most venomous fictional portrait was of the
journalist Steadfast Dodge, whose hypocritical celebration
of democratic equalitarianism could not mask his frustrated craving for power and prestige.[7]

In the face of these developments it might have been expected that with the disintegration of the old colonial gentry class the theory and practice of gentility would come to be identified with the nineteenth-century social-economic elite. The situation seemed ripe for a reconstitution of the older cultural affiliations under the auspices of new commercial wealth. To some extent this did occur; but a more significant development was the emergence of an independent gentry which looked to its own elite leadership and which formed a new alliance with the practitioners of high culture. For all practical purposes, gentility was now divorced from privilege and power and affiliated with the literary, artistic, and educational elites. It became the principal function of gentility in the nineteenth century to furnish the social identity for those engaged in high cultural activity. The alliance had profound effects upon both parties. The exchange of privilege for learning and creativity altered the gentleman's character. His growing sense of cultural responsibility strengthened the qualities of earnestness and sobriety, which in turn caused him to identify himself more closely with the religious and educational leaders. On the other hand, the creative person, in availing himself of the social role of gentleman, was obliged to conform to the social and moral norms prescribed by the gentry code. The effect of this commitment upon the cultural life of the nineteenth century was so pervasive as to have almost escaped notice, although in contrast with twentieth-century culture it should be apparent enough. The gentleman became the apostle of culture in a world of democratic capitalistic mobility.

Among the first tasks of the new gentry was that of conceptualizing American society in such a way that gentility would be found to have a distinctive place and function. Basic to their theory was a distinction between natural and artificial social order. An artificial order, such as the European, was composed of social classes based on such "unnatural" criteria as birth or wealth, and supported by the props of law or custom. In such an artificial order merit was largely irrelevant. In a natural social order, on the other hand, the only distinctions among men were those germane to their respective functions, reflecting all the personal differences of character, ability, and training. These "natural" differences might well result in practical distinctions as marked as those of the artificial order. But they were the consequence of the achievements of living men. Furthermore, the theory held that because these were distinctions based on human diversity rather than on artificial or arbitrarily imposed criteria, men would recognize and accept them as just and inevitable. Bonds of sympathy would unite men of different social stations because they would recognize their dependence upon one another's functions. Harriet Martineau had observed that only in America was universal mutual respect paid to man as man; and she indicated a principal reason for this when she added that to a remarkable degree social functions were interchangeable—the professional man was capable of supporting himself if necessary by manual labor, while the farm hand was usually a reading and thinking man.[8]

Emerson remarked that there was a natural rank order

in society in which every man had the place determined
by the "symmetry of his structure." Good breeding and
personal superiority always asserted their claims and were
recognized everywhere. A gentry was inevitable. This was
not unlike the modern view that elites are inevitable so
long as society requires the performance of certain functions.[9]

In a natural and equalitarian society there would be
a uniform standard of manners, "a quiet, dignified, and
manly deportment." Each individual would stand on his
merits as a man. The *American Quarterly Review* in 1837
professed to believe that America had no social class with
special political influence or privilege. Mere wealth had
no effect whatever when the people had determined upon
a given objective.[10] In such a society, gentility was a natural and not an artificial virtue. Where no hereditary
aristocrat existed to look down on him, the gentleman,
as Cooper remarked, stood supreme as the chief adorn-
ment of society.

The gentry believed that their notion of an individualistic democracy was wholly compatible with their pretensions to leadership. They assumed that the natural social
order would display all the gradations of status, with a
high and honored place for the gentry. Democracy did
not imply equality of condition. It would display all the
inequalities of condition that were native to human diversity. This was, of course, a philosophy of free competition
in a game in which the stakes were high—nothing less
than the individual's station in life. For the few who were
able and energetic the rewards were great; for the many

the prospects were meager. The gentry doubtless overesti-
mated the attractiveness of this philosophy to their fellow
Americans. Most men do not relish competition when the
odds are against them. They seek shelter from the storms
of life. Inevitably, the democratic majority would sooner
or later attempt to mitigate the rigors of competition by
using available political instruments to equalize the distribution of benefits. These benefits were psychological as
well as material—prestige, respect, a sense of self-satisfac-
tion. In spite of their genuinely democratic sympathies the
gentry preached a form of individualism too strenuous for
the majority, and when on occasion they sensed this they
undertook a critical reconsideration of their relationship
to the majority.

The gentry repeatedly affirmed that gentility was a natural condition, and that the gentry elite constituted a natural aristocracy of virtue and talent. William Tudor, the
founder of the *North American Review,* insisted that the
true principles of gentility were everywhere gaining ground
because of the acceptance of the doctrine of original equality. Talent and service now replaced birth as the basis of
rank.[11] Cooper even justified the exclusiveness of the gentry as appropriate to those of refined tastes. Such tastes
were the essence of civilization, and their preservation war-
ranted the formation of a special class of patrons.[12]

William Ellery Channing in 1823 emphasized the cultural responsibilities of the gentry. Nothing distinguished
a country so much as superior men, and thus far America
had expended too much labor on physical comforts to the
neglect of intellect. The great question was: what kind of

men did we breed? The prime function of the gentry was to elevate the national mind and character through intellectual activity. Because the mass was now accustomed to read, the power of the printed word was infinitely greater than in former times, and writing was now "the mightiest instrument on earth." As the custodians of this instrument the gentry were the repositories of the highest power, and on them the best hopes of society rested.[13]

THE RUSTIC SETTING

Although the tradition of gentility was deeply rooted in the past, a product of the Western cultural tradition, nineteenth-century gentlemen in America liked to think that gentility was in some special sense the indigenous product of their own social environment. To sustain this conviction they developed a theory that freedom and gentility were interrelated: the most immediate human response to the conditions of freedom was the appearance of a new and unique figure, the natural gentleman.

As a social type the natural gentleman reflected the romantic primitivism of the nineteenth-century imagination. He was presumed to be the spontaneous, unpremeditated product of a social environment uncontaminated by all the accretions of the traditional social order. The frontier provided an ideal set of images in which to depict the elements of this environment, although the areas surrounding the frontier—the wilderness to the west and the almost equally vast rural subfrontier region to the east—were also locales in which the nurturing influences of natural gentility could be readily found. It was thus no accident that someone like Cooper, preoccupied with gentility in its cultivated forms, should also display an intense interest in the natural gentleman. Cooper defined the type as the individual possessed of gentlemanly attributes of character without the cultivated refinements that came from membership in the social class of gentlemen. In other words, the natural gentleman had the moral qualities of gentility without the manners. In the Indian chief Susquesus, Cooper created a gentleman "in the best meaning of the word." The Indian possessed the "loftiness of a grand nature," developed under "the impetus of an unrestrained though savage liberty." [14] In a somewhat more sophisticated setting, the frontier of the white man's settlement, Cooper placed the most famous of his natural gentlemen, the scout Leatherstocking. The principal difference between the scout and the Indian as natural gentlemen was the scout's comprehension of the civilized world behind the frontier, and his humble acceptance of his honorable but highly circumscribed role in a larger hierarchy of gentility. In Cooper's mind, the frontier with the simplicity of its social structure contrasted with the complexities of civilization in the same manner as the natural gentleman contrasted with the cultivated gentleman.

The testimony of the writer of fiction was authenticated by the daily experiences of his contemporaries. While Josiah Quincy (1802–1882) was serving as personal aide to the governor of Massachusetts, it became his duty to receive President Andrew Jackson when the president toured

Massachusetts in 1833. The Whigs of that state knew Jackson only as a formidable barbarian, and Quincy, a superb specimen of the Boston gentry, undertook his assignment with deep distaste. But when they met, Quincy discovered at once that Jackson "was, in essence, a knightly personage,—prejudiced, narrow, mistaken upon many points, it might be, but vigorously a gentleman in his high sense of honor and in the natural straightforward courtesies which are easily to be distinguished from the veneer of policy." The qualities which most impressed Quincy were Jackson's sincerity, decision, honesty, and earnestness.[15] A later generation of cultivated gentlemen made a similar discovery of a natural gentleman in the White House, and thanks to their vigorous if somewhat belated celebration of his virtues Abraham Lincoln within a generation of his martyrdom came to be the most cherished exemplar of the natural gentleman America had produced.

The gentry elite consisted of those who articulated the code of gentility most effectively, and of those in positions of prominence who were looked to by the rank and file as exemplifying the ideals of the gentleman. This historical reconstruction of gentility inevitably focuses with disproportionate emphasis on the elite leadership because of their literary remains and social visibility. But it should not be forgotten that the leaders had a numerous following of anonymous citizens who subscribed to the code and in varying degree achieved a measure of dignity and refinement in their lives. Many older people still living can recall from childhood vivid recollections of the graciousness and charm of the local gentry of their respective neighborhoods. The elite, for their part, proclaimed solidarity with their following by celebrating the commonplace and indigenous sources of gentility. The natural gentleman and lady reinforced the rootage of gentility in the local scene, and set up a characteristic tension with the cosmopolitan tradition. Emerson may have revered Sir Philip Sidney, that great paragon of gentility, but he also cherished and respected his neighbor, farmer Hosmer, a worthy specimen of the natural gentleman.

William Cooper Howells, editor of small-town Ohio newspapers and father of the novelist William Dean Howells, indicated how anyone, regardless of wealth or training, could qualify for the honored status of gentleman:

There is refinement in whatever is well-finished—in all work where there has been pains taken in its execution. There is social culture wherever the mind has been trained to good and beautiful ideas. It is easy and within the power of everyone to be a gentleman or a lady. They may not have learned the conventionally prescribed manner or phraseology of standard social life; but if they act towards others upon the principle of "each esteeming another better than himself," or regarding the feelings and comforts of others, from a neighborly good will, they fill the true measure of the character. The words *"gentle man"* express the exact idea of the much coveted appellation. This fact does not warrant us in neglecting the polish of good training in manners, language or dress, for these add the beautiful to the good; or rather express in elegance the good which is admirable. The gentleman and the lady will always be recognized and appreciated for what they are, except by those who are ignorant of the quality themselves. . . .[16]

Henry Thoreau's famous experiment in living at Walden Pond may profitably be considered in terms of this commonplace tension between the moral and sociological dimensions of gentility. Thoreau was a sophisticated gentleman who deliberately reversed the conventional relationship between natural and cultivated gentility because he felt deeply about the loss or obscuring of basic values of life in cultivated environments. Bronson Alcott hailed him as "a sylvan man accomplished in the virtues of an aboriginal civility, and quite superior to the urbanites of cities." [17] Apart from the pervasive romantic primitivism of the nineteenth-century mind, American gentlemen returned to nature because they believed it to be the native environment of virtue. The American Adam, child of the wilderness, living outside of history and not knowing sin, was the natural gentleman.

In the course of her travels Harriet Martineau had frequently encountered "originals," usually rustics, whose character and manners had developed without the standardizing effects of class tradition or institutional restraint. They were eccentric characters unconscious of their eccentricity. The natural gentleman was often an original. As such he served as a useful symbol of protest against the artificiality of conventional manners. Writers of the later decades of the nineteenth century who specialized in local color witnessed the homogenizing effect upon manners that was exerted by urbanization, and sensing that originals were a dying race, recorded for posterity numerous portraits of the originals they had known.[18]

Emerson's heroic conception of the gentleman as a pioneer who explored new forms of social experience, unrestrained by convention, may well have reflected the influence of his friend and neighbor, the original Amos Bronson Alcott. This self-taught Yankee peddler had been assisted by his bitter failure as a Boston schoolmaster in sharpening the distinction between the conventional manners requisite to success and "the rustic awkwardness and simplicity of natural life." Alcott settled down in Concord, within walking and talking distance of Emerson, to live a life of proud and joyous poverty, refusing as a matter of principle to accept gainful employment. The journals of the two men contain abundant evidence of mutual stimulus and discipleship. Emerson's lecture on "Manners," with its distinction between forms and substance, which Alcott heard in April 1837, closely paralleled the invidious distinctions between cultivated and natural gentility which Alcott recorded in his own journal.[19]

On at least one occasion, Alcott dreamed (literally) of resuming his former occupation as peddler, and he seems to have given the matter serious thought in spite of the ridicule his wife and friends heaped on the idea. The chief virtue of peddling was the opportunity it afforded for conversation, which Alcott had come to recognize as his true calling. Brushing aside the objection that peddling would be beneath his dignity, he remarked in his journal that he would not hesitate to undertake whatever appeared to be his duty. "I see in the occupation of peddling many facilities for speaking that I could not enjoy in other relations. My epic would have a thread around which I could spin whatever of heroic action and utterance occasion should favor. It would be an *Excursion* realized in

life. My purpose would dignify my pursuit, and ennoble
me in the eyes of the simple and true." [20] To dignify a
humble occupation by a noble purpose was the essence of
natural gentility. And like Whitman and many another
American, Alcott made literal the notion of life as an excursion.

The stubborn individualism of the natural gentleman
was evident in Alcott's contempt for democratic ideologues
who found virtues in the mass while conceding that in-
dividually men were base. On the contrary, Alcott expected to find the devil in the midst of the mob, and God
within the seclusion of the single soul. "The Kingdom of
Truth is within, not out there in Church or State. *Vox
populi, vox diaboli.*" The best way for a man to prove his
democratic professions was to labor for a day or two beside
a plain working man in order to discover what they had in
common.[21]

One of the functions of the natural gentleman was to
resolve the distinctive American conflict between nature
and culture, between rusticity and manners. He was nature's nobleman, the hard-working, self-reliant farmer,
craftsman, or fisherman, whose natural graciousness en-
nabled him to perceive and acknowledge the legitimate
but not the spurious claims of cultivation. He stood between the two poles of civilization and wilderness savagery, and he combined the best moral and social qualities
of both. The fascination which he held for the cultivated
gentleman was apparent in the substantial modifications
of gentlemanly ideals which can be traced to his influence.
As early as 1825 a new social norm was apparent when

Theodore Sedgwick, high Federalist though he was, celebrated the happy union of labor, knowledge, and manners.[22] The traditional aristocratic emphasis on sports and
martial exercises was replaced in American gentility by a
new sense of the value of manual labor and skills. It was
no longer beneath the dignity of a gentleman to be skilled
in the use of tools, or to sit down at the dinner table, as
Emerson regularly did, with the field hands. In nineteenth-century utopian communities, whether actual or
fictional, the social ideal blended labor and learning, manners and service.

It seems clear in retrospect that the principal function
of the natural gentleman was to assist the new gentry in
reaching their own distinctive conception of gentility.
Both in his subordination of manners to character and in
his exemplification of the ideal possibilities of a free society, the natural gentleman illustrated the way in which
the tradition of gentility was to be shaped in American
usage. Edward Everett affirmed that the word gentleman
might be used meaningfully only with reference to a person of character, integrity, and intelligence.[23] Gentility
became synonymous, at least in the gentleman's own esti-
mation, with the good. And if a gentleman was to be
known by his manners, these also were honed down to
their moral core. The philosophy of good manners, observed George William Curtis in 1859, was simply this:
"a conviction that we ought to feel kindly and act charita-
bly toward everybody else. Bad manners are merely selfishness expressed in tones and conduct. Good manners are
charity in speech and action." [24] The democratic gentle-

man who embodied these wholesome and unpretentious maxims was a living testimonial to the triumph of Leatherstocking.

Although the nineteenth-century gentry emerged out of the disintegration of the old colonial gentry class, the gentry themselves preferred to entertain another view of their origins. They were preoccupied with current affairs rather than with historical events, and they liked to think of themselves as the spontaneous products of a free society. The principal source for the generation of natural gentility was the American "yeomanry," either farmers or craftsmen. Yeomen provided the reservoir from which the ranks of cultivated gentlemen were to be recruited. Early in the century, Edward Everett hailed the American yeomanry as "perhaps the most substantial, uncorrupted, and intelligent population on earth." Nearly a century later, Barrett Wendell repeated with approval the seventeenth-century maxim of Thomas Fuller, that "a good yeoman is a gentleman in the ore." [25] During the intervening decades these encomiums were regularly and dutifully repeated.

American yeomen were the indigenous products of the ethnic-cultural regions which Everett praised in his Phi Beta Kappa oration of 1825. These regions were the nurseries of those social qualities which the gentry prized, and with which they proudly identified themselves. Seaboard regions had been in process of formation since the seventeenth century, while in the West a couple of generations sufficed to give them their distinctive flavor. In his autobiography, Senator George Frisbie Hoar of Massachusetts expressed the pious conviction that no better example could be found of a pure and beautiful democracy than that which had existed in the town of Concord in the second quarter of the nineteenth century. While there had been no extremes of wealth or poverty, the gradations of rank which did indeed exist reflected personal merit and community consensus. The population, "of good English stock," was as permanent as that of any European region. Gentle blood flowed in the veins of many. "It is interesting to observe," reflected the senator, "how little the character of the gentleman or gentlewoman in our New England people is affected by the pursuit, for generations, of humble occupations, which in other countries are deemed degrading." Families engaged in manual labor were regularly producing individuals of ambition and ability who successfully made their way into the larger world of learning and refinement.[26]

Something of the way in which this was accomplished was revealed in the recollections of Lucy Larcom, the poet of the textile mills. Lucy grew up in the humble poverty of a farming and fishing community on Cape Anne. Her forebears had always "accepted with sturdy dignity an inheritance of hard work and the privileges of poverty, leaving the same bequest to their descendants." These humble yeomen had carefully preserved the religious and literary heritage of Anglo-American civilization. Poor though they were, the Larcom family had provided themselves with books and newspapers. Lucy's precocious literary bent was nourished by Watts's hymns, Shakespeare, Coleridge, Wordsworth, and Bryant. "The happiness of our lives," she recalled, "was rooted in the stern, vigorous virtues of the people we lived among, drawing thence its bloom and song and fragrance." [27]

Cooper's celebration of the Hudson and Mohawk regions included critical appraisals of the qualities and contributions of the British, Dutch, and Yankee elements of the population. Even newly settled country quickly developed its own distinctive regional cultures, notably in Ohio and Indiana. Robert Underwood Johnson, whose boyhood was spent in Wayne County, Indiana, recalled the literary interests of the local bench and bar when everyone wrote verses, and the recesses of court sessions were filled with talk of Byron and Scott. Regional loyalties were readily crystallized by the pervasive romantic worship of nature. As Alcott expressed it:

> The country is much to every young soul. How much it was to me I can never sufficiently feel. I am under the deepest obligation to it. It kept me pure. It soothed and refined my disposition. It was discipline and culture to me. I dwelt amidst the hills. I looked out upon rural images. I was enshrined in Nature. God spoke to me while I walked the fields. . . .[28]

The duty of the family, as the gentry usually conceived it, was that of transmitting the cultural heritage of the region to its children by providing the immediate environment in which they would grow up to a full realization of the potentialities of the regional culture. Pride of family or of gentry status was ordinarily subsumed within regional loyalty. The family should stand for what was best in the community. The notion of the family as the possessor of a special talent transmitted in the blood line rarely appeared before the end of the century. Pride of family usually meant pride in service to the community. The role of prominent families was not so much to divide the region between those of high and low degree—although there were always jealous carpers—as to unify it behind a tradition of public-spirited leadership. On numerous occasions the gentry from all parts of the country expressed their loyalty to their regional heritage. It was a heritage of the common folk and their sturdy, honest, self-respecting virtues. For a gentleman to claim descent from "good old stock" was honor enough. Lowell's *Biglow Papers* was a characteristic celebration of a gentleman's ethnic-regional heritage. Hosea Biglow was a letter-writing country bumpkin who composed doggerel verses on topics of the day, especially the politics of slavery. But the humor was meant to be only skin deep. Biglow might wear the costume of a clown, but underneath he was a sterling character, the native New Englander as homespun hero, to whom Professor James Russell Lowell was proud to be related as joint beneficiary of a cultural heritage.

The principal means by which the natural gentlemen of the yeomanry were transformed into the cultivated gentlemen of the gentry was formal education in the liberal arts tradition. Repeatedly, one encountered the poor boy who showed an aptitude for schooling, managed to go to college, and thus acquired the skills and interests which admitted him to the world of the gentry. Such an experience gave American gentility its strong professional, literary, almost classical tone. By bringing the gentleman into touch with the world of literature and learning, it made him a cosmopolitan. It also served to minimize the importance of family continuity. It was a common experience for men like Jared Sparks and John Gorham Palfrey to avail themselves of educational opportunity to rise to secure positions of gentry leadership, even in a town like Boston, where family antecedents were reputed to count so heavily.

· IV ·

THE GENTRY AND AMERICAN SOCIETY

IN THE TRADITIONAL CLASS-STRUCTURED SOCIETIES of Europe the gentry's status as a class of property and privilege carried with it a host of conventional routines of behavior and social attitudes. Traditions of class and family decreed that patterns of behavior were to be taken for granted. In America, however, where mobility prevailed and the class structure was inchoate, the rituals and routines of gentlemanly behavior were perpetuated only imperfectly and with the greatest difficulty. Even among gentry families of several generations' duration, styles varied appreciably and every household was to some extent unique. Under such fluid circumstances, even the most essential social relationships were clouded in uncertainty. Commencing with the members of his own family and proceeding to his clubs and formal cultural organizations, the gentleman had to establish new patterns consistent with the independence and equalitarianism that the Americans were taking for granted.

THE NUCLEAR FAMILY

In the early nineteenth-century phase of the mass society the home was the central social and cultural institution. The authoritative institutions of colonial society had crumbled. The colonial gentry class was gone, together with the British military and civil services and the established churches. At the same time, the institutions of the mature mass society of the twentieth-century—the dominating welfare-warfare state, the giant corporations, the labor unions, and the great educational "establishment"— had not yet emerged. Foreign travelers uniformly noted the absence of authority, both in actuality and in symbol. These transitional circumstances account for the great importance attached by contemporaries to home and family life as the principal props of civilization and order.

With the change from a class-structured society to a mass society the family underwent a corresponding change. The form of family typical of the mass society has been designated a nuclear family, a single-generation affair consisting of parents and dependent children. Such a family tended to be highly variable; it did not function effectively as a perpetuator of tradition. Its principal object was to prepare its children for careers of social mobility, and to the extent that it achieved this it created a radical discontinuity between generations. Limited though it was, the nineteenth-century family was nevertheless called upon to bear a heavy burden as the principal agent for securing social control.

The function of the nuclear family as depicted in gentry autobiographies was that of transmitting the regional cultural heritage, and of providing the all-important environment in which the child would grow up to a full realization of his heritage. The qualities of greatest importance were moral and spiritual rather than intellectual. Character formation was more important than the training of the mind, although this did not necessarily imply anti-intellectualism. The head of the family and principal income-earner was the father, although grandparents and other relatives often resided with the family. The father's authority as head of the household was still very great, extending to labor, religion, education, and family discipline. And yet the gentry consistently minimized the family as an authoritative determiner of status. Children were to make their own way in the world. Furthermore, talent and character might be found anywhere, and were to be honored wherever found. Early in the century, John Adams had declared that wherever distinction persisted in families through successive generations the choice of wives was the decisive factor, thus in effect tipping the balance from heredity to individual preference. While the gentry weakened the family by loosening the bonds between generations, they broadened the stage on which families acted to include regional, ethnic, and cultural responsibilities. The gulf between generations opened by the nuclear family fixed the perspective in which the typical gentry autobiographer viewed the course of his own career. He looked back on his childhood as from a great distance, while his success as well as his detachment served to invest his recollections with a warm glow of grateful memories. The fragments of his life fell neatly into chapters, his early experiences belonging to a past that was irrevocably closed.

In a democratic, socially unstructured society the family became the paradigm for all proper social relationships. Caroline Kirkland remarked that "home is indeed a little world; and in each household we see in some sense a resemblance to the society of which it forms a part." If love, truth, justice, and piety reigned at home, they would also prevail in society. But if pride, false pretenses, longing for excitement, and indulgence were tolerated at home, society would suffer from the same evils.[1] It was of the greatest importance that social order and stability be secured through the inculcation in the young of sentiments of deference and respect for parents. Seemingly, the Puritan doctrine of the sanctity of magistrates, driven out of politics by the democratic movement, had taken refuge in the home as its last bastion of defense. The authority of the parent, though it should be softened by love and veneration, was not to be questioned. On the other hand, the affection and consideration shown by parent for child (even indulgence, within permissible limits) corresponded to the kindly and comradely tone cultivated by the public official or employer in his relations with the citizen or em-

ployee. Democracy required the same subtle blend o
equalitarianism and deference that the gentry had always
extolled. Unfortunately, it was a difficult goal to achieve,
and throughout the century critics of American family life
regularly complained of the failure of parents to insist
upon receiving the subordination and respect owed to
them by their children. The latter, in turn, all too frequently displayed a painful lack of veneration and obedi-
ence.[2]

The cement that held the nuclear family together was
domestic love, a compound of sex, companionship, religion (woman worship), and exploitation (male dominance). Unlike the families of privileged classes, in which
marital choices were supervised by parents in terms of class
suitability, the nuclear family of the mass society rested
upon the sentimental preferences of the spouses, with a
minimum of parental oversight. Love justified the marital
relationship, and many apologists for the nuclear family
went so far as to say that marriage without love was scandalous, indeed adulterous. A more practical consequence
of loveless marriages was the growing divorce rate, which
mounted steadily throughout the century in the face of
stern religious and social disapproval.[3] It was no accident
that sentimental fiction should focus on the family. The
powerful force of sexual attraction, legitimized and domes-
ticated by marriage, was always in danger of bursting its
bonds and destroying the family. The principal tragedy
of this fiction, the broken home with its abandoned children, underscored the vulnerability of the nuclear family.

The brief life span of the nuclear family generated an

aura of sadness and nostalgia which is reflected in one of the minor episodes of American literary history. In 1867, Henry Wadsworth Longfellow had occasion to pay a visit to his young friend Thomas Bailey Aldrich. The Aldriches were recently married, and their small round dining table prompted Longfellow to remark that soon it would be necessary to add leaves as a growing number of young faces clustered about the table. But it would scarcely have been extended to its greatest size when one by one the faces would disappear as their owners took flight to build nests of their own. The leaves would be removed successively until in the end there would remain only the small round table with its two old faces. This cycle, said the poet, is "the sweet and pathetic poem of the fireside." [4]

A striking testimonial of devotion to the nuclear family at its best was provided by the theologian Horace Bushnell in his book *Christian Nurture,* one of the most celebrated religious works of the nineteenth century. Bushnell challenged the traditional evangelical Protestant doctrines of innate depravity and sanctifying grace by declaring that if a child were to grow up in the pervasive loving tenderness of a Christian family he need never know the condition of depravity nor the spiritual crisis of conversion. Bushnell rejected what he declared to be the excessive individualism of evangelical revivalism in favor of the corporate responsibilities of family, church, and community. The family was the basic organic unit of both church and society, the divinely constituted means of securing Christian character. A child who from his earliest years learned, as Bushnell himself had, to love the truth need not have a technical conversion experience. The fact that this romantic idealist placed so heavy a responsibility upon the family was striking evidence of his confidence in its stability and power. Such confidence was not, however, entirely consistent with Bushnell's nagging suspicion that the individualism of the mass society had seriously weakened the family.[5]

Similar ambiguities were apparent in discussions of the respective roles of the members of the family. Bernard Wishy has noted that as the authority of the father as head of the family weakened, the mother's role as the central figure in the lives of the children became more prominent, with the result that writers on family life became uncertain as to where the prime emphasis should be placed. When they addressed books on family management to parents they emphasized the mother as the center of home life, but when the same authors wrote for children they depicted the father as the authoritative head of the family. Sensing the weakening of family bonds, they wavered between sentiment and discipline.[6] The children were quick to take advantage of this situation, with the result that they were often accused of insubordination and lack of reverence for their elders. Caroline Kirkland placed the blame squarely on the parents, who, in their scramble for wealth and social distinction had made over the "old-fashioned, fundamental, patriarchal, God-given idea of the household" into a democratic republic where all were free and equal. In this way, worldly objects replaced family values, and home life for children became merely a time of preparation rather than a priceless end in itself.[7]

THE LADY AND WOMEN'S RIGHTS

Gentry families shared the characteristics of the nuclear family, and in a sense idealized them by proclaiming the canons of gentility to be universal norms rather than the exclusive possession of a class. Because it failed to achieve a distinctive class character, gentry family life experienced the typical shrinkage of the nuclear family, in which many social activities were abandoned to the "outside world," while the family itself became a refuge from the world. The social emancipation of the lady during the nineteenth century was an integral aspect of the shrinkage of family life.

The British historian Wingfield-Stratford has observed that there could not be a fully developed concept of the gentleman without that of the lady as well. In Eastern societies, where women had always been held in strict subordination to men, there could emerge only a second-class gentleman.[8] The "compleat gentleman" required the full play of social intercourse between the sexes; in this respect gentility was always a domestic phenomenon. The lady as well as the gentleman must be free to exploit her talents as a cultural amateur. The very notion of gentility or gentleness had to be nourished by a respectful and appreciative attitude toward women. This development did not come to full maturity before the nineteenth century, and in the United States it flourished only briefly at the end of the century.

In its earlier formulations the code of gentility focused

almost exclusively on the gentleman. The lady defined as one who rendered service to a queen or princess—one of the original meanings of the word—may have existed as early as the gentlemanly courtier, but as a social type she was less a person in her own right than a complementary figure to the gentleman. This reflected the universal subordination of women to men in Western culture prior to modern times. Only in the early nineteenth century did the lady begin to command attention in her own right apart from the gentleman.

Two phases can be distinguished in the social evolution of the lady. Prior to the end of the eighteenth century she remained subordinate to the gentleman, with scarcely an identity of her own apart from her status as a member of the gentleman's family. As the object for the exercise of the gentlemanly qualities of courtesy, kindliness, and benevolence she was supposed to display the corresponding virtues of submissiveness, discretion, and purity of character and conduct. Her principal function was to manage the gentleman's household and rear his children. The spinster was an unhappy figure, condemned to remain in the home of father or brother and perform semimenial tasks. The strictly observed division of labor between gentleman and lady was in fact a form of segregation which, although it preserved her status, placed the lady under restraints which required a century of strenuous efforts to throw off. Even as late as the 1830s, Tocqueville noted that in America the spheres of action allotted to the respective sexes were more clearly marked than in any other country.[9]

As long as the old colonial gentry constituted a social class, the lady's domestic role was underscored by strong feelings of the importance of family status and continuity. A gentleman concerned with perpetuating his name and family would naturally choose as his lady one who showed promise of being a good breeder, and who was herself socially well connected. Later, in the nineteenth century, the social-economic elite showed some tendency to perpetuate the older subordination of ladies in fashionable society. A finishing-school education was long deeméd sufficient for the young ladies of fashionable society. Similarly, in the antebellum South, where the old gentry class resisted the disintegration into functional elites which occurred elsewhere, the same tendency to perpetuate the subordination of ladies was observed. The southern lady managed the household and graced the drawing room, and if, as Josiah Quincy discovered, she proved to be surprisingly knowledgeable in the realm of public affairs, it was doubtless because she identified herself so completely with her husband's interests.[10]

The second phase of the lady's transformation began with the nineteenth-century separation of the gentry from the social-economic elite. This was an event of great importance for women, for it fixed the course of the social emancipation first of the lady and then of all women. When the new gentry became separated from the rich and fashionable, the lady began the process of establishing her own identity as something more than a mere foil for the gentleman. Her independence resulted in part from activities other than those of wife and mistress of the gentleman's household. The lady became successively a writer, teacher, public speaker, and social reformer. The social emancipation of women was doubtless decreed by all the complex forces of modern industrial civilization. But the pattern which the process was to take, and the values and expectations of the emancipated woman, were determined by the traditions and interests of the nineteenth-century lady. It was she who set out to deliberately embody the qualities which would make the world a better, more kindly, more wholesome, and more humane place through her influence. She then undertook to bequeath these characteristics to all women. Consequently, the spirit and the objectives of the larger movement for women's emancipation at the end of the nineteenth century were profoundly influenced by earlier definitions of the lady and her role in society.

The emancipation of women is usually understood in terms of the greater economic opportunities of urban civilization. Thus, according to David M. Potter,[11] the modern city emancipated women by presenting them with a variety of economic and social opportunities. Cities, however, have existed since earliest antiquity without emancipating their women; and women's industrial employment may be a far cry from emancipation, as any sweatshop employee would testify. In order to understand the emancipation of women it is necessary to recognize the emerging conception of womanhood as something of independent social value. This idea developed out of the social evolution of the lady, at a time when class distinctions and traditional family styles were breaking down. The nuclear

family characteristic of the mass society helped to emancipate the lady of the gentry elite, who in turn provided the
essential model for the emancipated woman.

The nineteenth-century nuclear family played a crucial
role in the historical development which led from the gentleman's lady to the modern emancipated woman. In a
world of social flux and rapid change, immense emotional
energies were invested in the celebration and defense of
the American home. Catharine Beecher claimed to be
privy to the Creator's intention that every man should
marry and raise a family. Thus the race would be perpetuated and the young trained in an atmosphere of self-
sacrificing labor and love.[12] The presiding genius, or
rather the guardian angel, of the home was the wife and
mother. If she performed her sacred duties effectively, she
could confidently send forth her menfolk into the world
secure from its dangers and temptations. For "their hearts
will be at home, where their treasure is; and they will re-
joice to return to its sanctuary of rest, there to refresh
their weary spirits, and renew their strength for the toils
and conflicts of life." [13]

The duties of the home were woman's paramount responsibility. If she neglected them by involving herself in
outside activities she was deserting the station to which
God and nature had assigned her. Let her recall that she
could serve the great interests of humanity far more effectively by supervising her own household than in any other
way. "In this age of excitement," warned Mrs. A. J. Graves,
"it is especially incumbent upon woman to exert her ut-
most influence, to maintain unimpaired the sacredness

and power of the family institution." [14] These admonitions were so widely respected that when Nathaniel P. Willis returned from a visit to London he remarked that the domestic restraints imposed on American married women were a serious obstacle to the formation of a cultivated and sophisticated society. The domestic seclusion of young married women—a "confinement" far more prolonged than pregnancy—had the practical consequence of remanding formal social life to young girls. The principal sufferers from this unnatural state of affairs were the young men, who were deprived of enlightening social contacts with older married women. What was missing from American society was the continuity between generations which could only be furnished, in Willis's opinion, by cultivated middle-aged women.[15] This was a specialized instance of the discontinuity between generations inherent in the nuclear family itself.

Let no one deceive himself into assuming that the woman who restricted herself to domestic duties was condemned to a life of drudgery. She could well be "the enlightened instructor and guide of awakening minds, her husband's counsellor, the guardian and purifier of the morals of her household." Her functions required great knowledge and skill, embracing as they did aesthetics, economics, ethics, labor relations, health care, education, and pediatrics. Such responsibilities justified a whole university organized exclusively to serve the particular needs of women, and Catharine Beecher labored heroically for forty years to bring such an institution into being.[16]

Opponents of women's rights generally took the position that women were different from men: they possessed a milder and gentler nature unsuited to activities outside the domestic circle. The complementary natures of the two sexes supported the family and assured its success. Our sympathy with the women in their struggle for independence often obscures the fact that many nineteenth-century women shared these views. Even Catharine Sedgwick, who emphatically repudiated them and urged women to achieve independence through education, nevertheless conceded that it would not be to their advantage to encroach upon male activities. She could not believe that women were destined to lead armies, serve in legislatures, vote, or sit on the judicial bench. "The work that is done quietly, and in seclusion, is as important as that which is manifested by collision and noise." The mother at home was the ultimate molder of male character; and the world would be a better place when men freely sought the counsel of educated and public-spirited women. This should be accomplishment enough to satisfy any woman.[17] The restriction of women to the domestic role had at least one unexpected consequence. While husbands occupied themselves outside the home with business, politics, and other practical affairs, their wives were free to cultivate the intellectual interests and tastes of their children. In a free society, it was constantly reiterated, every male child was a potential statesman, and they all would become active citizens. In order to accomplish her educational mission the mother must herself be well informed, well read, and in touch with the latest developments in science and the arts. "Out of all this fulness of knowledge she should com-

municate freely to her children, and labor by her conversation gently to draw her husband away from his contracted
sphere of thought, to enter with her upon a more extended field of observation and reflection." [18] In short,
while men devoted themselves to coarse, material matters,
women should cultivate the finer things of life. The segre-
gated female was thus able to dignify and ennoble her role
by accumulating about it all the familiar romantic and
sentimental associations of the nineteenth-century home
and mother. The lady's principal task was now defined
for her. Just as the gentleman attempted to articulate and
dignify the values of a democratic society, the lady sought
to elevate women and extol their cultural role. This educational objective accounted for the hortatory tone of the
flood of writings which she addressed to her sisters during
the course of the century. As the historian Barbara Cross
later observed, from Catharine Beecher in the 1830s to
M. Carey Thomas in the 1930s women were constantly
exhorting each other to foster and perpetuate high culture.[19]

Gentlemen commonly shared these sentiments with the
ladies, no doubt sincerely, even if we grant the relevance
of Andrew Sinclair's observation that such views were a
convenient substitute for justice and tended to perpetuate
women's inferior status.[20] Many men may have been inclined to agree with John Randolph of Roanoke that the
measure of liberty enjoyed by French women was both
the cause and consequence of the indifference of French
men. According to this view, if women were to leave their
own sphere they would jeopardize both their privileges

and their attractions.[21] In any event, the romantic image of woman as more refined, purer, higher, and more delicate was potent and relevant because the age demanded an antidote to the expansive and divisive social forces at work in American society.

The free society with its pervasive ideological rationalizations interacted with the tradition of gentility to produce the distinctively American images of the natural gentleman and the natural lady. The latter was the ideal figure who presided over the nuclear family. During the nineteenth century a vast literature traced and embellished her distinctive traits. As the stereotype became widely recognized and accepted women inevitably modeled themselves upon it, while men appreciated in their womenfolk approximations to the ideal type. In both fiction and autobiographical reminiscences were to be found countless portraits of the natural ladies who hallowed their homes and left their children with grateful memories.

The nuclear family was not only a highly vulnerable institution; it had the further disadvantage of making no satisfactory provision for unmarried women. It may be for that very reason that a higher proportion of Americans of both sexes marry than in other western countries,[22] but certain social circles have at times contained numerous unmarried females. During the westward movement, the young women of gentry families in the eastern seaboard states often failed to find suitable husbands, and for such spinsters the problem of personal or occupational security was a pressing one. Since the rearing of the young had been women's traditional occupation, the obvious career for the unmarried woman was that of teacher or nurse-maid. Catharine Beecher believed that the school should be an extension of the family, governed by the same principles of self-sacrificing labor and love. Unfortunately, training in pedagogical science was as unavailable as training in domestic science. What was needed was a good women's university where literary and occupational training would both be provided.[23] Opening her own school for girls in Hartford in 1824, and later another in Cincinnati, Miss Beecher lived to see higher education for women firmly established in the post–Civil War era.

The lady's first major step toward independence of the gentleman was to establish herself in the role of writer. A principal virtue of writing was that it could be done in the privacy of the lady's chamber where no one need see her engaged in so unladylike a pursuit. Mercy Otis Warren, whose patriotic verses later won her the honorary title of poetess laureate of the Revolution, encountered much disapproval for activity felt to be unbecoming to her sex.[24] Perhaps the first American woman to earn her living by writing was Hannah Adams, historian and anthologist, who died in 1831. She is said to have been the first woman to use the Boston Athenaeum for research, and for many years she was the only one.[25] But fiction quickly proved to be the most successful medium for the female writer. British sentimental novels of the eighteenth century provided the models, and the rapid growth of the literate mass furnished the consumers of the literary product.[26] By the middle of the century, four-fifths of the hard-core reading public were women, while those who provided the reading material for this public were clearly playing leading roles in the development of a mass culture. Successful writers like Catharine M. Sedgwick, Sarah J. Hale, and Harriet Beecher Stowe had a strong sense of their cultural responsibilities. Although ostensibly the lady addressed her reader as one woman to another, the prevailing tone and perspective of her work revealed her gentry affiliation and educational purpose.

The principal theme of the vast outpouring of sentimental fiction which fed the mid-nineteenth-century mass market was the broken home and the hardships of the children orphaned by it. The family depicted in this fiction was the nuclear family, precariously dependent on the continuity of a marriage. The inevitable trick of malign fate that broke the marriage, destroyed the home, and orphaned the children was the most heartbreaking tragedy conceivable.[27] The uneasiness revealed by this obsession with domestic insecurity was but one symptom of the more pervasive gentry concern with the instability of the mass society.

Speaking in public, seemingly a trivial matter in itself, represented another step toward social emancipation because it symbolized repudiation of the lady's traditionally passive and secluded role. If she were going to behave shamelessly it might as well be in a good if controversial cause; the earliest acts of self-assertion often occurred in connection with antislavery or women's rights activities. The social affiliations of the lady in question usually determined the degree of radicalism implied in public speaking. For Quaker ladies with their peculiar tradition of

female involvement, the act was less challenging than for
a woman like Julia Ward Howe, who risked the disapproval and ridicule of her fashionable friends and whose
own husband, staunch reformer though he was, attempted
to discourage what he must have felt to be an act detri-
mental to worthy causes.[28]

The popular doctrine of woman's superior moral refinement and sensitivity may well have served as a rationalization of her social subordination, but it also had another
and quite different effect. If indeed her moral perceptions
were keener than those of men, should she not be more
sensitive to the injustices and inhumanities that stained
the face of American life? How else is one to account for
the active leadership of women in the great reform causes
of the day? Women must have believed what was being
said about them, and set out to behave in a manner consistent with their public character. Within the space of a
few decades women occupied prominent places in such
reform movements as antislavery, temperance, prison reform, pacifism, legal reform, and education. Among the
women, it was the ladies who took the lead in these activities, their sense of propriety and dignity giving to the
reform movements a restrained and accommodating character.[29]

It was inevitable that in the various victims of discrimination and injustice women should recognize themselves,
and should launch a determined drive to eliminate the
legal discriminations against married women which prevailed in most states. The pioneer champions of women's
rights had to proceed cautiously in order to avoid the

appearance of challenging the integrity of home life. The sentimentality surrounding the home, combined with fears for its safety, produced a protective loyalty to home life to which even the most vigorously assertive advocates of women's rights had to bow. The traditional subordination of the lady to the domestic functions assigned to her was certainly a handicap to emancipation, but it was not to be denied. The strategy of the pioneers of women's rights was not to repudiate the domestic role but to find a way to transcend it. Rather than attack the family their first objective was to realize the full potentialities of women within it. They could capitalize on the sentimentalization of the wife and mother by stressing the perfection of her domestic traits. They were themselves married women for the most part, and it would not have occurred to them to question the morality and pieties of monogamy, of which they were notable exemplars. (The notorious Fanny Wright and Victoria Woodhull were scandalous exceptions, whose antics were a source of embarrassment and mortification to the responsible women's rights leaders.) It was appropriate that the first organized drive for women's rights should focus on legal discriminations against married women. Underlying the movement was the assumption that when a married woman achieved legal recognition of her rights as a person, she would no longer be a vassal to her husband, and would be free to play the conjugal role with greater dignity and assurance.

The first step, then, toward emancipation was to exploit the sentimental stereotypes of the home already prevalent. "Home is the empire, the throne of woman," as a gift book published in 1844 put it.[30] Woman might be physically weaker than man, admitted Sarah J. Hale, but she was stronger morally, and this strength was enhanced, like steam in the cylinder, by confinement in the home. Caroline Kirkland affirmed that even though she remained at home, eschewing commerce and politics, woman "by cultivating every faculty" was drawing into her hands immense powers. By venturing out into the world she would risk the dispersion of these powers. While such traditional institutions as class, church, and stable community life crumbled under the impact of the mass society Americans fell back upon the home as their last refuge and support.

Working within this tradition but vigorously repudiating its morbid sentimentalism were such healthy-minded reformers as Catharine E. Beecher and Julia Ward Howe. Lyman Beecher's daughter went about the country tirelessly expounding the principles of the new "domestic science" of home management—a complicated subject in times when there were few appliances and no packaging. Ranging from food, hygiene, and exercise to costs, domestic manners, and the management of servants, Miss Beecher sought to rationalize the functions of the homemaker, thereby dignifying and elevating them. The practical dividends of mastering domestic science were spelled out by Mrs. Howe. Every woman of reasonable intelligence, she insisted, should be able to manage her household and still have time left over for the higher things of life. If three hours daily were available one could study art, literature, and philosophy. If one hour, philosophy or a foreign language. If only fifteen minutes, one could still read the Bible with commentary plus a verse or two of the best poetry. With such opportunities available, the household was indeed "a kingdom in little, and its queen, if she is faithful, gentle, and wise, is a sovereign indeed." [31]

The drive for legal rights produced such satisfying results that after the Civil War Catharine Beecher advised women to forget about suffrage and concentrate on securing laws like the New York married woman's property act of 1848, which tipped the traditional balance in women's favor: what was the husband's was now also the wife's; but what was hers was no longer his. Miss Beecher was taking a long step into the twentieth century.[32]

The ladies who had provided the pioneer leadership in the struggle to secure a larger scope for the independent activities of women and who had fixed the moderate, dignified tone of the movement were unable to maintain control over it. A second generation of leaders, more militant and less respectful of the ideals of the lady, introduced the principles of feminism. As the word itself suggested, feminism (i.e., womanism) was a forceful assertion of the interests and aspirations of all women. It may have grown out of the activities of ladies, but as it developed it belligerently rejected the tradition of gentility in the name of equality and independence for women.

The lady had never challenged the traditional social role ascribed to sex. She had always believed that her sex determined her distinctive social qualities as mother and homemaker, and as the patroness of morality, delicacy, and ideality. She celebrated marriage as the institutional setting in which her most important and most suitable role was played; and she regarded divorce as a deplorable if not scandalous confession of failure. Feminists, on the other hand, vigorously repudiated the sexually prescribed social role. They strenuously insisted that there were no significant distinctions between men and women except the biological. For convenience's sake there might be a practical division of labor, perpetuated in part by traditional male dominance, but there was nothing in the nature of womanhood to justify such a division. Let sex be reduced to its biological essentials: procreation and pleasure. The bloomer and other adaptations of male attire were visual symbols of this drive to minimize social distinctions between the sexes. The feminist attitude toward marriage was at best ambiguous. Marriage and family responsibilities were options to be weighed without prejudice against other career alternatives. Marriage must be compatible with feminine freedom, and divorce must be available without stigma. The new feminism was epitomized by Victoria Woodhull, with her free sexual life and her confident invasion of the masculine world of publishing and finance. Historically, the possibilities of emancipation were first suggested by the ladies, but the forms which emancipation was to take in the twentieth century were largely determined by the feminists.

The "New Woman" of the turn of the century was to be a blend of the feminist and the lady. The same processes of diffusion and attenuation that spelled the demise of the gentleman were also apparent in her. Women of the upwardly mobile middle mass seized upon the convenient mixture of freedom and style to produce a new social type.

At least some among the last surviving generation of

gentlemen were not favorably impressed with the social qualities of the new woman. Robert Grant, a Boston jurist and novelist, penned a bitter fictional portrait of her in a now-forgotten novel, *Unleavened Bread* (1900). As a probate judge for thirty years, Grant had ample opportunity to observe the emergence of the new woman in the context of changing patterns of family life. A member of the overlapping sector of elites with firm connections in fashionable, political, and intellectual circles, Grant observed mass mobility with characteristic distaste. The central concern of his novel was upward social mobility in America, making it a companion piece to William Allen White's *A Certain Rich Man,* Dreiser's *The Financier,* and Robert Herrick's *Memoirs of an American Citizen.* Grant found that the new woman was as likely as a man to contract the disease of social ambition. The appalling thing about his central character, Selma White, was that her ambition did not focus on any fixed or ultimate objective. It grew from moment to moment, attaching itself to more lofty goals as her opportunities enlarged. It was pure ambition unalloyed with particular purposes, hence its repulsiveness. In the course of the pursuit of her ambitions she used and destroyed a succession of well-meaning men who were unlucky enough to cross her path.

Selma was wholly unaware of her evil nature. She was proudly conscious of being the new American woman, dignified by her rights, smug in her high responsibilities to beautify the city, to clean up politics, to elevate the tone of cultural life, to enrich home life. Because she was wholly unprepared to accomplish any of these objectives, she easily confused her personal ambition with worthy social ends. Grant knew, of course, that such destructively selfish creatures could appear anywhere, but he insisted that the specific forms of evil were peculiarly American. The men had engrossed themselves so exclusively in business that women had rushed in to fill the cultural vacuum. Ambition and envy, the motivating forces of mobility, made unqualified women resentful of their superiors, and turned them into unconscious hypocrites.[33]

One of the major objectives of the Progressive movement at the turn of the century was to complete the process of the emancipation of women. In fairness to Grant, it should be noted that he wrote at a time when the process was still far from complete. Legal equality had been achieved, but the status and role of women were not yet so redefined as to give satisfying meaning to equality. The history of women in America has some similarity to the history of Negroes. Each step toward true equality uncovered a new and more subtle form of discrimination. This discovery was so frustrating as to make one forget that real progress had been achieved. The new woman was like the robber-baron of the Gilded Age who muscled his way through the business world with impunity because public and private rights were so ill-defined. She was making a shambles of social life because she had not yet learned how to make constructive use of her newly won freedom, and because she resented the discovery that freedom in itself was of little value without useful and satisfying roles to play.

As a probate judge, Grant had been in intimate contact

with those aspects of family life that involved the law. With the coming of a mass society and the disappearance of social classes the family remained the principal institution for social stability. Countless Americans had sensed this fact, and had erected around the family elaborate defenses of sentiment, precept, and religion. The chief object of the nuclear family in the mass society was to prepare the children for independent careers of upward mobility. To provide the necessary "inner direction," a blend of discipline and freedom had to be provided in the home. The father was the legal owner of his minor children, while the mother furnished a tender refuge from the rigors of the law. As the bonds of the family were steadily loosened during the nineteenth century, the growth of personal freedom occurred largely at the expense of the father. During Grant's tenure on the bench the courts had tended increasingly to settle custody cases in terms of what was found to be the "best interests" of the child, rather than respecting the traditional rights of the father. At the same time, the rapidly rising divorce rate (one divorce for every nine marriages by 1916) furnished ample evidence that the family would survive only at the pleasure of the spouses. Grant foresaw a matrilocal family composed of mother and minor children through which a succession of husbands flowed, a situation he characterized caustically as "the nationalization of husbands." [34] The family may have been an institution of central importance to the mass society, but it was also proving to be one of the most vulnerable.

Unleavened Bread also touched upon the issue of culture conflict in the mass society. Nineteenth-century America produced its own literate-mass culture of newspapers, dime novels, saloons, sports, songs, and gossip. Increasingly commercialized, mass culture was purveyed by a largely anonymous elite of producers who were essentially entrepreneurs. The traditional high culture continued to flourish in its cultivated but narrow circle; while the old pre-literate folk culture of voice and ear was steadily pressed back into regional and ethnic backwaters and enclaves of the elderly and the very young, where it slowly began to wither away. The conflict between mass culture and high culture was expressed in the mass contempt for the kind of specialized and refined aesthetic standards maintained by high culture. Grant's fictional midwestern city of Benham was depicted as the site of an ongoing conflict between a coarse and tasteless mass culture and a nascent, struggling high culture that was supported by a small but influential alliance of elite groups. As the city grew in size and wealth its cultural ambitions expanded accordingly, New York architects who had been trained at the Ecôle des Beaux-Arts being imported to design the business buildings and pretentious residences that were springing up.

Under the prevailing conditions of rapid growth and mobility the simple distinction between mass culture and high culture proved inadequate to describe the complexities of the cultural situation. There were vaguely defined cultural levels analogous to social stratification levels, but "cultural mobility" analogous to social mobility obscured the boundaries between levels. A crude method of coping with this situation is provided by the introduction of an intermediate cultural level, designated by Edward Shils as "mediocre culture," or by Dwight Macdonald as "midcult." [35] A distinctive feature of the middle cultural level was its emulation of the forms of high culture. Whether in music, art, literature, religion or other areas of high cultural activity each form had a corresponding expression at the middle cultural level. These were, however, cheap imitations at best. Just as the upwardly mobile mass man aspired to status in the social-economic elite, creative individuals aspired to high cultural achievement and status in the cultural elite. Unfortunately, many lacked the talent to succeed; others were corrupted by the much larger financial rewards of the commercialized mid-cultural market. Many forces in the mass society conspired to bring about this corrupting effect, often in ways of which the creative person was wholly unaware.

One of the first to comment on this development had been E. L. Godkin, editor of the *New York Nation,* the principal organ of gentry opinion. Reflecting contemptuously on the sordid Beecher-Tilton scandal in 1874, Godkin called attention to the emergence of what he called a "chromo-civilization," a cheap imitation of the real thing, symbolized by the chromo-lithographs of Currier and Ives. A flood of newspapers, fiction, lyceum lectures, and freshwater colleges had diffused a thin veneer of sophistication over a large number of people who now presumed themselves cultured and capable of new solutions to the perennial problems of religion, morals, and social relations. Ignoring traditions and the wisdom of the past they were running off after their own false prophets and reducing society to chaos.[36]

Selma White's cultural ambitions paralleled her social aspirations, and were equally vulgar and destructive. She had commenced at the bottom, culturally speaking, at a women's club luncheon where the entertainment was furnished by a young woman who whistled, an accomplishment that Selma found highly edifying. Going on to higher things, she was soon advising the architect Wilbur Littleton to design the kind of tasteless, eclectic buildings that would appeal to Benham's wealthy clients. Littleton, who was dedicated to high standards, was literally driven to his death in the futile attempt to reconcile her demands with his own artistic ideals.

The absence of taste was the central deficiency of the middle culture as Grant analyzed it. An instinctive preference for the gaudy and pretentious would be defended by a contemptuous rejection of the criteria by which high cultural authority was identified and standards maintained. Here the covert conflict between mass and high culture became open and explicit. Although the middle culture professed to emulate the standards of high culture, in fact it despised them. Much was made by Grant of the function of patriotism as an unconscious device for asserting the authority of mass tastes and preferences. Mass taste was best because it was American; to question it was unpatriotic. This was especially aggravating to the gentry, whose cultural cosmopolitanism transcended national boundaries. Patriotism was easily made to justify provincialism.

But the most corrupting feature of the mass society was

its pervasive commercialism. Everyone wanted to make money. There was little comfort for the gentleman in recognizing that this was the necessary psychological precondition for a consumer-oriented society. Wilbur Littleton put his finger on the gentry dilemma when he remarked that the temptation to be avoided above all else was to sell oneself for money. One must be true to one's principles and standards even though it meant poverty. Admittedly, it was very difficult for a gentleman to discharge his traditional responsibilities (and thus be true to himself) without at least some money, and it was becoming ever more difficult. Nineteenth-century gentility had not been an economic phenomenon primarily, although it did presuppose an economic threshold. Earlier in the century, the threshold was readily surmounted by individuals possessed of the other essential gentlemanly attributes. Genteel poverty was a widely recognized if not highly honorable status. Wide disparities of wealth had been tolerated within gentry ranks.

A rather abrupt change in the economics of gentility which occurred at the end of the nineteenth century may be taken as a special case of Richard Hofstadter's "status revolution." [37] At this time it became increasingly difficult to ignore the universal commercialization of the mass society. Bronson Alcott's lordly contempt for earning a living was no longer relevant. Robert Grant addressed himself to this problem in 1895 in a series of magazine articles on how to live like a gentleman on $10,000 a year. A decade earlier the Grants had kept four good maids for total wages of $62 a month, with an annual family budget of between $6,500 and $7,500. Now, within the space of a decade, three amenities the gentry had previously taken for granted, servants, spacious housing, and superior private schooling for their children, were jeopardized by the rising cost of living. Grant could only counsel his friends to accept these deprivations with good grace, and to cultivate the art of plain living and high thinking. Caught between a rapidly growing social-economic elite of wealthy business and financial men on the one hand and a vulgar mass on the other, the gentry were rapidly being squeezed out.[38]

English civilization during the nineteenth century had managed to produce within its traditional class structure a gentry cultural elite that had been the country's crowning glory. Would American democratic society of the twentieth century be able to do as much? Robert Grant believed that the answer would be found in the disposition of the mass, which would inevitably create its own elites. Ominously, it had already produced a social-economic elite composed largely of stockbrokers, mere dignified gamblers with nothing but money to distinguish them. At the same time, the mass was destroying gentility, and Grant was willing to concede that perhaps it was just as well. And yet there must be a high-cultural elite of some kind if there were to be a civilization worthy of the name. Would the mass honor and reward it, or abuse and strangle it? This was to be the great question for the twentieth century.

CLUBS

To the extent that it functioned as a refuge from the world, the nuclear family was unsuited to the social needs of gentility. The salons and country houses which served the social and cultural needs of the continental and British gentries never developed in America. N. P. Willis's dream of an "after-growth" of fashionable society in which talented and refined ladies and gentlemen would come together without pomp and ceremony never materialized in New York, even though the talent was there, waiting to be gathered. The qualified and accommodating hosts who alone could have made such a society possible rarely came forward, notable exceptions being George Ticknor and James T. and Annie Fields in Boston, or, later in the century, Dr. J. G. Holland and Mrs. Vincenzo Botta in New York.[39] The gentlemen were consequently driven out of their homes in search of a more satisfying social life.

In the cities where the gentry congregated in sufficient numbers, clubs became the social centers of nineteenth-century gentry culture. These were usually dinner or supper clubs restricted to the male sex, and as such were hardly an adequate substitute for the salon. The earlier clubs provided a convenient meeting ground for the overlapping interests of social-economic and gentry elites. Here the differences in life styles of the two groups could be minimized.

Between 1836 and 1844 a representative gentry group including Emerson, Alcott, Theodore Parker, and Frederick H. Hedge had been meeting informally in one another's homes for "Symposia," discussions of scholarly and philosophical topics. When Emerson visited England in 1847–1848 he discovered the immensely superior style of British gentry social life. He reported enviously: "They have carried the art of agreeable sensations to a wonderful pitch; they know everything, have everything; they are rich, plain, polite, proud, and admirable, but, though good for them, it ends in the using." He was determined that the gentry of Boston should enjoy similar amenities, and he proposed to his friend Samuel Gray Ward a Town and Country Club, where scholars and poets of Concord and Cambridge could meet men of affairs in circumstances of ease and refinement in the metropolis. Ward was a broker with good social connections. He had traveled in Europe with Ticknor and enjoyed wide contact with the gentry and social elites.[40]

The Town and Country Club, organized in 1849, quickly proved too ponderous and too ambitious to realize the Emersonian objective. Fifty-seven distinguished Bostonians attended the organization meeting and promptly fell into a dispute over the proper blend of social and intellectual ingredients. Since the principal purpose was to hear papers presented by members, it seemed inappropriate to some to restrict the membership to gentlemen. William Lloyd Garrison, Thomas Wentworth Higginson, and James Freeman Clarke argued for the eligibility of women; and Garrison, for blacks as well. Emerson had no objection to a clubable black, but he drew the line at making the club "a saloon for ladies." Parker further pointed out that some members might wish to smoke, which of course would be impossible in the presence of ladies. Perhaps the clinching argument against women was offered by Elizur Wright, who observed that to admit women might create jealousy among those members' wives not invited to join. By vote of thirty to twelve, a motion to make women eligible for membership was defeated. Blacks were made eligible by an agreement to interpret the constitutional term "men" to include men of all races. Ambitious plans for permanent club rooms, a library, and a café quickly proved to be beyond the means of the eighty-one members. Attendance at monthly meetings rapidly dwindled; and within a year the club was dead.[41]

A few years later, in 1855, Horatio Woodman, a Boston lawyer, revived the plans of Emerson and Ward on a more modest but durable scale. The Saturday Club was to be a private affair with a small, carefully selected membership drawn from the intellectual and commercial elites. A lighter note would be sounded, with no papers or formal discussions. The principal criterion for membership—aside from civilized interests, which were taken for granted—was to be "clubability," the happy combination of qualities that made a man good company. Emerson himself, according to Richard Henry Dana, Jr., was eminently clubable: "Emerson is an excellent dinner-table man, always a gentleman, never bores, or preaches, or dictates, but drops and takes up topics very agreeably, and has even skill and tact in managing his conversation." Alcott, on the other hand, despite his formidable conversational powers, was too ponderous and pontifical, and Ward had to maneuver adroitly to circumvent Emerson's wish to include him.[42]

The club met on the last Saturday of each month, at 3:00 P.M., at the Albion Hotel (later at the Parker House), for a seven-course dinner washed down with sherry, sauterne, and claret. The original eleven members, in addition to Woodman, Ward, and Emerson, included Dana, Louis Agassiz, John Sullivan Dwight, Ebenezer R. Hoar, James Russell Lowell, John Lothrop Motley, Benjamin Peirce, and Edwin P. Whipple. Subsequent additions to the membership included many other prominent names of the New England Renaissance, together with such leaders of the social-economic elite as John Murray Forbes, Thomas Gold Appleton, and Martin Brimmer. The club had no formal organization, no speeches, and rarely even a general conversation. Agassiz always sat at the head of the table, apparently by virtue of his immense vitality and good fellowship —"fat and plenteous as some successful politician" was Emerson's admiring characterization. Agassiz fully satisfied the Emersonian conception of gentility with his capacity to meet peasant, mechanic, or fine gentleman with equal propriety.[43] The staid old New England culture now had its own agreeable sensations which ended in the using.

The success of the Saturday Club inspired a host of imitators. There appeared, inevitably, a Friday Club, a Thursday Club, and a Wednesday Club. Among the more distinguished was The Club, also a dinner and conversation society, organized in 1868. Its original membership of fourteen included Henry and William James, Henry Adams, Oliver Wendell Holmes, Jr., William Dean Howells, John Fiske, and Thomas Sergeant Perry. In Moorfield Storey's carefully understated opinion it produced the best conversation in Boston.[44]

The overlap of economic and gentry elites was more extensive in Boston than in other seaboard cities, and several clubs managed to combine representatives of both groups in their membership. It was Emerson who proposed John Murray Forbes, the railroad builder, for the Saturday Club, and the mutual admiration of the two men was cemented in the marriage of their children. Agassiz and Longfellow each made second marriages into the economic elite. Such alliances helped delay the two groups' tendency to draw apart, a tendency which by the end of the century was nevertheless apparent to all. While the social-economic elite became ever more self-assured and powerful, gentility dwindled away into ineffectuality. In the end, club life reflected this divergence, each club being identified primarily with one group or the other.[45]

In New York, the Sketch Club, inspired by Irving, and Cooper's Bread and Cheese Club furnished the precedents for the considerable number of gentry clubs which appeared during the course of the century. The most influential was the Century Club, founded in 1847 by Lewis Gaylord Clark, the publisher, and Frederick S. Cozzens, a merchant. Its object was to promote "the cultivation of a taste for letters and the arts and social enjoyment." In addition to such prominent writers, artists, and professionals as William Cullen Bryant, Ashur B. Durand, Henry W. Bellows, Parke Godwin, Edwin Booth, and David Dudley Field, the membership included John Jacob Astor, A. T. Stewart, the merchant, and David D. Colden. During the post–Civil War period it was, according to Henry Holt, the most active center of culture in New York. The National Academy of Design, the Metropolitan Museum of Art, and the American Museum of Natural History all had their origins in discussions at the Century

Club. Virtually everyone of distinction in literature, art, or science was a member.[46]

Because the commercial and professional element in Washington was small, and the city had no deep cultural roots of its own, the club movement came late, and never flourished. The outstanding club was the Cosmos Club, founded in 1878 by a group of scientists employed in government bureaus. Among the nonscientific members were Henry Adams, Thomas Nelson Page, Ward Thoron, the banker, and Levi Leiter, a Marshall Field partner. The club never attempted to attract the social elite, who congregated at the Metropolitan Club; nor, surprisingly enough, did it attempt to bridge the gulf between culture and politics. The distinguished geologist G. K. Gilbert candidly admitted that the standards of clubability applied to applicants from the sciences were never as rigorous as those applied to nonscientists. The scientists would thus profit, hopefully, from the civilizing influences emanating from the nonscientific members. "Our own outlook has been broadened," Gilbert concluded, "our angles have been rounded, our conceit has been moderated, and in general we have been humanized by the good society we have enjoyed." [47] Whenever clubs functioned in this fashion they were one of the effective means for the dissemination of gentility.

THE ACADEMY

Clubs represented local and spontaneous responses to the need for fellowship, but they were of little value in promoting the claims of gentility to the respect and support of the community at large. For this purpose some other kind of organization was necessary, and no satisfactory solution was ever found. The colleges were probably the most effective instruments for the dissemination of gentry culture, but the colleges were too scattered and, in the end, too weak and sensitive to local pressures to resist the imperious claims of mass culture. High culture in several European countries was supported officially through national or royal academies for the arts and sciences, membership in which was a great honor reserved for the most distinguished intellectuals. Certain Americans eyed these academies enviously as devices for strengthening and preserving cultural traditions threatened by vulgar innovations. A local precedent was furnished in 1863, when Congress incorporated the National Academy of Sciences for the immediate purpose of mobilizing the scientific community for more effective support of the Union war effort. In the following year, Charles Sumner introduced in the Senate simultaneous bills providing for the incorporation of a National Academy of Literature and Art, and a National Academy of Moral and Political Sciences. Each body was to consist of fifty self-perpetuating and self-governing members named in the bills, and charged with the responsibility of promoting the arts and social sciences. The Senate, after hearing a few terse comments about creating "a close corporation of mutual admirers," conclusively tabled the proposals.[48]

It was perhaps an ironic symptom of the deterioration clouding his later years that Emerson, the great prophet of

individualism, should have been one of the active instiga-
tors of Sumner's bills. In concerting plans for the National
Academy of Literature and Art with Lowell, Holmes,
Dana, and George W. Curtis, Emerson wrote to Longfellow that the worthy objects of such an institution should
include (1) the conservation of the English language; (2)
judgment upon matters of taste and fitness in literature;
(3) the condemnation of frauds and pretenders.

> Custodians of sense and elegance—these colleagues are
> to be,—in literature. They would be the college of ex-
> perts, to which the Government might sometimes wish to
> refer questions touching Education, or historic forms or
> facts. They would perhaps suggest to the Government
> the establishment of prizes for literary competition. . . .
> We all agreed that the simple meeting of an Academy
> under the inspiration of national aims, would tend to
> quicken the power and ennoble the aims of all the
> members.[49]

The matter was raised again four years later in the
columns of the *New York Nation*. This time it was proposed to organize an "Institute" with an affiliated network
of local academies for science, art, or literature. The principal object was to provide a means of communication for
intellectuals who, unlike tradesmen, manufacturers, or
politicians, all of whom had such organizations, were almost completely isolated from each other. Nothing was
said now about government sponsorship. Indeed, the open
hostility of the *Nation* to the trends of popular culture was
wholly incompatible with the idea of public sponsorship.
Its editors believed that the "mob spirit" counted too heav-

ily in the arts of America as well as in its politics, and they hoped that an Institute would end the tyranny over art and literature established by common schools and newspapers. It would accomplish this, hopefully, by infusing a philosophic spirit and enlightened will into the mass.[50] These discussions of the organization of gentry culture invariably took for granted the educational and disciplinary responsibilities of the gentry toward the mass.

When at last gentry culture did achieve organization on a national level it was already moribund, and the achievement was meaningless. The American Social Science Association, formed in the post–Civil War years for the purpose of representing the gentry point of view on social and public issues, took the initiative in 1898 to organize a National Institute of Arts and Letters, consisting of 150 (later 250) writers, artists, and composers. One of its leading spirits, Edmund Clarence Stedman, proposed the formation within the Institute of a smaller body which would represent the best achievements and exert the most desirable influence on American culture. The result was the American Academy of Arts and Letters, organized in 1904. The first academicians to be elected were William Dean Howells, Augustus St. Gaudens, Stedman, John LaFarge, Mark Twain, John Hay, and Edward MacDowell. A subsequent group included Henry James, the architect Charles Follen McKim, Henry Adams, Charles Eliot Norton, the sculptor J. Q. A. Ward, the critic Thomas R. Lounsbury, Theodore Roosevelt, and Thomas Bailey Aldrich. Founded at a moment when the tide of modernism was already beginning to engulf gentry culture the Academy proposed to foster the highest standards in a country dedicated to the average. John Hay told Robert Underwood Johnson that an academy was more necessary in a democracy than in an old-world monarchy because traditions and standards were weaker, and the arts and letters more subject to the tyranny of vogue. Johnson agreed that while the Academy should be democratic, it should stand firmly on the conviction that knowledge and experience should guide. Probably not all the academicians would have gone so far as to insist with Stedman that the Academy should enforce dignity in manners as well as in literary style, but the prevailing tone was certainly traditional and conservative. The earlier failure of gentry liberalism was now confirmed in the failure of genteel culture.[51]

WILLIAM DEAN HOWELLS

Among the more revealing gentry portrayals of American social life were those of the novelist William Dean Howells. The principles of literary realism of which Howells was a leading practitioner obligated the writer to describe the current scene as faithfully as possible. "Let fiction cease to lie about life; let it portray men and women as they are, actuated by the motives and the passions in the measure we all know." [52] The American writer would of course deal with American materials. His subjects would be plain, ordinary people, the six-sevenths of the population that constituted the mass. The realist's obligation was not simply one of accurate reporting. He also acknowledged a profound moral obligation to articulate the values and qualities of democratic society. This was the principle that chiefly distinguished the realists from the later naturalists. In a famous passage, Howells celebrated the civilization in which "there is no 'distinction' perceptible to the eye that loves and values it." The beauty and grandeur of American life were its "common" qualities, and the artist who would flourish in such a society must learn how to cultivate the common touch.[53]

Inevitably, realistic fiction would be in considerable measure autobiographical. Many of Howells's novels contained material based on personal experience, and the fictional characters were often portraits drawn from life. One of the novelist's friends cautioned that anyone who sought Howells's friendship must be prepared to be clapt into a book by the "novelist-photographer." [54] The writer himself should never pretend to write from any other point of view than his own. If he wrote very much he could not help but reveal his character and opinions to the reader. The realistic writer faithful to his principles was committed to the measure of accuracy and sympathetic detachment which, according to the handbooks of historical method, should make him an ideal eyewitness to the past. Much can be learned from Howells's novels about American society in the Gilded Age, as seen from the gentry point of view.

Two great facts, according to Howells, dominated American life in the postbellum decades: vertical social mobility, and sharp social stratification. Mobility and stratification were the warp and weft of American life. But they negated each other; and caught in the conflict between them

Howells's characters were either destroyed or ground down like pebbles on a rocky beach. A third element in Howells's sociology of the Gilded Age was the dramatic contrast between the small village and urban environments. Rural village society was homogeneous and socially unstratified, the home of the traditional moral and social virtues. A recurrent device of the novelist was to project the innocent and wholesome countryman, devoid of invidious social discriminations, into the big city environment and to witness there the inevitable awakening, which was always painful and sometimes tragic. The cities Howells knew and wrote about were Boston and New York. In them he found the abundant evidence of marked social stratification recorded in his novels.

The study of social stratification was the more intriguing because the dominant democratic ideology did not recognize or sanction social distinctions. On the contrary, it sponsored the popular mythology of upward social mobility and the self-made man. It assumed that ability and money would open all doors. The result was that privileged social groups were denied the legal distinctions and overt symbols of status that characterized the traditional classes of Europe. Forced to sustain themselves by their own efforts, without public support, social classes in America took on something of the character of private associations in which the members made the rules and controlled admission. The coterie in which acceptance was most sought after could afford to be the most exclusive.

A distinctive feature of the American stratification system has always been the absence of generally accepted terms of designation for its various status groups. Students who attempt to describe it systematically have been compelled to devise their own vocabulary. The exceptions to this generalization, so far as Howells was concerned, were to be found at either extreme of the stratification system. At the bottom of the scale were two clearly distinguishable "classes," servants and laborers. At the top of the scale was the social-economic elite, referred to by the novelist in its social aspect as "Society."

The latter term was an apt one in that members of Society dedicated themselves in extra measure to the cultivation of the arts of social intercourse. Society liked to think of itself not only as the class of the affluent, but as the principal bearers of the burden of culture, of moral and aesthetic refinement, and of intellectual interests. In Howells's day its members were building their mansions, endowing the libraries and art galleries, founding the symphony orchestras, and entertaining with a lavishness hitherto unknown. The gentry had been thrust aside, and American social processes were now clearly focused on the social-economic elite.

The members of Society were, as the term itself suggests, highly articulate. Whatever their other traits, they were able to verbalize their relationships and interests in subtle and minute degrees. The development and practice of this skill was their principal activity. The capacity for articulation is in some sense the essence of socialization. Society was the acme of the American social structure, not simply because its members were rich and powerful and self-satisfied but because they were free to cultivate the civilized arts of social intercourse as were no others. Howells often dramatized this fact by confronting members of Society with individuals from other social strata. These contacts were usually awkward and mortifying to the individual from the lower social stratum. The incommensurability of classes was a favorite theme.

The capacity to articulate was to give full expression to the personality. The novelist had only to allow the members of fashionable society to speak for themselves in order to display them adequately to the reader. Individuals from other strata lacked this capacity, and Howells generally respected their deficiency; he did not undertake to say for them what they could not say for themselves. Rather, he allowed character and motive to unfold with the action of the story itself. The Social class, then, realized itself fully in conversation, while the middle mass could only ease the burden of frustration by acting. Hence the dynamic and creative role of the American mass in social change. In Howells's novels inarticulate country people possessed a firmness of character that gave them rugged strength. They were inner-directed. Members of Society, on the other hand, tended to be flabby and ineffectual. They could talk around every subject and discharge their psychic energies in conversation. The tension between word and deed that ran through Howells's fictional portraits of the Gilded Age was soon to receive therapeutic treatment in Dewey's instrumentalism.

Money alone was not enough to qualify its possessor for admission to fashionable society. He must also have the requisite degree of social refinement. A recurrent theme with Howells concerned the painful abrasions suffered by the newly rich but socially untutored in their contacts with members of Society. As Howells saw it, the distinctive American tragedy was the bitter isolation and frustration that was the lot of the self-made man, the demigod of popular mythology, when as a result of his business success he renounced his lowly social origins only to find himself confronting a new social world that could not assimilate him even if it would.

Because a candid public admission of status differences was suppressed by the democratic ideology, "social anonymity" was a common phenomenon. People met one another not only as strangers personally but also socially. Their first problem was to identify each other socially. Identification was the key to the status situation, especially for Society. Acceptance by Society was gained through identification by a member in good standing, much as in admission to an exclusive club. Whenever an individual was moving outside his usual orbit the uncertainties of identification were pervasive. How should one treat the stranger: familiarly, as an equal? Condescendingly, as a social inferior? Or respectfully, as a superior? Members of Society were the most expert in making these discriminations, since a large part of their training had been devoted to detecting the little identifying signs of social status. Countrymen, on the other hand, were generaly oblivious of them. Howells was skillful in his choice of settings where the anonymous social encounter occurred. Railroad stations, transatlantic packets, summer resort hotels, and college campuses all furnished the public occasions when strangers were thrown together and presented with the necessity of establishing one another's social identity.

Between Society at the top of the scale and servants and laborers at the bottom was the great middle mass. If the mass is to be designated a middle class, as Henry Steele Commager has suggested,[55] it was certainly the most amorphous of classes. As portrayed by Howells it was little more than a temporary transitional stage between humble origins and anticipated admission to Society. It was a mere function of mobility, composed of men on the make. It was that portion of American society that eluded analysis in social class terms.

A striking characteristic of the upwardly mobile mass men in Howells's novels was their complete social isolation. They had no friends, and their lives were without significant social dimensions. They had a humble past, glowing aspirations for the future, but a singularly meager present. Surrounded by the members of their immediate families they were adrift on a social sea, like shipwrecked mariners on a raft. They knew their desired destination, but the reader knew that their chances of reaching it were highly uncertain. The contrast in Howells's work between the socially isolated mass man and the convivial member of fashionable society could not be more sharply drawn.

The novelist's feelings about the atrophied social condition of the mass were certainly ambiguous. He readily acknowledged that the restless energy and determination of the ambitious mass man had made America what it was; and he mercilessly exposed the effete indolence and snobbery of fashionable society. Nevertheless, the curse of social ambition exposed all the coarse vulgarity and ignorance of the social climber, who stood fully exposed to the scorn of the reader.

Howells anticipated the modern sociological dictum that the family is the basic unit of the social status system. Whatever the status of the head of the family, the other members assume that position and associate with other families of the same status. Howells's social novels were always family novels, concerned with the consequences of mobility for family relations. The isolation of the socially mobile family was caused by its detachment from its original social environment, often underscored by a change in place of residence. Those who proved to be less adaptable suffered the most. Although it has often been remarked that women are socially ambitious and stimulate social mobility, this was not Howells's view of the American woman. It was always the man who was ambitious, even when the ambition was for other members of his family. The woman was depicted as the homemaker. Her role was to provide domestic support for the more gregarious, predatory, mobile male. In *A Modern Instance,* the reprehensible bounder Bartley Hubbard abandoned his wife and child to pursue his private ambitions. The deserted wife was in turn befriended, ironically enough, by members of Boston's fashionable elite, who were not only genuinely touched by the woman's plight but who also knew that she would not presume on their friendship by making social demands. The relative stability of American family life was reflected in the clear division of functions between the spouses. Howells stubbornly refused to recognize the signs of family transformation that lay all about him. In a social world in which everything else was in flux the solidity of the family stood out in the novels as a rock in a weary land.

The peripheral status of the gentry was clearly apparent to Howells. Gentry intellectuals in his novels generally stood apart from the activities of other social groups. They were detached and mildly alienated observers of the American scene. It was through the eyes of journalists, artists, or clergymen that the action of the novel was often seen. Like that of the medieval clergy, the status of these gentry types gave them access to various social strata where they could observe and report events. By means of such a spokesman the novelist could move back and forth between mutually exclusive social circles. In *The Landlord of Lion's Head* the action was seen through the eyes of an artist who became interested in the career of the son of a country innkeeper. The artist could follow the boy to Harvard, chronicle his clumsy and abortive venture into Boston society, and finally escort him back to the inn, a sadder and wiser man. The most familiar example of the gentleman cast in the role of reporter was the journalist Basil March, a character who reappeared in several of Howells's novels and who was closely identified with the author himself. As a self-portrait, the character of March, with its blend of kindly condescension and ineffectuality, provides a revealing insight into the frustrations of the gentleman in the rough, bustling commercial civilization of the Gilded Age.

The close similarity between these fictional gentry spokesmen and Howells himself can hardly escape the reader's attention. Howells's own rise from printer's devil

to the honored role of dean of American letters exemplified
the peculiar kind of mobility available to the genteel intellectual. His realistic literary principles and his comprehensive democratic sympathies were an excellent embodiment
of the qualities of the gentry at their best. His sense of detachment was readily apparent in the remark that so far as
the novelist was a man of the world he was the less an artist; he was apparently of the classes and really of the
masses. It would have been difficult to put more succinctly
the ambiguities of the gentry status.

If social stratification set the stage on which men acted
in Howells's novels, social mobility furnished their motives
and patterns of action. A recurrent theme concerned the
rebuffs that beset the aggressive and energetic individual
who through ability and hard work was able to acquire
wealth and seek acceptance by the social-economic elite.
Such rejections were an ironic commentary on the popular
mythology of success. One of Howells's deepest convictions
was the belief that newly made money was morally corrupting to its possessor. Pride and arrogance were un-
leashed; people were pushed around and dealt with
unscrupulously. In view of the newly rich man's corruption the reader can find little sympathy for his frustrated
social ambitions. On the other hand, those characters who
acknowledged the objective reality of status differences
and were content with their own status were able to meet
the contingencies of life most successfully. Their outlook
and expectations conformed to reality. In Darwinian terms,
they were best adapted to the social environment.

In a familiar passage from *A Hazard of New Fortunes,*

Basil March described the moral deterioration that all too frequently accompanied the making of money:

> I don't believe a man's any better for having made money so easily and rapidly as Dryfoos has done, and I doubt if he's any wiser. I don't know just the point he's reached in his evolution from grub to beetle, but I do know that so far as it's gone the process must have involved a bewildering change of ideals and criterions. I guess he's come to despise a great many things that he once respected, and that intellectual ability is among them—what *we* call intellectual ability. He must have undergone a moral deterioration, an atrophy of the generous instincts, and I don't see why it shouldn't have reached his mental makeup. He has sharpened but he has narrowed; his sagacity has turned into suspicion, his caution to meanness, his courage to ferocity. That's the way I philosophize a man of Dryfoos's experience, and I am not very proud when I realize that such a man and his experience are the ideal and ambition of most Americans.[56]

And yet, in spite of everything that might be said about the hazards of social mobility, it would be inaccurate to deny that the rich by and large did succeed sooner or later in gratifying their social ambitions. This was the historic destiny of the social-economic elite. The vulgar new rich were the raw material for fashionable society, and the period of tutelage was becoming ever shorter. In the good old days, it had taken a generation or two; but now, an insider ruefully reflected, a mere social season was sufficient. After all, the influence of money was very difficult to resist: "Money prizes and honors itself, and if there is anything

it hasn't got, it believes it can buy it." Even the most determined snobbery wilted in the face of such complacence.

The classic study of the trials and tribulations of social
mobility was *The Rise of Silas Lapham*. Lapham's financial
rise and fall was paralleled by his abortive social career,
and each phase revealed a crucial defect of character: un-
scrupulousness in business and vulgar social ambition.
Fortunately, however, he had not succeeded in wholly
stifling his sturdy New England conscience. At the height
of his success, that conscience impelled him to come to the
aid of a former business associate whom he had ruined, and
the act, as he suspected, proved to be his financial undoing.
The moral and financial crisis purged Lapham of his pride,
and at the end he was found where he had begun, a
small village businessman, but now humbled in spirit and
contented with his lot. For Lapham, as for so many of
Howells's characters, coming to terms with life involved
acceptance of one's social status as a kind of birthright.

Lapham's social aspirations had centered on a daughter
whom he hoped to marry into a socially prominent Boston
family, the Bromfield Coreys. His heavy-footed invasion of
Boston society was routed at a preposterous dinner party
given by the Coreys, where Lapham, being unaccustomed
to wine, drank too much and made a fool of himself. The
occasion furnished Howells an excellent opportunity to
dramatize his sense of the incommensurability of social
strata. Corey's guests recognized in Lapham an authentic
American type, shrewd, blunt, and powerful, but crude,
narrow, and wholly devoid of the arts of cultivated social
intercourse. His social failure was decreed with crushing

finality, and his financial failure following shortly thereafter seemed almost anticlimactic.

Although social mobility was repudiated in Lapham's
rejection by fashionable society, it was at least partially
confirmed in the romance of the children. Young Tom
Corey, who had had no intention of exemplifying Veblen's
conception of the leisure class, had gone to work for Lapham's paint concern and had successfully wooed the boss's
elder daughter (not the younger, as Lapham had expected).
The elder Corey reflected sadly on the American gentleman's preference for working, and for marrying across
class lines. But it was significant that he seems to have
made no effort to prevent the marriage. In any event,
Lapham's financial failure and retirement to the country
robbed the marriage of much of its social significance, since
it no longer involved the social acceptance of the Lapham
family. The young couple conveniently went off to Mexico
where Corey was to represent the company, now in other
hands. His parents indulged the hope that while his bride
could hardly expect to become an American lady, she
might at least acquire some measure of Latin finish.

Howells was one of a large group of American writers
of the Gilded Age whose happy recollections of childhood
experiences in a rural village were incorporated in their
fiction. The contrast between rural and big city ways of
life was more than an ideological convention for them; it
was a matter of personal experience and conviction. They
had participated in one of the major forms of spatial movement during the nineteenth century, and the contrast between rural simplicity and urban complexity furnished a

perspective from which they viewed the problems of urban civilization.

Movement from country to city figured prominently in Howells's novels. The relatively unstructured, socially homogeneous village community that he recollected from his boyhood in Ohio provided a baseline for all of his sociological projections. Several of his more memorable characters exemplified the strict moral code, the sturdy self-respect, and the shrewd capacity of the countryman. It was Lapham's conscience, after all, that governed his fate in the crucial moment. Lemuel Barker, a kind of admirable Creighton, was also true to his conscience even though it impelled him to renounce his rising fortunes in Boston and return to the farm.

Howells disclaimed any intention of idealizing the rural way of life. He was fully aware of its drabness and poverty. Barker, one of his experts on the subject, observed that rural life was for those who had neither hope nor ambition. Contrary to a common assumption of city dwellers, the village was less charitable than the city, if only because it had fewer opportunities for the exercise of charity. Nevertheless, rural America remained for Howells the stronghold of the traditional moral and social virtues of the democratic ideology.

During the last fifteen years of the nineteenth century, Howells became deeply disturbed by the industrial conflicts that erupted in a wave of violence and bloody strikes. His sympathies were entirely with the laborers. He vigorously protested the conviction and execution of the Haymarket anarchists in 1886. Bellamy's utopian novel *Look-*

ing Backward and Laurence Gronlund's pioneer socialist treatise *The Cooperative Commonwealth* were read with enthusiasm. He even tried his hand at the utopian novel with *A Traveler from Altruria*. To his friend Mark Twain he characterized himself as "a theoretical socialist and a practical aristocrat."

Howells's growing concern with social justice and economic conflict was not so much the result of a changing point of view as it was a logical development of his earlier outlook. Had he been less impressed with the virtues of stability and the obstacles to upward social mobility, he might well have been, like most Americans, more complacent in the belief that social advancement embodied the promise of American life. Social radicals had always recognized this expectation to be the chief barrier to the formation of class consciousness. Because he was disenchanted with mobility Howells was able to project himself imaginatively and sympathetically into the problems of laboring people, knowing that they had no choice but to bear their burdens stoically.

There never seems to have been much doubt that the practical aristocrat would in the end triumph over the theoretical socialist. Howells repudiated revolutionary violence as the solution to existing social injustices so long as legal means of recourse were available. Even more significant, socialism was declared to be deficient because it left out of account the Christian principle of suffering for the sins of others. What Howells condemned was not a stratified society of mutually exclusive classes. That was inevitable. He condemned the false social ambition that caused men and women to be discontented with their lot, and to divert all their energies to the mad scramble for status.

For the gentleman uncertain of his own status, stability was the social condition most to be desired. In such novels as *Silas Lapham, A Modern Instance,* and *The Landlord of Lion's Head* the characters of whom the author approved and whom he treated sympathetically were those who found their places socially and reconciled themselves to them. They revealed an integrity of character and self-sufficiency that enabled them to withstand the temptations of ambition. The ideal of stability was preached most eloquently in *The Minister's Charge.* Lemuel Barker, the able and ambitious farm boy, renounced a promising career in the city because he realized that the working girl he had innocently befriended and to whom he felt himself committed would not be able to keep pace with him. The Unitarian minister, Sewell, through whose eyes the story unfolds, applauded the "wisdom of resignation," especially in one so young. In the final analysis, social ambition was antisocial. The individual's place in life should be determined not simply by his own efforts, but by the totality of associations that entered into his experience.

Howells could not leave American society permanently divided into mutually exclusive social strata without some overarching bond that would unite all in universal brotherhood. He formulated this bond in the ideal of complicity: the realization that we are all involved in one another's fate. Sewell devoted a sermon to the subject.

> No man he said, sinned or suffered to himself alone; his error and his pain darkened and afflicted men who never

heard of his name. If a community was corrupt, if an age was immoral, it was not because of the vicious, but the virtuous who fancied themselves indifferent spectators. It was not the tyrant who oppressed, it was the wickedness that had made him possible. The Gospel—Christ—God, so far as men had imagined him—was but a lesson, a type, a witness from everlasting to everlasting of the spiritual unity of man.[57]

This spiritual unity should at least soften if it did not dissolve the social barriers that divided men and made them indifferent strangers to each other.

In his analysis of American society in the Gilded Age Howells was groping his way toward a concept of mass society. He found the amorphous middle mass to be flanked by satellite classes: the fashionable economic elite and gentry above, laboring and servant classes below. In several novels he concentrated upon the isolated, essentially antisocial character of the mass man. This antisocial quality was attributed, ironically enough, to the vertical social mobility which caused men to cut themselves off from their fellows in persuit of personal, selfish advantages. Mobility was in turn sanctioned by the dominant ideology of successful achievement. Howells was able to arrive at such a subversive analysis of American life because the traditional gentry values were becoming increasingly irrelevant.

· V ·

GENTRY POLITICS

AMERICAN POLITICS in the eighteenth century had been dominated by the old gentry class. Holding a near monopoly of elective and appointive offices and functioning as the American counterpart to the privileged classes of Britain, the old gentry took for granted their central role in the political process. The Revolutionary War began the social and political transformation which, in half a century's time, destroyed the old gentry and its "politics of status," and securely established the new democratic mass society with its "politics of opinion." The new era was symbolized by Jackson's inaugural celebration, at which triumphant democrats in muddy boots climbed on the chairs, broke the dishes, and postured in classical revolutionary style. Richard Hofstadter has equated the rise of democratic politics in the 1820s and 1830s with the demise of gentry influence. The democratic attack on gentility was so successful that the Whigs, heirs of the gentry Federalist tradition, were perforce compelled to imitate it, and when they did so, "the gentleman as a force in American politics was committing suicide." [1] Hofstadter was referring, of course, to the old colonial gentry class, which outside the South had indeed ceased to exist. But his analysis did not take into account the surviving influence of gentility in the new mass context, nor the peculiar character of the several elites in which the social interests of the mass society received their principal expression. Although the new gentry elite exercised virtually none of the practical power of the old gentry class, it did inherit something of its prestige as the custodian of venerated social norms. Gentlemen consequently continued to play a prominent role in American politics throughout the nineteenth century, long after their identification with gentility had become if anything a liability rather than an asset with the electorate at large.

In a sense, the concerted Jacksonian attack on "aristocracy" was flogging a dead horse. The old gentry class had disintegrated, and the new social-economic elite was still pitifully weak and insecure. Perhaps at no other time in American history was economic power so widely diffused as in the 1830s. Nevertheless, the attack on aristocracy was a strikingly effective political maneuver. It demonstrated that success in mass politics consisted in finding a popular issue which would appeal to mass prejudices. Gentility was still so closely identified in the popular mind with wealth and social prestige that the gentry would inevitably be victimized by the attack on aristocracy.

As a cultural elite only indirectly identified with social or economic interests, the nineteenth-century gentry did not fall neatly into particular political categories. After the fall of the Federalist party, no party presumed to claim the kind of monopoly on public spirit and civic virtue which was the only contribution to political life that the gentry claimed as its distinctive function. Protestations of superior virtue were intolerable in a political society where all had potential access to power, and gentlemen were increasingly thrown on the defensive by popular annoyance with pretensions of superiority. Nevertheless, although they were denied a political organization of their own, many gentlemen remained deeply involved in politics. Federalists and Jeffersonian Republicans, Democrats and Whigs, Free Soilers, Native Americans, and Republicans all included gentry leaders in their ranks. Because of their general commitment to democratic values and their cosmopolitan outlook, the gentry's influence, although usually imperceptible, was everywhere an elevating and accommodating one.

The political dispossession of the gentry was the common fate of several nineteenth-century elites representing functions formerly monopolized by the old colonial gentry class. Democratic politics produced its own political elite composed of professional politicians who were fully prepared to bargain on equal footing with all comers. As politics came to reflect numbers it was perhaps inevitable that the "interests" should range themselves outside politics and learn how to exert pressure on the politicians. The gentry became in effect one of many special interests, no longer a force *in* politics, but often effectively bringing force to bear on it. The reform movements of the antebellum decades which were so effective in modifying American institutions had an almost solid gentry leadership. The technique of reform was to work outside the formal party and political structures by organizing pressure groups and mobilizing public opinion until irresistible pressure was brought to bear on governmental agencies. The gentry learned to be highly adept in the use of these techniques.

Traditions die a lingering death, even under adverse circumstances. It is noteworthy how powerfully the gentry tradition continued to color nineteenth-century democratic politics. Not until the rise of the proletarian politics of the new immigration after the Civil War was there a frontal attack upon respectability as the proper garb of politics. The gentleman remained highly desirable as a public front for political organizations long after gentility had ceased to have more than a faint, diffuse effect upon public life.

Throughout the nineteenth century, gentlemen held political office at all levels, especially in the seaboard states where the gentry were concentrated. Of the 31 governors of Massachusetts during the century all but 2 were clearly identified with the gentry, 24 of them being college graduates (including 14 Harvard alumni). In the last two decades of the century, every Massachusetts governor was a college graduate, all but one of them from Harvard. All but 4 of the 27 United States Senators from Massachusetts were college graduates. Two of the non-college Senators were the influential Radical Republicans, Henry Wilson and George S. Boutwell. The latter, although he held no earned degree, could boast an honorary LL.D. from Harvard, awarded in part for distinguished services to education as secretary to the state board of education. The 31 mayors of Boston were similarly dominated by gentry with Harvard affiliations.

While Columbia graduates were not equally prominent among the major office holders of New York State, the proportions of college graduates were almost as large as in Massachusetts: 14 of 33 governors and 23 of 33 United States senators were college graduates. Even among prominent Tammany Hall leaders, where one would hardly expect to find gentry influence, 13 of 31 leaders selected for their historical prominence proved to be college graduates.

In Connecticut also the gentry played an impressive role in public life: 22 of 35 governors during the nineteenth century were college graduates, 18 of them from Yale. Of 29 United States senators 19 were college graduates, 15 from Yale. The gentry influence was less prominent in Pennsylvania politics, with only 6 of 21 governors being college graduates, the first of them elected in 1855. Of 31 United States senators 12 were college graduates. It is apparent that University of Pennsylvania alumni did not play roles in state politics comparable to those of Yale or Harvard alumni, and that gentry families were less inclined to concern themselves with statewide affairs.

In the four midwestern states of Ohio, Michigan, Illinois, and Missouri a similar check of governors and senators reveals a fairly uniform pattern of slightly less than half college graduates or attendants. Rather more of these had attended college after mid-century than before. In Virginia and South Carolina, on the other hand, the educational credentials of office holders were more impressive. Twenty-four of Virginia's 34 governors were college graduates, and 20 of her 33 senators. Of South Carolina's governors 26 graduated from college, while 8 more attended for varying lengths of time. Twenty-two of her 33 senators also graduated. The data from the Southern states strengthens the impression that while the South lagged behind in popular education her old gentry class succeeded in perpetuating its political monopoly well into the nineteenth century.

While gentry politicians won their share of elective offices, they were even more successful in securing appointive offices, where special skills as well as prior political service were so often prerequisites. Sidney Aaronson's study of the social and economic status of appointees to high federal office under the John Adams, Thomas Jefferson, and Andrew Jackson administrations is highly suggestive. High percentages of the cabinet officers, ambassadors, ministers, Supreme Court justices, and territorial governors appointed during those administrations were recruited from gentry ranks. That John Adams should have made his appointments from the wavering ranks of the old gentry class is not surprising; but that Jackson, reputedly the innovator of democratic spoilsmanship, should have drawn as heavily upon the newly emerging gentry elite is more notable. A near monopoly of high federal appointive offices passed from the remnants of the old eighteenth-century gentry during the Adams administration to the new gentry elite under Jackson. While fewer of Jackson's appointees came from distinguished families, an appreciably higher percentage of them were self-made professional men, affiliated with learned societies and educational institutions, including many former teachers and journalists. About half of them were college graduates at a time when only 2 percent of the population received any higher education. These choice positions did not go to gentlemen simply by virtue of their social status. Over 80 percent of the appointees in each of the three administrations had had previous political experience as officeholders. These facts provide impressive testimony to the extensive overlapping of the gentry and political elites. Although Jacksonian politicians may have talked about the democratic virtues of rotation in office, the pressing claims of the gentry to the top positions were not to be denied. The Jacksonian revolution seems to have comprised rather the opening of minor offices to the patronage system, a practice resisted by previous administrations.[2]

Similar gentry involvement is found in representative administrations of the later nineteenth century. However unsavory the reputation of the Grant administrations (1869–1877), the extent and quality of its gentry representation is impressive. Fourteen of 23 cabinet members were college graduates. Among them was Hamilton Fish, Secretary of State, former governor of New York and senator, a "gentleman of the old school," later to serve as president of the New York Historical Society and chairman of the Columbia University board of trustees. Benjamin H. Bristow, Secretary of the Treasury, long active in Kentucky politics, won the acclaim of the Liberal Republicans by his reform and efficient administration of the Treasury. William A. Richardson, who preceded Bristow in the Treasury, was a distinguished jurist, legal scholar, and editor of the United States Statutes. An eminent succession of Attorneys General included Ebenezer R. Hoar, a distinguished Massachusetts jurist; Amos T. Akerman of Georgia, an ex-Confederate turned Republican; Edwards Pierrepont, whose names signified his descent from the theologian and the founder of Yale; and Alphonso Taft, founder of the distinguished Cincinnati political family. The Secretary of the Interior, General Jacob D. Cox, lawyer and former governor of Ohio, had a high reputation in gentry circles for his general knowledge and legal acumen. Without formal education but with gentry approval for their integrity and competence were George S. Boutwell of the Treasury and Marshall Jewell, Postmaster-General, who opposed the administration in the Star Route scandal.

Grant's principal diplomatic appointments included several gentlemen of comparable distinction. Minister to Austria-Hungary was John Jay, grandson of the Federalist, prominent in the civil service reform movement, a lawyer and historical scholar. Among Jay's successors in Vienna was Edward F. Beale, a Naval Academy graduate described by Charles Nordhoff as "a sparkling combination of scholar, gentleman, and Indian fighter." Elihu Washburne of Maine, a self-made lawyer, journalist, Congressman, and historian, served as minister to France. The historian George Bancroft was succeeded in 1874 as minister to Germany by his nephew John C. B. Davis, who had previously served in the New York legislature, then as Assistant Secretary of State, and who would later serve as a judge on the United States Court of Claims. John Lothrop Motley, also a distinguished historian, served briefly as minister to Great Britain before differences with the administration over its Santo Domingo policy forced his resignation. James Birney, son of the antislavery leader James G. Birney, served as minister to the Netherlands after a long career in Michigan politics as legislator, lieutenant-governor, and judge. George H. Boker, a poet and playwright, succeeded Marshall Jewell as minister to Russia. Finally, Caleb Cushing capped a distinguished career in law, politics, and diplomacy as minister to Spain. Clearly, then, in spite of what Henry Adams felt about the impossibility of a gentleman serving in the Grant administration,[3] the fact was that a good many of them did so; although it was also true that some became entangled in the web of corruption, while others were forced into retirement.

The election of Grover Cleveland in 1884 was marked by the Mugwump rebellion of the liberal Republican gentry against their party's nominee, James G. Blaine. But the gentry representation in Cleveland's first cabinet was less impressive than in Grant's, while the influence of high finance was much more apparent. Thomas F. Bayard, Secretary of State, William C. Endicott, War, and Lucius Q. C. Lamar, Interior, were eminent representatives of the gentry interest, but the distinctive tone of the cabinet was established by the financiers and corporation lawyers like William C. Whitney, Secretary of the Navy, and Charles S. Fairchild and Daniel Manning of the Treasury. Cleveland's diplomatic appointments were divided between gentry and social-economic elite, the latter being represented by Perry Belmont, minister to Spain, Lambert Tree, Russia, and Robert Roosevelt and Isaac Bell, the Netherlands.

The facts of continuing gentry involvement in public life throughout the century suggest that a distinction should be made between the availability of gentlemen as individuals for public service and the existence of a distinctive gentry program. The personal characteristics of the gentleman made him suitable for public service regardless of the fact that gentlemen often disagreed on matters of public policy. So long as the community prized those characteristics it would continue to look to gentlemen for leadership in all its organized social and political activities. By the time of World War I, however, respect for gentlemanly qualities had become so attenuated that gentility ceased to be an appreciable factor in public life.

Apart from these general considerations, there was a more explicit gentry interest that can be traced, at times obscurely, through the course of nineteenth-century politics. With the emergence of a mass society and the fragmentation of the old gentry class into a number of functional elites, the new gentry elite was free to apply its distinctive code of manners and morals to public life. The code emphasized independence, integrity, honor, self-respect, self-denial, and public spirit. Gentlemen could disagree among themselves on issues of policy and still enjoy mutual esteem so long as they remained loyal to the common substratum of gentry values. Prior to the War of 1812, the Federalists liked to think that they had a monopoly on gentility, and were prepared to ostracize gentlemen like Elbridge Gerry, Perez Morton, and John Quincy Adams for identifying themselves with the Democratic-Republicans. The assumptions of the old gentry governing class survived as late as 1808 in a man like Judge Theodore Sedgwick, who defined Federalists as "those who alone from education, fortune, character, and principle are entitled to command." [4] Such imperious assertions of superiority looked to a vanished past, and were out of keeping with the temper and convictions of the newly emerging democratic politics. Gentlemen continued to assume leadership roles not by virtue of any prescriptive right to command, but because the community associated gentry qualities with public leadership. In the language of mass theory, the political and gentry elites overlapped.

The identification of gentility with public spirit and leadership was apparent in the circumstances surrounding the entrance of Edward Everett into politics. A Harvard graduate and pastor of the Brattle Street Church in Boston, Everett was the first American to earn the doctorate at a German university (Göttingen, 1817). He returned to Harvard in 1819 as professor of Greek literature and served also as editor of the *North American Review*. Secure status in the overlapping group of gentry and social-economic elites was achieved by marriage to a daughter of Peter Chardon Brooks, socially prominent and wealthy Boston merchant. Everett announced his political aspirations in an address to the Harvard Phi Beta Kappa society in 1824. The address was an eloquent statement of cultural nationalism in which the orator indicated how the indigenous vitality of autonomous cultural regions would interact with social equalitarianism to stimulate intellectual life. That such a topic discussed under such auspices could be expected to result in political advancement was itself impressive indication of gentry influence in politics. Everett was in fact to enjoy a long career in various state and national offices. It was his misfortune to live at a time when the slavery issue was to furnish the measure of a man's accomplishment, and by this test Everett fell short. Although personally opposed to slavery, he sought to evade it as a political issue, and the course of events passed him by.

From the perspective of Reconstruction times, a writer in the *New York Nation* in 1867 attributed the political demise of the gentleman to a mental and moral decay which first showed itself in the slavery crisis, and of which Everett's career might well be symptomatic. The writer, probably Godkin, believed that a change had occurred at about 1840. Prior to that time, the gentry had been highminded, progressive, and public-spirited, even if conservative in taste and social outlook. But thereafter, gentlemen became increasingly timid, aping the Southern and European gentry and diverting their attention from politics to religion. They had conducted themselves with "such a shocking want of manliness, courage and truthfulness that good clothes and polished manners got to be associated in the popular mind with moral turpitude and mental imbecility." The last gentry representatives in the White House, according to the *Nation,* had been Pierce and Buchanan, those paragons of ineffectuality. The gentleman's failure to commit himself early and firmly to the Union cause properly invited his condemnation.[5]

The *Nation* was more concerned to stir the gentry out of their post-Civil War lethargy than to provide an accurate appraisal of their prewar history. Loyalty to the Union had in fact been the sentiment that transcended gentry uncertainty on the slavery question and unified gentry ranks in the 1850s. Prior to that time, many gentlemen had figured prominently in the antislavery movement, although there was certainly no consensus on the matter, and individual antislavery leaders courted various forms of disapproval for speaking out. Wherever there was extensive overlapping with the social-economic elite a potent restraint upon social radicalism existed. When Charles Sumner took up the antislavery cause the homes of Boston's fashionable society where he had previously been welcomed were closed to him.[6] His gentry associates, however, stood by him. Among the leaders of the Free Soil Party in Massachusetts were such prominent gentlemen as Samuel Gridley Howe, Charles Allen, Richard Henry Dana, and Samuel Hoar. In such company, Henry Wilson, a mechanic and erstwhile shoemaker's apprentice, stood out as one of the few nongentry leaders in the movement. Although the Republicans of Massachusetts were to draw many of their leaders from these Free Soilers, they were to be joined by an equally distinguished group of former Whigs extolled by George Frisbie Hoar as "men whose private and public honor was without a stain." [7]

EDWIN LAWRENCE GODKIN

A leading gentry spokesman who addressed himself to the political and social issues of the Gilded Age was Edwin Lawrence Godkin, founder and editor of the *New York Nation*. Godkin had been born in Ireland, of English ancestry, in 1831. His father was a dissenting clergyman whose support of home rule had deprived him of his parish and driven him into journalism, a career his son was to follow with distinction.

Educated at Queens' College, Belfast, the young Godkin was exposed to the full force of British liberal social philosophy. His prophet, he later recalled, had been John Stuart Mill; his daily food, Bentham and the historian George Grote. He had studied political economy as a predictive science consisting of the knowledge of what man as a producing and consuming animal would do if left alone. Had Godkin attended an American college he doubtless would have received much the same kind of instruction. Many years later, as he looked backward from the turn of the century, he noted how political economy had changed during his lifetime. It no longer claimed to be a science, but was now merely a body of technical know-how designed to aid men in making themselves more comfortable by means of governmental assistance.[8]

Young Irish liberals like Godkin looked to America as

the promised land where the principles of laissez-faire were being proven in practice. They defined "democrats" as those whose hopes and sympathies were not bound up in a party or class, but who worked for the welfare and progress of humanity. In Godkin's case, his liberalism was further sharpened by his study of the reactionary despotisms of central Europe. Going to London in 1851 to study law, he instead became interested in the abortive revolutionary movement in Hungary. He wrote a history of that unhappy country the central theme of which chronicled the struggle between emergent liberalism and reaction. In 1854 he was in the Crimea, reporting the war there for a London paper.

Already, however, Godkin had had his eye on the United States as his ultimate destination, and he arrived in New York in 1856, still intending to practice law. A chance encounter with the landscape architect and publicist Frederick Law Olmsted again diverted him. Olmsted had recently completed a first-hand investigation of American slavery, and was in the process of publishing an account of it in his *Journey in the Seaboard Slave States*.[9] He urged Godkin to retrace his itinerary through the South. In doing so, the newcomer was brought face to face with the glaring discrepancy between the democratic ideology of freedom and the reality of chattel slavery.

In New York City, Godkin confronted a second major American paradox. He was probably familiar with the view of Mill that it was the virtue of representative government to bring the general standard of intelligence and honesty in the community to bear upon public problems. Representation invested the virtue and wisdom of the best members of the community with more power and influence than did other forms of government. On the other hand, it also tended toward collective mediocrity in direct proportion to wider extensions of the suffrage. In the United States, the philosopher observed, the more highly cultivated individuals no longer sought elective office because of the certainty that they would not be elected.[10] Godkin found that this was indeed the case in New York. Local government was in the hands of blatantly corrupt and disreputable politicians who provided utterly inadequate public services while looting the public through very high taxes. Godkin knew that European cities enjoyed infinitely better administration, and yet the gentry of New York stood aside with fastidious disdain while suffering themselves to be dispossessed.

Out of these sobering discoveries of the defects of American democracy grew the convictions which diverted Godkin from the private pursuit of a profession to the public career of a journalist. He resolved to establish a journal of opinion which would rally the gentry to a keener sense of their public responsibility and serve as a mouthpiece for the gentry point of view. The Civil War prevented immediate implementation of his plans, but as soon as peace was restored Godkin launched the *Nation* on $100,000 borrowed from sympathetic investors who assured him of complete editorial freedom. In a journalistic world of poor newspapers and quarterly and monthly magazines ill-suited to the discussion of public issues Godkin offered a weekly "paper" which proposed to discuss current politics, letters, art, and social affairs. It was a major journalistic achievement, developing a formula that survived for a century in weekly and bi-weekly magazines and profoundly influenced the monthly and quarterly journals as well.

Godkin never envisaged a mass circulation for the *Nation*. He wanted only to influence the informed and responsible leaders of opinion. That these leaders should voice the gentry point of view reflected Godkin's conviction that gentry leadership was vital to the success of a democratic society. Although he knew the leading public figures of the day, his closest personal associates were such gentry figures as Charles Eliot Norton and James Russell Lowell. William James asserted that Godkin had a more pervasive influence on public opinon than any other writer of his time—by which James must have meant the circles in which he himself moved. In fact, the magisterial tone commonly sounded in the columns of the *Nation* could have been congenial only to those readers who shared gentry assumptions. A less enthusiastic reader than James once observed that Godkin could make even virtue seem repulsive.[11]

Godkin's role was to develop the social philosophy of liberal humanism. Writing to his friend Norton in 1865, he affirmed his highest allegiance to liberty and civilized values. Democracy were merely a fallible means to these great ends. If, for example, the majority were to vote for socialism, Godkin would unhesitatingly take up arms against the majority. The Southerners had just been put down because their aims were believed to be injurious to the ends of liberal society. The suffrage should properly be withheld from the freedmen until they were ready for it.

History showed that thus far only one race had been capable of sustaining self-government.[12]

Because of his willingness to subordinate democratic means to liberal ends it was possible for Godkin to take a realistic view of the origins of democracy in class conflict, and of the continuing relevance of democracy to the articulation of social conflicts. He detached the theory of democracy from its eighteenth-century matrix of natural rights and grafted it onto a post-Marxian theory of class conflict. He reminded his readers that the eighteenth century had distinguished inalienable civil rights from the political right of suffrage, which was a matter of mere expediency. But the nineteenth century had committed itself fully to universal suffrage as a right. Democracy was the wave of the future, and Godkin was confident that for better or for worse all civilized nations would be democratized. The revolutionary implications of democracy should be candidly acknowledged: democracy meant government by poor men. Its perennial problem would be to prevent the corruption of the legislator (a poor man) by the rich man.[13]

Viewed in the currently fashionable Darwinian terms, it would appear that through the successful democratic revolution the poor had survived the class struggle and had emerged as the "fittest." They would understandably define progress as the making of such changes in their environment as would assure their continuing power and success. One could confidently expect, therefore, that democratic government by poor men would continue to sponsor the kind of political program which in the past two centuries had greatly increased the population of Europe and enhanced its comforts. The poor would use the state as a means to assure their survival as the fittest. This was Godkin's version of the politics of class struggle.[14]

The distinctive feature of Godkin's liberalism was the assumption that there would always remain a division and conflict between the rich and the poor. Politics could not alter this ultimate fact. The liberals were not revolutionaries in the Marxist sense; they did not believe that a stratified society could be replaced by a classless society. Democracy was not to be the means by which the poor would overthrow the rich. It was merely the means by which they would alleviate their miseries at the expense of the rich.

The democratic society envisioned by nineteenth-century liberals was characterized by intense competition and unrestricted vertical social mobility. The aspect of mobility in which they were particularly interested centered on recruitment of the gentry elite, especially by means of education. They knew that the price of liberty was inequality. The less able and energetic who constituted the mass should willingly accept leadership by the various elites. Indications of mass restlessness or envy were to be deplored. Democracy meant equality before the law, and equality of opportunity; not equality of condition, or the imposition of mass standards of taste. Repeatedly, Godkin affirmed the necessity of gentry leadership. There had never been a time, he believed, "when it was more necessary to assert boldly the value of education, and the authority of training and culture in matters of government." [15] The assertion of the rightful claims of intelligence in the manage-

ment of public affairs was to remain a persistent item in
the liberal creed from Godkin to John Dewey and Walter
Lippmann.

Godkin reminded his readers that the sources of national
greatness and progress were to be found in the small number
of leaders—the boldest thinkers, the most ardent investi-
gators, the most prudent, careful, and ingenious workers
—in successive generations. Such reminders were doubtless unpalatable to an age that gloried in mere numbers,
but Godkin was no man to shrink from stating an unpop-
ular truth. Because leaders might originate in any rank of
society the problem of identification and utilization was a
perennial one, and various methods had been used in different times and places. In the United States, the recent
tendency had been to equate leadership with the capacity
to make money. But Godkin believed that Americans were
already becoming disenchanted with leadership by the
rich, and were prepared for a salutary turn to leaders of
trained competence in their respective fields. The practical
symbol of such a leadership was formal education. The
colleges and universities should gather and focus the materials from which American leadership in the twentieth century was to be drawn.[16]

In some respects this was a shrewd forecast of the changing qualities of American leadership. Leaders would indeed display ever-lengthening educational pedigrees. But
educational experience was in itself less important to Godkin than the personal and intellectual qualities of gentility
which he always associated with formal higher education.
He took it too readily for granted, perhaps, that the col-

lege-trained person was a man of character and mental culture as well as ambition. He did foresee and warn against the watering down of educational values which would inevitably accompany the dissipation of energies in the face of mounting costs and enrollments. But apparently he did not perceive the subtle changes which were undermining the academic roots of gentry culture, changes which would leave to the colleges occupational and professional rather than social relevance.

It was widely believed in Europe as well as among the American gentry themselves that their political dispossession was due to the unwillingness of the American mass to accept their leadership any longer. Godkin, who professed to have studied the matter closely, refused to accept this explanation. In every instance of public repudiation of a gentry political leader he found a persuasive personal reason for the rejection. Many potential gentry leaders disqualified themselves by declaring the rough and tumble of politics to be beneath their dignity. Gentry failure was of their own making.

In his search for an explanation of this failure of nerve Godkin turned to the history of gentility. He noted that a major element in the tradition running back from the southern slaveholder through the medieval manor lord to the classical Greek aristocrat appeared to be institutions of servitude fixing the qualities of what Godkin called "the high-toned gentleman." The last survivors of this breed had just been destroyed by the victorious forces of democratic mass society. While he did not have the effrontery to suggest that the destruction of the slaveocracy had been a mistake, Godkin did observe that it might be useful to look closely at the better qualities that appeared whenever slavery and civilization were united in the same society. After all, one need not apologize for analyzing the traits of such slaveholders as Washington, Jefferson, Madison, and Calhoun. What most impressed Godkin in these high-toned gentlemen was their moral energy. Of especial relevance for his contemporaries was their insistence upon playing an influential role in public affairs, their sense of honor and public spirit. They towered like giants over the penniless shysters who were crawling through the ward caucuses to Capitol Hill in the Grant era. The slaveholding southern gentry were in fact the last surviving representatives of the old eighteenth-century gentry.

In any event, the high-toned gentleman was gone, to be succeeded eventually, Godkin hoped, by "the gentleman of democracy," whose traits were not specified in detail but who would presumably exemplify the best features of the new order. In the meanwhile, an interregnum of vulgarity prevailed, a "paradise of bad manners." Godkin accused his gentry contemporaries of a cowardly lack of self-respect. "Too much impudence is borne with in the Northern States. . . . Instead of incontinently chastising the vulgar ass who chances to call us evil names, we sidle away from him, perhaps smile upon him with a placating air." The mass had humbled the gentleman and was forcing him to defer to mass types, to the servant, the hackman, and the railroad conductor.[17]

Inevitably, the democratic gentleman who was to provide future leadership was conceived by Godkin less as a product of democratic conditions than as a critic of them. The gentry were to remain the custodians of high culture, and culture, Godkin always insisted, was the result of mental and moral discipline.

It comes of the protracted exercise of the faculties for given ends, under restraints of some kind, whether imposed by one's self or other people. In fact, it might not improperly be called the art of doing easily what you don't like to do. It is the breaking-in of the powers to the service of the will; and a man who has got it is not simply a person who knows a good deal, for he may know very little, but a man who has obtained an accurate estimate of his own capacity, and of that of his fellows and predecessors, who is aware of the nature and extent of his relations to the world about him, and who is at the same time capable of using his powers to the best advantage. In short, the man of culture is the man who has formed his ideals through labor and self-denial. To be real, therefore, culture ought to effect a man's whole character and not merely store his memory with facts. Let us add, too, that it may be got in various ways, through home influences as well as through schools or colleges; through living in a highly organized society, making imperious demands on one's time and faculties, as well as through the restraints of a severe course of study. A good deal of it was obtained from the old Calvinist theology, against which, in the days of its predominance, the most bumptious youth hit his head at an early period of his career, and was reduced to thoughtfulness and self-examination, and forced to walk in ways that were not always to his liking.[18]

Godkin's democratic gentleman was the product not of a social or economic class, but of a cultural tradition. This tradition organized human energies in the service of great moral and cultural ends. Godkin found the meaning of America in the struggle for culture. The real class struggle was not economic, but a cultural class struggle. His emphasis on the moral check signified a philosophy of restraint in the face of the myriad temptations of vulgar materialism. It is not difficult to understand how critics of genteel culture should have picked out this element of Puritanical restraint and converted it into the caricature of Victorian prudery. Godkin's definition of culture as discipline and his implicit division of mankind into a disciplined elite and an undisciplined mass anticipated by half a century the similar distinctions made by Ortega y Gasset in his *Revolt of the Masses*.

Godkin refused to share the prevailing complacent optimism of the Gilded Age. The public life of the period was understandably depressing. Very little progress in the political arts had in fact been made since Roman times, in his opinion. Admittedly, modern man enjoyed the advantages of representative government, public education, and some knowledge of political economy, but Godkin minimized the importance of these achievements. Modern cities were still inferior to those of the Romans in cleanliness, sewage disposal, and recreation facilities. Confronted by the municipal problems of New York or Chicago, his contemporaries stood as helpless as had the Roman oligarchy before the mob in the last days of the Republic. Modern imperialists were inferior to the Romans in civilizing barbarian peoples. Such improvements as had occurred in modern times were the product of nonpolitical forces.[19]

Godkin was one of the first of the gentry to insist upon the necessity of administration by experts. Representative legislative assemblies may have been adequate for simple agricultural communities, but they could not cope with complex urban industrial conditions. "What with ignorance, haste, want of training, and the distractions of an infinite variety of details and of multifarious conflicting interests, legislation is becoming in every legislative body in the world often rather a positive hindrance than a help to healthy progress, and a sapper rather than strengthener of public morals." [20] The next great revolution in politics would provide some device for giving prompt and scientific expression to the popular will. This would suggest some form of direct democracy such as initiative and referendum. But the mass should restrict itself to the enunciation of the basic objectives of public policy, leaving the details of implementation and administration to scientifically qualified civil servants.

The current interregnum in gentility was analogous to the Dark Ages separating classical from modern civilization. In both cases, a civilized people stood at bay before a barbarian world. The modern situation differed from the classical only in that the barbarians were not outside a geographical boundary marking the limits of the civilized world; they were the mass of the population within it. Like the Romans, the gentry who had produced the art, literature, science, and civil polity of modern civilization could no longer keep the barbarians out. The mass was in the process of dispossessing the cultural elite. It was inevitable that many of the gifts, graces, and ideals of gentry civilization should be lost forever.

Godkin nevertheless found some consolation in his vision of the democratic gentleman who would reestablish civilized values on a more secure and permanent foundation. The aims and outlook of the high-toned gentleman had been too narrow and parochial to embrace the challenge of democratic aspirations. His fate should remind men that Providence cares little for individuals or classes or races, but everything for mankind. He was now discovering, just as Rome had found, that so long as any portion of the human race lagged behind, further progress was impossible. In the moment when he was forced to share, when indeed his work was trampled under foot, he would realize that no one creates for himself alone. Progress must be diffused sooner or later among all. Godkin therefore counseled his friends not to despair:

> We shall, doubtless, now pass through a period of much ignorant fermentation; we shall see a great number of old experiments repeated, with the old and well known result; a great many old discoveries re-discovered, and a great many attempts to embody in legislation wild anticipations bred and nourished through generations of ignorance and privation. But then we know that no conquest of the human intelligence will again be lost; that the records of human experience are beyond the destroyer's reach; that the hold of science on human thought will never again be relaxed; that all that is best in human thought will find every day readier expression and wider influence; and that, whether the end be far or near, it is certain.[21]

THE LIBERAL REPUBLICANS

The steady decline in gentry political fortunes was marked less by the withdrawal of gentlemen from high public office than by their increasing visibility and by their self-consciousness as a vulnerable elite. The low moral tone of American politics in the Gilded Age presented a challenge to which the gentry could not fail to respond. The scandals of the Grant administration precipitated a gentry reaction which culminated in the Liberal Republican movement of 1872, and at the same time crystallized the political program which provided liberalism with its positive content. Although the two themes may be separated for purposes of analysis they were inextricably intertwined in fact.

The idea that a public office is a public trust, and that the officeholder should observe high standards of integrity, impartiality, and honesty in conducting public business was a product of the gentry tradition. It was the application to public affairs of the same code of conduct that governed the gentleman in his private life. Gentry domination of eighteenth-century politics had been commonly justified on the ground that gentlemen were best qualified to govern precisely because they respected and practiced these principles. At the same time, the possession of wealth by the officeholder was presumed to remove the temptation to exploit the office for personal profit. This consideration underlay the proposal of Franklin and others that officeholders should serve without compensa-

tion. With the coming of democracy with its spoilsmanship, rotation of placemen in office, and the subordination
of the public interest to the business of machine politics,
the worst fears of the old gentry seemed to be realized. A
major function of the gentleman in nineteenth-century
politics was to restrain and civilize these primitive democratic impulses.

The principles of personal honor and integrity were
directly related to the gentry political program of the post-
Appomattox years. Free trade, sound money, and civil
service reform were generally defended at least in the first
instance on moral grounds. The gentry position on reconstruction of the South also reflected its distinctive point of
view. Reconciliation rather than vindictive oppression
should be sought by withdrawing troops, granting amnesty
to Confederate leaders, and refusing to build Republican
strength on the votes of freedmen. However mixed the
motives of Radical Republicans in enfranchising the
Negroes the gentry rejected them all. To use the Negro
vote for partisan purposes was unworthy, while the idealistic motive of guaranteeing political and civil rights to
the freedmen seemed premature and unwise. Many gentry
followed Godkin in his old-fashioned view of suffrage as
a privilege for which the Negro voter should be properly
qualified. Generations of servitude had been hardly a suitable preparation for the responsibilities of citizenship.
Disinterested though their motives may have been, the
gentry were certainly short-sighted in failing to foresee the
consequences of turning the freedmen over to the tender
mercies of the southern whites. No gentry voice was raised

in protest when in the years after 1877 southerners elaborated the new system of segregation and caste subordination to replace chattel slavery. Indeed, the northern gentry were almost pathetically eager to accept southern assurances that the Negro would be "protected" in his civil and constitutional rights.[22]

Nowhere else were the limitations of the gentry political intelligence more vividly apparent than in the failure to defend the civil and political rights of the freedmen. Godkin, who had chided the gentry for their earlier evasion of the slavery issue, now saw no inconsistency in abandoning the freedman until such time as accumulated experience in freedom would render him fit for active citizenship. Had the gentry rallied behind the Radical program and insisted upon enforcement of Negro rights under the Fourteenth and Fifteenth Amendments it is conceivable that the southern caste system with all of its tragic consequences might never have emerged. Lacking the gentry flair for dramatizing the moral content of public issues, and indeed largely indifferent to them, the Radicals could not see beyond the manipulation of Negro votes for partisan purposes, and the public quickly tired of radical reconstruction.

Their obvious desire to evade the race problem was in part at least a function of the political strategy of effecting an alliance with the southern gentry. Although the existence of such a group was largely a figment of the northern imagination, enough Southerners of the gentry type did exist to support the hope that in combination the gentry of both regions could effectively advance national reunion.

Robert Underwood Johnson proposed that the Southerner Thomas Nelson Page should promote reconciliation by writing a novel setting forth the respective virtues of the two regions. Page responded with *Meh Lady; A Story of the War,* in which the sectional variants of the gentleman were set over against each other in florid counterpoint. James Russell Lowell went so far as to say that the entire object of the North had been to preserve the Union, and that emancipation had been merely incidental.[23] While no effective political or social combination emerged from these overtures they did serve to divert gentry attention from civil rights and the problems of the freedmen.

The personal disinterestedness of the post-war gentry was sometimes carried to pathological extremes. The younger John Quincy Adams, oldest of the famous sons of Charles Francis Adams, was five times an unsuccessful Democratic candidate for the governorship of Massachusetts. Although no one would accuse any Adams of pursuing a political career out of motives of personal profit, this member of the family was compulsively eager to insist upon his purity of motive. When his father offered condolences after one of his defeats the son replied:

> As to the trouble, pain, and expense of my politics, I hope that you do not think that I did it for a reward. I do trust that you know me to be sincere when I say that I do not wish, and would shun, any political honors. Once and for all understand me—do—when I assure you on my honor, that absurd as it may look, I took my line last fall solely from a sense of duty and because I felt that the time demanded that an insignificant person like

myself do his little d——est. I see now that you consider
my views Quixotic—but I neither expected nor hoped
for success nor desired notoriety or applause—if it had
been a winning cause I would not have touched it.[24]

Such fastidiousness contrasted strongly with the more realistic outlook of the prewar gentry, whose political hero,
Daniel Webster, openly accepted princely gifts of money
from wealthy admirers without tarnishing his god-like
qualities in gentry eyes.

The defensiveness and sense of vulnerability underlying
Adams's disavowal of winning causes had a sound foundation in political fact. As popular respect for gentility was
replaced by veneration for money, the political influence
of the social-economic elite overshadowed that of the
gentry. Wealthy men in increasing numbers sought political careers, especially in the United States Senate, to which
election by state legislatures obviated the necessity of
going through the arduous routine of a popular election.
Gentlemen, on the other hand, found increasing resistance
to their claims to public leadership, especially among recent immigrant groups for whom local traditions had little
meaning. An event that symbolized the new political
climate occurred in 1868, when Massachusetts Republicans sought to elect Richard Henry Dana, Jr., author of
the celebrated *Two Years Before the Mast,* to the Congressional seat held by the adventurer General Ben Butler.
Fancying himself a man of the people and sponsoring
various reform causes, Butler sensed that the time was ripe
for an open attack on the political pretensions of gentility.
Mercilessly he ridiculed Dana for his white gloves, fine

manners, proud ancestry, and aristocratic preferences. Dana was paralyzed by such tactics, and the people easily outvoted the bondholders.[25] Lowell's indignation boiled over as he gloomily wrote to John W. Field that the gentleman must stand silently by while his ideals were subjected to contemptuous ridicule.[26]

Something of this mood of despair permeated the ranks of the gentry when they finally abandoned hope of reforming the Grant administration and openly rebelled against the regular Republican party organization in 1872. The elements of the Liberal Republican program had been well established before the prospect of Grant's renomination brought the rebellion to a head. Gentry opponents of the high tariff, led by Edward Atkinson, David A. Wells, Horace White, Carl Schurz, and Godkin, had formed the American Free Trade League in 1869 and had worked hard to defeat protectionist candidates in the Congressional elections of 1870. They had been active advocates of civil service reform since the end of the War. The widely publicized departure of gentlemen from the administration overshadowed the fact that many more remained in their places. By 1871, a number of local organizations of antiadministration Republicans had sprung up around the country.[27]

The rebellious Republicans who answered the call to the Cincinnati convention on May 1, 1872 included many disgruntled politicians who could hardly be identified with the gentry or their program. Opposition to Grant was the factor that united them. The assembly was of necessity an "open" convention of delegates recruited in various ways and reflecting a variety of tensions and issues in several states. In most states self-appointed committees selected the delegates; in others, general invitations to attend were issued publicly. Few of the delegations were instructed or controlled by party organizations.[28] Carl Schurz, the principal gentry spokesman, told the convention in his keynote speech that the people demanded not only good intentions but "superior intelligence, coupled with superior virtue." [29] The gentry delegates were confident that their candidate for the presidential nomination, the elder Charles Francis Adams, would represent these qualities with distinction, and they underestimated the strength of those who favored a practical politician who would deal with the various factions and perhaps have a chance of defeating Grant. As the balloting began, Adams was the strongest of several candidates, but he lacked the votes to win at the outset, and after five ballots his supporters disintegrated in confusion. Adams himself, in the best gentry tradition, scrupulously refrained from giving his admirers encouragement or support, either publicly or privately.[30] The winner was Horace Greeley, a maverick journalist and publisher wholly unacceptable to the gentry, as much for his character and eccentricities as for his support of a high tariff.

The defeat of Adams was a crushing blow to gentry aspirations. They felt themselves to have been the victims of wily politicians who had manipulated the convention in order to defeat its legitimate purpose. In the wake of their failure to control an open, unorganized convention they floundered to the other extreme and discussed the desirability of holding a closed convention of carefully selected "notables." Schurz suggested to Godkin that fifty to one hundred men of recognized standing in the political and social worlds be invited to a meeting at which Adams's name could be safely placed in nomination. A conference to discuss this possibility was held in New York on June 20, six weeks after the Cincinnati debacle, but a decision was wisely made not to put forward a third Republican candidate.[31]

Why did the gentry liberals carefully nurture the public image of themselves as high-minded but gullible gentlemen hoodwinked by crafty politicians when in fact the politicians seem to have had no more confidence in Greeley than they, and when the politicians had been equally incapable of controlling the delegates at Cincinnati?[32] The explanation doubtless lies in the pervasive sense of futility and decay that gripped the gentry of the Gilded Age. The romantic image of the gallant gentleman going down to inevitable destruction with flags flying, was widely indulged by those who sensed the growing disrepute of gentry values among the mass of the population.

Not all the gentry yielded to this mood of despair, however. Younger and more vigorous men continued the struggle for reform. One of these was Henry Adams, editor of the *North American Review* and assistant professor of history at Harvard, who still found time for frequent political trips to Washington and for fund-raising in an unsuccessful attempt to purchase a Boston newspaper in order to secure a reform mouthpiece in the Hub. Looking ahead to 1876, Adams joined with his brother Charles,

Carl Schurz, Sam Bowles of the *Springfield Republican,* and young Henry Cabot Lodge to organize liberal support for the presidential candidacy of Schurz or Benjamin Bristow. Grant would be unavailable in 1876, but the liberals feared the possibility that James G. Blaine or Roscoe Conkling might obtain the Republican nomination. Mindful of their bitter frustration in 1872, they felt that the best strategy would be to pressure the Republican convention into nominating a reform candidate. In one respect the liberals were stronger in 1876 than in the previous campaign. Because the Republican image was tarnished by scandals, and the Democratic opposition promised to be more vigorous, they were now in a better position to make their demands heard. Schurz realized this, if all the others did not. A conference of liberal Republicans organized by Schurz, Theodore Dwight Woolsey, Horace White, Lodge, and others, and carefully controlled by them, was held at the Fifth Avenue Hotel in New York on May 15 and 16, 1876. Its object was to pressure the Republican convention into nominating a reform candidate. An "Address to the People" drafted by Schurz declared that the liberals would not support a candidate who would not pledge himself to end corruption and to assert his independence of party managers. The candidate must be a man of proven integrity. Independent action was not preferable, but the liberals threatened to take it if their conditions were not satisfied. Pressure of this kind proved to be more effective than the rebellion of 1872. Neither Schurz nor Bristow received the Republican nomination, but the convention chose Rutherford B.

Hayes, who was acceptable to Schurz and to most of the gentry liberals. Hayes in turn acknowledged the value of this gentry support by appointing Schurz and William M. Evarts to his cabinet.[33]

During these later decades of gentry decline the high-water mark of political influence was probably reached in 1876. Although the Mugwump movement of 1884 is better known than the previous gentry rebellions against party regularity, its outcome in the election of Cleveland was at best an ambiguous indication of gentry political strength. Republican reform clubs had been active for several years in states like New York and Massachusetts, where politicians of the stripe of Conkling and Butler seemed particularly obnoxious to gentry sensibilities. These clubs let it be known that they would bolt the party if Blaine were to receive the Republican nomination in 1884. When their worst fears were realized the liberals transferred their support to Cleveland, although the well-organized reform clubs provided a potential basis for liberal Republican political action.

Mr. Dooley's celebrated definition of Mugwumpery— mug on one side of the fence, wump on the other—touched the heart of the gentry political dilemma. Following the nomination of Blaine, the Massachusetts Mugwumps proposed to support an independent Republican candidate, but they were overruled by the New York Mugwumps, who preferred to work for the nomination of Cleveland by the Democrats. Only if an unacceptable Democrat were to be nominated would the New Yorkers consider an independent candidate of their own. No one seems to have taken seriously Charles W. Eliot's call for a new national party with a promise of permanence. The nomination of Cleveland determined the dubious course the Mugwumps were to follow.[34]

So long as the liberals had supported independent candidates of their own they could continue to lay claim to the honored name of Republican, no matter how offensive they might be to their stalwart brethren. But once they crossed over to support the Democrat their political identity became suspect. Party loyalty could no longer be a part of their political creed. The more perceptive of them realized that thenceforth they must make their way as independents.[35] Theodore Roosevelt and Henry Cabot Lodge refused to take this course, doubtless persuaded that the political careers they were determined to pursue could best be advanced through party loyalty. The practical wisdom of this view became only too apparent in 1896, when the conservative Cleveland gave way to the radical Bryan. The issue as the gentry now saw it was not merely morality, as it had been in Blaine's heyday, but socialism and the integrity of the Constitution itself. Trapped in this hopeless dilemma the former Mugwumps could either support the pathetic "Gold Democrat" ticket, which meant in effect to vote for McKinley, or remain silent. The course of "bolting" and "scratching" which they had pursued since 1872 had finally reduced the gentry elite to political impotence.[36]

PATRONAGE AND PARTY POLITICS

The political dispossession of the gentry in the years after Appomattox was not to be accepted without a struggle. George William Curtis went about the country lecturing all who would listen on the responsibility of educated men to furnish the public with leadership. They must not withdraw in the face of popular contempt for their pretensions to special competence. They should remember that the Founding Fathers had been educated gentlemen, and that more recently it had been the gentry of New York who had rescued the city from Tweed. Indeed, it was a prime function of the educated citizen to define the proper limits of the powers of the majority, while acknowledging its legitimate authority.[37]

The securing of individual liberty was for Curtis, as for Godkin, the ultimate object of government. Throughout history, liberty had been made more secure by restricting executive power. This had been the great lesson of Anglo-American political experience from the Magna Carta to the Petition of Right and the Declaration of Independence. Under modern democratic conditions it was the political party that controlled the executive power by virtue of its management of the executive succession. The security of liberty under law therefore required that public-spirited citizens actively engage in party politics. This was the only alternative to control by selfish, venal, and ignorant politicians. Educated men must shoulder duties that were often wearisome and distasteful—attendance at caucuses and committee meetings, the assumption of duties and expenses, and the willingness to stand for public office. Practicing what he preached, Curtis engaged himself actively in politics. Several times an unsuccessful reform candidate, he struggled hopelessly against the well-oiled New York Republican machine managed by Roscoe Conkling.[38] The latter, who affected an acidulous mock-gentility in his public manner, was especially offensive to gentry sensibilities.

Gentry who, like Curtis, were drawn into politics out of a sense of public duty found themselves grappling with a system in which patronage had introduced mercenary considerations of the most blatant sort. It seemed to them that the spoils system corrupted the very foundations of government by shifting the focus from a contest over policies to a struggle for office and patronage. As Curtis put it, "the consequences are unavoidable. The moral tone of the country is debased. The national character deteriorates. No country or government can safely tolerate such a surely increasing demoralization." [39] The outcome of this conviction was the major gentry activity of the later nineteenth century, the crusade for civil service reform, in which Curtis played a leading role. As a member of the Civil Service Commission established by President Grant in 1871, and the author of its first report, and later as President of the National Civil Service Reform League, Curtis kept up a constant drumfire of exposure and criticism which helped to extend and strengthen the merit system in the public service.[40]

Civil service reform was a cause uniquely suited to the

gentry status and outlook. As libertarians unable to unite upon a positive political program they could nevertheless rally solidly around an issue involving administrative procedure. The corruption and inefficiency so patent under the spoils system challenged the gentry values of integrity and public spirit, and the moral issue touched the gentleman on one of his most sensitive spots. In Curtis's words:

> what we affirm is, that the theory which regards places in the public service as prizes to be distributed after an election, like plunder after a battle, the theory which perverts public trusts into party spoils, making public employment dependent upon personal favor and not on proven merit, necessarily ruins the self-respect of the public employees, destroys the function of the party in a republic, prostitutes elections into a desperate strife for personal profit, and degrades the national character by lowering the moral tone and standard of the country.[41]

Less significant, perhaps, but thoroughly objectionable to gentry taste was the unseemly scramble for places which occurred with each change of administration. Curtis quoted with approval Josiah Quincy's complaint of 1811 about the "clamors of the craving animals at the Treasury trough here in the Capitol. Such running, such jostling, such wriggling, such clambering over one another's backs, such squealing because the tub is so narrow and the company so crowded!" [42] The remedy for these abuses was a merit system of public employment which would use the attractive device of examination as a test of fitness. The principle of competitive examinations open to all citizens had been incorporated in the original Civil Service Reform bill of 1865 sponsored by Representative T. A. Jenckes, like Curtis a prominent member of the Rhode Island gentry. It was necessary for proponents of examination to explain repeatedly that it was not intended to favor educated people, in spite of the well-founded popular suspicion that such people would enjoy an unfair advantage over less literate competitors. Speaking for the Civil Service Commission, Curtis insisted that since there was an unmistakable connection between ignorance and vice it was only appropriate to favor a practice which encouraged education, promoted efficiency, and raised the character of applicants for public employment.[43]

Ben Butler shrewdly observed that civil service reform was a matter of vital importance to the Outs, and of supreme indifference to the Ins. The gentry were out, and without being wholly conscious of the irony, they strenuously sought in the name of the public a reform which would greatly strengthen their position. If gentlemen could obtain places in the civil service by merit and be protected from removal for patronage reasons they could serve the public without demeaning themselves by political huckstering. By the same token, the area in which political parties were supreme would be narrowed, while the scope of efficiency and merit would be correspondingly extended.

But the ostensible concern of the gentry was the public welfare, and their interest in reform led to a thorough-going critique of party politics. The ultimate evil of the spoils system was that it entailed the corruption of the political party, diverting it from its proper object. The

special class of patronage officeholders, deliberately swollen
by sinecures and inefficiency, had now captured political
power through party control. Their object was not the
national welfare, but the welfare of the party. "Party
spirit, from the first," Curtis warned, "has been the terror
of republics." [44] Once it had become the instrument of
patronage the party ceased to concern itself with legitimate matters of public policy.

Curtis knew of only one serious objection to civil service
reform. It was that parties were necessary to representative
government, and that to do their work effectively they
must be able to appeal to motives of self-interest, since all
government was presumed to rest on a system of rewards
and punishments. Curtis held that some public offices were
policy-making offices and others not. Only the former were
properly subject to party control. Jefferson's party had not
been built upon patronage; and bitter though the struggle
had been, the victory over the Federalists had not eventuated in wholesale removals from office. Although he traced
the origins of the spoils system to Jackson, Curtis repeatedly insisted that it was for all practical purposes a modern
innovation. The Founding Fathers had shown their moral
courage by heroically resisting spoilsmanship.[45]

Educated men knew from their study of history that
sooner or later every republic had been seized by the party
spirit, the "master passion" which had substituted party
welfare for the national welfare. For a decade following
Appomattox, Republican stalwarts had waved the bloody
shirt in attempts to convince their fellow Americans that
party regularity was synonymous with patriotism. Henry

Adams was to make this the central theme of his novel *Democracy*.[46] The individual was required to surrender his judgment and integrity to the dictates of party discipline on the threat of being branded a disloyal renegade. Curtis believed he was witnessing the emergence of single-party dictatorship, a "permanent revolution." To avert this danger the informed and public-spirited citizen must insist upon his independence. In this spirit the Liberal Republicans had broken with the Grant faction in 1872 and in 1884 had bolted to Cleveland.

The political dilemma of the latter-day gentry was well illustrated in Curtis's ambiguous attitude toward party government. He conceded that parties were necessary to select candidates and crystallize issues. They should be responsive to the popular will. Unfortunately, however, parties tended to nurture "machines" consisting of the oligarchies of professional politicians who lived off emoluments of place and exercised absolute control of their parties. "The machine has no public purpose, no faith in private honor or integrity or patriotism." In New York State, where Curtis fought the machine for years, its power lay in the ward associations where delegates to the party conventions were chosen. Party regularity was the criterion for admission to the associations, so that able but independent Republicans were disfranchised from the outset. After such manipulation the formal election was merely a "Bonapartean plebiscite." The machine politician nurtured by such a system had no conception of the public interest; his sole objects were personal power and profit.[47]

It seemed to Curtis that the superstition of divine right

had passed from the king to the party. Treason and rebellion against such tyranny was the only true conservatism. Two counterrevolutionary weapons were available to the gentry. One was scratching and bolting, devices which were occasionally used in New York with but little effect. The other was civil service reform designed to deprive the machine of the power of patronage. Curtis believed that without spoils of office with which to reward the faithful, the machine would collapse. The party would then perforce revert to its true function of providing the leaders who would form and guide public opinion. These leaders would, of course, be gentlemen, men of patriotic intelligence capable of swaying great masses of men "as the moon draws the waters of the sea." [48] The gentry of Curtis's generation still professed to believe that if public opinion actually governed, they were capable of shaping that opinion.

OUTSIDE THE PARTY SYSTEM

The interrelated issues of political independence and partisanship, morality and efficiency in public office, civil service reform and scientific management of public enterprises all marked the wavering influence of the gentry elite in American public life at the end of the nineteenth century. The subtle diffusion of gentility throughout the population endowed these issues with a relevance they would not otherwise have claimed, while at the same time the public was brought to share in values which had earlier been the more exclusive concern of the gentry. The reason

underlying the gentry retreat from politics toward an
asceptic conception of scientific administration was revealed by Moorfield Storey in 1889:

> The conditions of society have changed. The prizes of
> life are no longer political. The methods by which in
> most cases nominations are obtained and elections car-
> ried are inevitably distasteful to a sensitive man.[49]

But there still remained important public services which
the gentleman was uniquely qualified to render. There
was a growing demand for highly trained administrators
to manage the rapidly growing public agencies of the
emerging welfare state. This demand fathered the notion
of a scientific elite functioning in the public interest but
outside organized politics. The personnel of this elite
was scattered through the federal bureaus and agencies,
and in Washington found its social rallying point in the
Cosmos Club, organized in 1878. One of the principal objects of civil service reform was to foster and motivate this
elite. As Whitelaw Reid remarked, popular government
was entitled to be the beneficiary of "the finest culture and
the highest intellectual power available." [50]

Another role the gentleman could play outside the traditional bounds of politics was that of nonpartisan municipal
reformer. Both in numbers and in influence the gentry
remained strongest in the cities, where the national party
divisions were often irrelevant to local issues. In his presidential address to the American Bar Association in 1894,
Moorfield Storey defined the gentry independent's role in
politics as essentially educational. Through press, pulpit,

and platform he could still hope to reach and influence the public. His impulse for sociability could be turned to useful account through the organization of city clubs, public forums, and citizens' unions which would serve as effective centers of reform activity.[51]

Formal education in the twentieth century no longer stood for a unifying culture, as it had formerly professed, but increasingly for a segregating expertise. When William Howard Taft in 1906 reminded educated men of their public responsibilities he found it necessary to speak to them as political outsiders. He advised them that if they were to be successful in politics they would have to learn how to rub elbows with laborers and saloon-keepers, convincing such influential political types that gentlemen did not hold themselves above the common herd. Such special influence as the educated man might claim stemmed only from his fund of information and acquired knowledge of public affairs. Successfully managed, these contacts would broaden his sympathies for the mass and correct the biases of the classroom. Advice of this kind reflected the ambiguities of social relationships in the mass society. The elite man might be superior with respect to his elite function, yet he must accommodate his superiority to the equalitarian expectations of the mass. The latter-day gentry generally proved to be either unwilling or unable to make this accommodation. A few gentry families managed to survive in twentieth-century American politics, notably the Tafts and the Roosevelts, but the distinctive development of the new century was the emergence in politics of the social-economic elite. Taft anticipated this development when he noted the rapid increase in the number of large fortunes at the beginning of the twentieth century. These fortunes would be available to support young men willing to devote themselves to the public service. England had long reaped the advantages of having such a class, which had done wonders "for the high tone of their public men." When rich Americans similarly came to a sense of their civic potentialities a great step would have been taken toward elevating public life.[52] But no such opportunities seemed to beckon to the well-educated. Taft had addressed his advice to Yale men, and the time would soon come when Josephus Daniels would similarly speak of the political handicap of a Harvard education.[53]

Gentility had always provided a standard for personal character. Those who felt deeply about it placed character at the center of their thinking about social matters. In politics the most important question was what kind of political leadership did the system produce? Did it display integrity, high moral character, ability, and public spirit? If not, the country was in trouble. While they were also interested in issues, the gentry reached no consensus that could sustain an organization of their own. The issues they felt most strongly about were those closely related to character, such as civil service reform, corruption, and tariff and currency questions, in all of which moral principles seemed to be at stake. With the passing of the gentry, judgments as to character ceased to have much importance in American political life. Issues came to have an almost exclusive relevance. No one seemed to care much about the moral character of a politician so long as he did what was wanted of him. The twentieth-century science of public relations with its expert management of public images tended to homogenize everything in a gray moral neutrality. Under these circumstances a curious reversal of roles occurred. Educated and professional descendants of the gentry became largely preoccupied with issues and oblivious of character, while the mass revealed an intuitive feeling for character and often made its political discriminations on this basis.

It was apparent by the end of the nineteenth century that a distinctive gentry position on political issues was impossible. Although the gentleman's successor, the intellectual, might continue to serve a useful function as a critic of party politics, his role was inevitably restricted to criticism. Without organization his power was limited, and organization implied regularity. Politics, like other practical affairs, involved compromise. The politician must subject himself to the necessary measure of party discipline. These requirements implied a more pliable temperament than the tradition of gentility had nurtured.

The gentry contribution to American political life was nevertheless a significant one. The attenuation and diffusion of gentry manners at the end of the nineteenth century had its parallel in the universalization of gentry conceptions of public service which underlay the idealism of the Progressive era. The idea that the state had a vital stake in the welfare of all its citizens was but the next step beyond the notion that the officeholder was a disinterested servant of the public. This progressive gospel of service and efficiency was essential in making the idea of the welfare state palatable.

· VI ·

ANCIENTS
AND MODERNS:
AN EDUCATION
CONTROVERSY

IN 1883, twenty-seven years after his graduation from Harvard, the younger Charles Francis Adams returned to his alma mater to report on the effectiveness of his education in preparing him for the kind of active life he had been leading since his graduation. Soldier, journalist, public servant, railroad executive, business promoter and land speculator, few men had a broader practical acquaintance with American life in the Gilded Age than did Adams.

More in sorrow than in anger, he informed the Phi Beta Kappa Society that as a place to prepare young men for the struggle of life Harvard had been a resounding failure. "Superstitions and wrong theories and worse practices" had imposed insuperable handicaps on the young graduate, and it was little consolation to know that the other American colleges had been equally derelict.[1] Moreover, during the generation since Adams's graduation, the Western world had been dramatically transformed. The transportation and communications revolutions had annihilated space and brought masses of men into instantaneous contact with each other, triggering the release of enormous mental and physical energies. Advancing science was rapidly displacing the older authorities; and as they responded to these forces it seemed to the thoughtful observer that the civilized nations were rapidly becoming one people. Above all, the conditions of modern life required that each individual who would amount to anything must master some specialized field of competence. Nothing was penalized more severely than superficiality.

One of Adams's principal complaints was that the college had done and was still doing nothing to prepare the student for this situation, or to equip him with a useful or relevant skill. It had insisted upon allocating a substantial part of his time to acquire a superficial acquaintance with two dead languages, while ignoring the necessity of mastering English and modern foreign languages. In an age of science only a meager introduction to any of the sciences was available. Adams had no objection to a thorough classical education as such, but he insisted that a liberal education should have modern as well as ancient sources, and that a student should if he wished have an opportunity to immerse himself in modern thought. Repeatedly, Adams referred to the gulf which had opened up between the world and the college: the world required thoroughness and practicality; the college nurtured superficiality and impracticality.

The symbol of everything that was deficient in collegiate education was Greek. By requiring this difficult and esoteric language for admission, the college prevented the schools from teaching anything thoroughly. Once admitted, the student would continue to devote a substantial portion of his time to this language, although he would rarely acquire a sufficient mastery of it for effective use. Around this "college fetish" the pedagogues had erected their defensive rationalizations. The study of Greek was said to provide severe intellectual training; to strengthen the memory; to provide incomparable discipline; and to impart to the student a subtle, precious residuum which would give its possessor a unique intellectual distinction.

Adams declared all this to be arrant nonsense. The study of Greek was in fact harmful to the extent that it failed to engage the observing and reflective faculties. It was absurd to claim that the kind of training that came from mathematics or physics was to be had from Greek. Adams insisted that he had no quarrel with the values of the liberal arts. He found them in modern as well as classical languages and literatures, and he contended only for the student's opportunity to choose his sources. As a practical compromise he proposed to the college authorities that they require Latin and English for admission, plus either Greek or two modern languages. He shrewdly observed in conclusion that the sanctity that hedged the classics was the only surviving patent of nobility possessed by the gentry in a world experiencing rapid democratization.[2]

Adams's remarks were something of a bombshell in the educational world, and received wide attention and comment. Although Charles William Eliot had been president of Harvard for more than a decade before Adams spoke out, and had been working toward the kind of reform Adams had in mind, the old order in collegiate education was still firmly entrenched, and the two parties, Ancients and Moderns, had yet to come publicly to grips. The controversy precipitated by Adams quickly spread beyond Harvard to the other major colleges, and resulted, after a decade of discussion, in substantial changes both in admissions requirements and in curricula. The principal casualty, as Adams had proposed, was to be the study of Greek.

The American colleges of the early nineteenth century were nominally supported by the religious denominations which had founded them, notably the Congregationalists and the Presbyterians. In fact, however, the curriculum was usually geared more to the liberal arts than to religion. Greek and Latin led not so much to the New Testament and the Church Fathers as to the arts and philosophy of pagan antiquity. The colleges were as much the property of the gentry as of the denominations, although the educational alliance between the two groups was so close that the distinction was rarely made. Josiah Quincy, who had

been President of Harvard when Adams was an undergraduate, had, in the words of his son, sought to make
the college "a nursery of high-minded, high-principled,
well-taught, well-conducted, well-bred gentlemen." [3] Andrew Jackson, the natural gentleman, had displayed the
proper attitude toward gentility when he admonished his
ward to obtain an education and thus achieve the respect-
able status of scholar and gentleman.[4]

The connecting link in the alliance between piety and
gentility was moral character. However much the evangel-
icals may have prized the dogma of sin and redemption, in
their role as educators they put prime emphasis on the
moral qualities requisite to a life of freedom and responsibility in a fluid society. For their part, the gentry, among
whom religious piety was often unobtrusive, responded by
imbuing the American concept of gentility with qualities
of earnestness and solemnity hardly found in European
notions of gentility. Ideality, indeed, became the common
gentry substitute for religion. Henry Adams in his younger
and less cynical mood had voiced this sentiment when he
confessed to a wish to be a man of the world, even a man
of pleasure, "and yet be something wiser, nobler, better." [5]
By virtue of their role as recruitment centers for the gentry
the early nineteenth century colleges were in a strategic
position to strengthen and perpetuate the strain of moral
earnestness.

The fully developed genteel culture of the later decades
of the nineteenth century represented the intellectual tradition of liberal humanism. Its principles and values were to
be found in a great body of literary works reaching back to

classical times. The wisdom embodied in these writings provided the most penetrating analyses of the human condition. The insights of Aristotle into political problems, for instance, were as fresh and relevant to the nineteenth century as to the times in which they were first conceived. Humanists assumed that human nature was always the same, and that to whatever extent education might assist the individual to understand himself, the great works of the past would provide inspiration and guidance.

An important role in determining the tone of gentry culture was played by such academic scholars as Longfellow and Lowell, who introduced generations of college students to the wisdom of Dante, Cervantes, Shakespeare, and Montaigne. A practical consequence of the humanistic point of view was reverence for the authority of texts. The wisdom of mankind was largely contained in the great books, which every educated person should know. The attitude of mind inculcated by this tradition was one of deference to authority. The prescribed text was the Word; and the teacher was an authoritative figure because he presided over the dispensation of the Word. The qualities of mind most to be admired were memory, verbal skills, and grammatical logic. Gentlemen were expected to study a common body of subject matter with little specialization. Scientific schools and technological institutes had grown up apart from and in an inferior status to the liberal arts colleges.

Because human nature was always the same, human experience was essentially repetitive. Genteel humanists rejected as naïve the more flamboyant forms of belief in

evolutionary progress. They were, of course, too sophisticated to reject evolutionary science as such, but they stubbornly refused to interpret human history in the currently
fashionable terms of development. In the long run, science
raised more difficult problems for gentility than did religion. Since the time of Bacon science had emphasized research and the discovery of new knowledge. Science was a
growing body of fact and principles, not merely an authoritative and essentially completed corpus of truth. The gentry usually failed to perceive this aspect of science. E. L.
Godkin complained to Henry Holt that "science killed the
imagination" by shrinking the immensity of experience
to dimensions susceptible to mechanical investigation.[6] He
assumed that the result would be to stifle literature, art,
and religion. The failure to accommodate science to gentry
culture had serious consequences. Ultimately, it was the
scientist as investigator who displaced the gentleman as
scholar.

THE SCIENCES AGAINST GREEK

Although Adams's challenge to the old order was ostensibly
addressed to his alma mater it was in fact accepted as an
attack on American collegiate education in general. The
champion who came forward to defend the Ancients was
President Noah Porter of Yale. Porter was a Congregation-
alist clergyman who had been professor of philosophy and
theology before becoming president in 1871. The Yale he
knew and strove to perpetuate offered the student a com-
munal experience, stiffened with moral purpose and dis-

cipline. The college encouraged the cultivation of strong bonds of sentiment and loyalty among classmates, achieved in part through class consciousness and class conflict—in an academic but not a social sense. It was assumed that in the intimacy of college living the students learned as much or more from each other as from their instructors. George Santayana, who visited Yale in 1892, neatly caught the difference between the two colleges when he reported that Harvard was a gentleman's college, whereas Yale made gentlemen.[7]

According to Yale's educational philosophy, the course of instruction should proceed from exact studies and memory training (languages and mathematics), to philosophy and the broad cultural subjects, such as the natural and social sciences and history. All students should study the same subjects, since the object was to train an educated gentry, not to prepare students for a vocation. The discipline of hard and unpleasant work was indispensable. As Porter admonished, "the student often most needs the discipline to which he is least inclined." The study of Greek and Latin was deemed ideal both for disciplinary and intellectual purposes. It was the classics that gave the Bachelor of Arts degree its universal content and relevance. Modern knowledge, on the other hand, could readily be picked up in the course of life. "A hard and positive narrowness of mind," Porter warned, "is the besetting danger of the science and literature of the present day." In any event, the limitations of time would not permit the addition of much specialized modern subject matter to the traditional curriculum.

Porter conceived of the college teacher in the image of the old-fashioned schoolmaster. He should teach with authority, take a personal interest in his students, and color the subject matter with the projection of his personality. Teaching rather than scholarly activity was the prime duty of the faculty. Porter might have conceded that in principle both functions should go together; in fact, however, he saw little necessity for a university to do the various things necessary to make research a reality.[8]

The entire curriculum of courses at Yale in Porter's day could have been listed on a single page of the college catalogue. The principal subjects were Greek, Latin, mathematics, and rhetoric. Somewhat less time was devoted to history, social science, physics, and French or German. One term only was reserved for courses in logic, astronomy, psychology, moral philosophy, history of philosophy, chemistry, geology, law, and jurisprudence. It was assumed that the mind consisted of the faculties of memory, reason, imagination, taste, and will, and that these faculties were to be developed through regular exercise. Although the curriculum was impressively comprehensive the subject matter was in fact covered only superficially. It was a rare student who could read Latin or Greek with ease.

Although Porter's defense of the traditional curriculum and pedagogy was ostensibly a reply to Charles Francis Adams, it was in fact directed at Charles William Eliot. Adams might be able to stir up public discussion, but it was Eliot who was in a position to affect the course of collegiate education. Eliot had become president of Harvard in 1869 after studying chemistry in Europe and teaching at the Massachusetts Institute of Technology. He had seen at first hand how the continental universities had been revitalized by the scholarly activity of their faculties, and he was possessed by a vision of the fruits that would spring from the union of discovery and learning. His curricular reforms were a by-product of this vision.

If the standards of liberal arts education in Eliot's day were low, those of professional education in law and medicine were even lower. His greatest accomplishment as an educational administrator was upgrading professional education to postgraduate status, and bringing it under unified management with the undergraduate liberal arts college, thus establishing the distinctively American type of university. As late as 1884, a majority of American professional men engaged in the practice of law, medicine, engineering, public service, and journalism were not holders of Bachelor of Arts degrees. Only among the clergy were liberal arts graduates in the majority. Eliot was strongly persuaded that liberal arts education was not safe in a country where the majority in the professions were not educated in the liberal arts. His solution was to make college prefatory to professional training; and to achieve this, the content of the liberal arts curriculum would have to be broadened and modernized.[9]

Eliot did not envision a sharp distinction between college and professional faculties. He assumed that the law and medical professors would offer courses to undergraduates, and that the "liberal" spirit would permeate the entire university. Several decades were required to accomplish these reforms, which encountered stubborn opposition both within and outside the Harvard faculty.

Although Porter was to accuse Eliot of failure to define what he meant by a liberal education, the latter's views seem in fact to have been stated clearly enough in his inaugural address of 1869 and reiterated frequently thereafter. There were four principal "methods of thought": those of language, mathematics, science, and faith. By the age of twenty-five, the student should have encountered each of these, and in addition should have studied one of them intensively. Eliot declined to say that any one of them possessed greater value than the others. He merely declared that the ancient prescribed curriculum had ignored differing traits of mind among students. He also proposed that the preparatory school should introduce the student to the principal fields of knowledge in order that the college student would already know what he liked best and was best suited for. The implementation of such a program would require a considerable broadening of college admissions requirements. The elective system of studies in college, with which Eliot's name was to be chiefly associated, was simply a provision for progressive freedom in the choice of courses following the prescribed curriculum of the freshman year. With what in retrospect seems like innocence Eliot insisted that all of the subjects offered for elective study should be liberal disciplines, as distinct from utilitarian or professional subjects.[10]

The freeing of the college from the dead hand of the classics was to be Eliot's chief claim to fame as an educational reformer. But he also moved decisively to sever the alliance between gentry and clergy insofar as that alliance rested on the joint control of the college. Some of the strongest passages of his inaugural address were directed to the distinction between the scholarly search for truth and "the authoritative inculcation of what the teacher deems true." The latter was doubtless appropriate in a seminary for priests, but it was not consistent with the spirit of the university. "The worthy fruit of academic culture is an open mind, trained to careful thinking, instructed in the methods of philosophic investigation, acquainted in a general way with the accumulated thought of past generations, and penetrated with humility." Although he might soften the blow by affirming that thus the modern university served Christ and the Church, the fact was that Eliot had irrevocably sundered the traditional bond between religion and learning.[11] Whether the gentleman as scholar unaided by the priest would be able to control the educational machine was a question which would soon be decided.

If the watchword of the Ancients was "discipline," the battle cry of the Moderns was "freedom." In the warfare of ideas who could doubt the outcome of such a conflict? Eliot took it for granted that elective freedom was to be restricted to the proper subject matter of the liberal arts curriculum—the arts and sciences—and would not include vocational subjects. The exercise of such freedom by students with differing interests and aptitudes would result in strengthened motivation and a firmer grip on the subject matter. One consequence was to exchange the full range of the traditional curriculum for greater concentration on chosen elements within it. Individual subjects were now better taught and more intensively studied. But the student often remained ignorant of certain of the liberal disciplines, and he sometimes failed to study the things necessary to pursue his own interests in full measure. Freedom in education implied an awareness and concern for individual differences. Eliot understood the appropriateness of such an educational philosophy in a democratic society. He was attempting to do for higher education what John Dewey was about to do for elementary education.

By posing the issue as one of scholarship versus culture Eliot had put the Ancients on the defensive, and greatly increased their bitterness. He had had the temerity to suggest that not only did English afford a far richer literature than Greek, but that the modern languages were now the vehicles of scholarship without which few subjects could be pursued exhaustively.[12] Porter could only reply that the study of the classics "exacted a discipline" that English could not furnish. He stubbornly reaffirmed the ancient definition of liberal education as "that kind of culture which tends to perfect the man in the variety and symmetry and effectiveness of his powers, by reflection and self-knowledge, by self-control and self-expression, as contrasted with that which brings wealth or skill or fame or power." [13]

Because it was apparent that Greek would be the principal casualty of the elective system, it was essential that the Ancients defend its central place in the liberal arts curriculum. The defense was undertaken by Porter's Yale colleague, George P. Fisher, historian and theologian. Fisher conceded that Greek no longer had the importance it had had in Renaissance times; but it was still essential for a broad and complete culture. Just as mathematics was necessary for understanding the sciences and the physical world, so a knowledge of Graeco-Roman history and civilization was necessary to understanding man and his place in modern society. Without Latin and Greek such a knowledge would be second-hand. The roots of the present were deeply embedded in classical antiquity, and without a knowledge of such roots the educated person would no longer share a cosmopolitan culture.

> In general, it is the increase of mental force, the refinement of sensibility and of perception, the facility in the use of the faculties, whether strictly rational or esthetic, which constitutes the main end and aim of culture. When this result is not attained, the best fruit of education is missed.[14]

ELIOT AND MODERN EDUCATION

The Yale faculty was by no means solidly united behind President Porter and the traditional curriculum. A powerful champion of the Moderns appeared in William Graham Sumner, a professor of political economy and sociology who had already crossed swords with Porter over the assignment of student reading in Herbert Spencer. Sumner's appraisal of the educational situation was similar to that of Adams, and it was couched in equally pungent language.

In no other civilized country, Sumner declared, was "mandarinism" in education so strong as in the United States. Nowhere else did youths and their parents look upon a college education as the gateway to membership in the gentry elite of supposedly "educated" and "cultivated" persons. "A few gentlemen with strong prejudices and limited experience of life" controlled the colleges, and through their admissions policies the schools as well. These mandarins carefully perpetuated the notion that what was useful was vulgar, and that the esoteric attainments of the classical curriculum were the adornments of a closed caste.

Like Adams, Sumner had a strong sense of the revolutionary impact of science upon modern civilization. The colleges of the previous generation had failed to keep pace with new knowledge, thanks to the monopoly exercised by the Ancients. Drastic educational reform was necessary, and if the price was to be the demise of gentility itself, Sumner was prepared to pay that price, perhaps because of his implicit assumption that much of what was best in the gentleman would survive in the man of science.

In any event, the classical education was now outmoded by the sciences, by modern logic, by critical historical study, and by political science and civil law. With a contemptuous glance in Porter's direction Sumner observed that the mentality of dogmatic certainty nurtured by the ancient curriculum and pedagogy was a definite handicap to college administrators. At once timid and autocratic, they knew exactly what should be studied, in what amounts, and in what order. Sumner confessed that it had cost him years of labor to overcome the deficiencies of his classical training. Its intellectual processes had been neither clear nor rigorous. It had provided him neither with useful methods of study nor the proper attitude toward work. A training which had been essentially literary, grammatical, and metaphysical had inculcated bad intellectual habits, such as reverence for the authority of the text rather than for the truth, excessive veneration for literary form, and love of paradox.

Sumner proposed that the university teach everything that anyone wanted to know. The student should be free to choose his own subject matter. But once chosen, the nature of the subject would dictate what must be done in order to achieve its mastery. The one rule should be that everything must be done thoroughly. Sumner emphatically rejected as false and superficial the ancient maxim that the student should be acquainted with the general principles underlying all things. It was "false and stupid" for a university to presume to decide what everyone ought to know. The philologist would certainly need classical studies, but the scientist could equally certainly do without them. "The vile doctrines of anti-culture" flourished in modern society just in proportion to the degree to which gentry culture had become precious and artificial.[15] A generation later, after the controversy had already become academic, Sumner's erstwhile student, Thorstein Veblen, was to carry this argument a step further by showing how the moribund Ancient curriculum had been taken over by the social-economic elite, which would thus adorn its brows with the faded laurels of gentility.[16]

Sumner was singularly insensitive to the social dimensions of the conflict, but with the decisive defeat of the Ancients it quickly became apparent to other observers that the gentry were a principal casualty. Without a distinctive curriculum to place its stamp upon the graduate, the college no longer functioned to produce gentlemen. By 1897 it was apparent to Professor Harry Thurston Peck of Columbia that one could no longer assume the university man to be a gentleman and a scholar. Now that all subjects were of equal importance and equally available to the student no bond of common intellectual experience united university men in brotherhood.[17] The mob had invaded the campus and leveled it down to social mediocrity.

After the battle had been lost, the surviving gentlemen were tempted to indulge in nostalgic dreams of an earlier and better time when a common liberal education had nurtured a special class, a sacred band, whose influence for sanity and serenity had been out of proportion to its numbers. From this caste had come the founders of the Republic, and, indeed, those responsible for every great accomplishment in history. Peck went so far in his disillusionment as to question the wisdom of universal education. Education meant ambition, and ambition meant discontent. By educating all its citizens the state merely condemned most of them to unhappiness. Everywhere one could observe the masses seething with restless discontent, ripe for the agitator. Let education be restricted to the unhappy few! A true university should produce an intellectual elite, a small highly trained patriciate which would dominate society and control public life. Such a caste would be possible if the universities would only concentrate their energies on the humanities and liberal arts.

Eliot, however, was by no means persuaded that the transformation of the university spelled the demise of gentility. No one was more persistent in attempting to reconcile gentry values with changing educational needs. From the inaugural address of 1869 to the last speeches of 1911 he returned repeatedly to the theme. His own public interests had always conformed closely to the common gentry pattern. A political liberal with Mugwump leanings, he supported free trade and civil service reform. Like so many gentlemen of the 1880s and 1890s he interested himself in municipal reform. Through the activities of his son Charles Eliot, the landscape architect, he became involved in the conservation movement. He was sufficiently sympathetic to labor to support collective bargaining, but he drew the line at the closed shop and once designated the scab as an "American hero." [18]

Eliot's object was to modernize the concept of gentility by adapting it to the needs of a democratic society. He adhered to the gentry tradition in his emphasis on the importance of public education in preparing young people for the responsibilities and opportunities of citizenship in a free society. To the gentry, democracy had always meant freedom of opportunity to realize one's potentialities, and the outcome was a society of great diversity. The schools must prepare the young to participate effectively in a mobile society, counteracting the divisive effects of mobility by inculcating in the students a respect for talented leadership. While recognizing that individual differences among students would result ultimately in differing status positions, the schools should at the same time teach the great truth that social as well as individual well-being depended on ethical principle. "Selfishness, greed, falseness, brutality and ferocity are as hateful and degrading in a multitude as they are in a single savage." [19]

Eliot squarely confronted but could not resolve the educational dilemma which the gentry had always faced. They all acknowledged that the fundamental object of democratic education was to lift the entire population to a higher plane of intelligence and behavior. But it must also respect individuality and recognize individual differences of ability and aptitude. The vague democratic desire for equality should be sternly suppressed. The particular capacities of individual students should be ascertained as early as possible, and elective options should be introduced into the school curriculum at least as early as the fifth grade in order to serve these aptitudes.

In his attempt to reconcile these divergent needs Eliot anticipated the progressivism of Dewey. The great truth of democratic society should be firmly implanted in the mind of each child, namely, the mutual dependence of individuals upon one another. This truth could be effectively taught by studying the basic economic processes of the community.[20] The study of history would confirm the essential unity of the community and the dependence of successive generations upon their predecessors. At the same time, however, Eliot refused to compromise with the scholarly emphasis on subject matter. The first twelve years of schooling should introduce the student to all the main divisions of knowledge: languages and literature, mathematics, science, history, drawing, music, and manual training. All students should acquire a capacity for exact observation, description, and reasoning, the prerequisites for every form of intellectual activity. In 1897, when Eliot expressed these views, the high schools were still primarily college preparatory schools, enrolling only a small portion of the school-age population, and the great debates over the intellectual capacities of the average student were still in the future.

Because he shared the growing conviction of the gentry of his generation that representative democratic institutions were incapable of coping with the complex issues of an urban industrial society, Eliot's theory of education emphasized the importance of inculcating in the young a due respect for the work of the expert. American experience since 1877 had shown that legislatures were incapable of dealing successfully with problems of taxation, currency, and public works. Such matters needed to be managed by qualified experts working within broad guidelines established by elected representatives. Democracy would not be safe until the people understood that government must be conducted on the same principles as a successful private business. Above all, schoolchildren must be taught to recognize and venerate the "democratic nobility" from which these experts were to be drawn, the men and women whose intelligence, taste, and devotion to the public welfare set them apart as the most valued class in the community. In a democratic society this nobility was the product of a fine inheritance, careful education, and a rich experience. From its example the student would learn that service to others was the surest source of personal satisfaction.[21]

The democratic nobility were, of course, the gentry. Eliot devoted considerable attention to the functions of gentility in a democracy and to the methods by which a gentry elite was to be perpetuated. Inevitably, manners were a central issue. Manners in a democracy should be more uniform than in a feudal or military society, and of a high average quality. Eliot acknowledged that many forces were working to debase manners. In the urban setting it seemed doubtful that the home, school, and church could continue to play their traditional roles in fixing good manners. Corrupting influences now emanated from street gangs, athletic teams, and the "smart set." In the face of these challenges, the importance of the gentry as custodians of the highest standards could not be overemphasized. Among them, at least, it should be possible to preserve the traditional distinction between manners and breeding. Fine homes and a distinguished social milieu would continue to provide the environment in which standards of learning, service, and manners would flourish.[22]

Eliot was determined to adapt the traditions of gentility to the leadership needs of a democratic society. In dedicating Harvard to the nurture of such a leadership he insisted that the spirit of the university was intensely democratic. If it was true that "you could always tell a Harvard man by his manners," it was also true that at their best these were democratic manners. The changes in gentility brought about by democratization were all for the good. These changes reinforced such qualities as generosity, serenity, and considerateness. The gentleman was still a man of power, but the modes of his activity reflected the adroitness with which results had to be achieved when arbitrary command had become passé.

As an educated man the latter-day gentleman must be familiar both with the scientific method and with some branch of human learning. In him the passion for knowledge and the passion for service must fuse. By physical exercise and the cultivation of some form of manual skill the gentleman would testify to the importance of a fluent interaction with the physical world. As a leader and a man of action Eliot's gentleman would exemplify the perennial truth that "the solid satisfactions of life are won only through labor." [23] In Theodore Roosevelt, with his "strenuous life" and his comprehensive democratic social sympathies, Eliot's Harvard produced an excellent example of the democratic gentleman.

Eliot's thinking revealed the dilemma faced by the gentry with respect to higher education: how to preserve gentry culture and at the same time meet the educational demands of the age? Eliot believed that he could improve the quality of higher education; and there is no doubt that he succeeded in specializing it. But he also believed that he could preserve the values of gentry culture by adapting them to the needs of a democratic society. In this he failed, as several of his more perceptive contemporaries remarked.

By the turn of the century, the Harvard historian

Ephraim Emerton observed sadly that the qualities of gentility and scholarship were no longer regarded as "necessarily combined or as forming two essential parts of a single complete and beautiful whole." Neither ideal had been abandoned, but they seemed to have become separated from each other. The traditional education of a gentleman had been liberal rather than professional. It had provided a certain body of knowledge, a kind of power of thought and expression, and a sense of the largeness and beauty of intellectual life. In America, the gentle life had implied a devotion to intellectual culture rather than the pursuit of a practical calling. It seemed to Emerton that German scholarship and the rapid growth of interest in science had dealt a fatal blow to the genteel tradition.[24] Emerton knew that in England gentility had been largely confined to a social class, to which the universities were merely appendages. In America, where no such confines were recognized, the colleges and universities themselves came to bear an increasing share of the burden of maintaining gentility. By the First World War, Henry Holt would note that "culture" was largely restricted to the teaching class, a sufficient indication of its anemic condition.

Frederick J. Stimson also believed that Harvard had lost its traditional capacity to equate learning with social status. He assumed that in the middle of the nineteenth century Harvard professors had been men of national reputation, who were respected as such by their students and who lived in a style befitting their status. By the end of the century, however, their social and economic status had

deteriorated to the point where students could only conclude that there was something servile about high thinking.
Living in poor homes without servants, the faculty no
longer met their students on terms of social equality. For
all his efforts to reinvigorate gentility Eliot had only succeeded in cementing the relationship between poverty
and learning. It was not surprising to Stimson that the
sons of the newly rich should have seen nothing to disabuse
them of their contempt for mere scholars.[25]

· VII ·

THE HERITAGE OF
TOCQUEVILLE

THE GENTRY with whom Tocqueville had conversed in the 1830s had revealed a deep ambivalence toward the emergent democratic movement. Although they endorsed social and political equality in principle, they were distressed by the fact that their distinctive social values were ignored or rejected, and that their pretensions to leadership—except, perhaps, in New England—were generally spurned. Their experience suggested a more critical, realistic theory of democracy than was available in either the Jeffersonian or Jacksonian versions. Tocqueville himself had laid the foundations for such a theory with his examination of the sociological and political consequences of equality. In subsequent decades, as the distinctive characteristics of the mass society became more apparent, a succession of gentry commentators contributed to the elaboration of a theory that reached full fruition only in the mid-twentieth century. The present chapter will trace the successive steps in the development of mass theory.

HENRY ADAMS

Tocqueville's most distinguished American disciple, Henry Adams, was born in 1838, three years after the publication of *Democracy in America*. The divergent paths of American political society and its gentry elite were dramatically illustrated in the history of the Adams family. The first two generations produced Presidents of the United States. The third produced a distinguished Congressman and diplomatist who was widely regarded to be of presidential timber, although he never attained the office. The fourth generation, which was Henry's, produced four men, all very able, one of whom ran repeatedly but always unsuccessfully for the governorship of Massachusetts. Another briefly held a state appointive office. The remaining two, including Henry, never held public office of any kind. The Adams family history epitomized that of the gentry. As the century advanced, the gentry became ever more refined and fastidious. Their tastes and interests restricted them by preference to a highly specialized and exclusive cultural milieu. Thus, although Henry Adams always retained an absorbing interest in politics, he was bored and repelled by politicians. When E. L. Godkin said that the political failure of the gentry was due to their own deficiencies he might well have had Henry Adams in mind. Adams could not adapt himself to the democratic politics of the Gilded Age, which was, to be sure, an era of very low political morality and vast corruption. During the 1870s, he worked energetically if unsuccessfully to fashion Liberal Republicanism into a viable political movement. Thereafter, he moved his residence to Washington and amused himself with the conceit that he was a confidential adviser to men in power.

America produced no finer example of the gentleman in all his latter-day perfection than Henry Adams. He made his whole life a studied work of art. Henry Hobson Richardson designed his home in Washington, which he filled with Japanese vases and the art of Reynolds and Blake. Saint-Gaudens and Stanford White executed the famous memorial to Mrs. Adams in Rock Creek Park. Adams's flair for self-dramatization seemed to predetermine the course of his life. Following his wife's tragic suicide, which confirmed his reclusive tendencies, he turned the remainder of his life into an elaborate ritual of mourning. For such a gentleman, democratic principles were a matter of intellectual conviction rather than of personal preference.

It was also intellectual conviction that forced upon Adams his concern with science. The best minds of the time all acknowledged the obligation to explore the relevance of science to their own particular concerns. Students of social and public life were often led to various forms of naturalistic social philosophy. Scientific methods of organizing and manipulating data, or the conception of problems in terms of analogies drawn from biological or physical science, seemed to promise fruitful insights into historical and current affairs. Adams had early interested himself in the uniformitarian geology of Charles Lyell. Louis Agassiz and Clarence King were among his closest friends. Later in life he consulted Willard Gibbs on thermodynamics, and made some fanciful applications of the phase rule to history. The social evolutionism implicit in his early essays on Anglo-Saxon law and the history of women was confirmed by his reading of Lewis Henry Morgan's *Ancient Society*.

While serving as secretary to his father at the London legation during the Civil War, Adams carefully read Tocqueville and John Stuart Mill, "the two high priests of our faith." These commentators on the current scene helped Adams fix the characteristics of the modern era in a historical evolutionary framework. Their critical appreciation of the strengths and weaknesses of democracy was congenial to opinions held in the Adams family since the days of John Adams. All shared the conviction that democracy was inevitable, but that it threatened to rob man of his individuality by submergence in the mass. Tocqueville had asked whether democracy and freedom could continue to coexist after the frontier phase of American history had passed. Henry Adams, who reported that he had taken Tocqueville as his model, determined to study the historical origins of the mass society in America.[1]

Three themes dominated the naturalistic interpretation of history at the end of the nineteenth century, each of which was woven into the texture of Adams's thinking. One was the social evolutionary development of mankind from primitive simplicity to modern civilized complexity. In interpreting this process the historian might employ either the Darwinian analogy of a struggle for existence with survival of the fittest, or the Lamarckian notion of use inheritance. An alternative to the biological analogies was the use of physical concepts such as mass, inertia, and equilibrium. Auguste Comte and John W. Draper had proposed the application of these concepts to social problems, and Adams made increasing use of them as he grew older. The third theme concerned the relationship between mass and elites. For various reasons the study of leadership in a mass society proved to be an uncongenial one for social scientists committed to equalitarian values, while the historians, many of whom continued their traditional preoccupation with political leadership, were not always coherent about the mass context in which leadership functioned. In his attempts to cope with this problem Adams employed insights which for many years remained unappreciated.

Following a series of papers on varied topics in early and recent history, in 1879 Adams published his first major historical work, a *Life of Albert Gallatin*. This was followed by a biography of John Randolph, in 1882; and an unpublished biography of Aaron Burr, portions of which were incorporated in other works. These biographical studies paved the way for the monumental *History of the United States of America During the Administrations of Thomas Jefferson and James Madison,* published in nine volumes in 1889 and 1890. In these works Adams was to incorporate the convictions and insights into the nature of the mass society which had initially been suggested by his study of Tocqueville.

The former teacher of Anglo-Saxon law could appropriately turn to the study of American history because of its eminent suitability as a social science laboratory. As Auguste Comte had held, the laws of social change were most readily to be discovered in large societies, "where secondary disturbances have the smallest effect." Adams was persuaded by Tocqueville that the United States was perhaps the only country where it was possible to witness the natural and tranquil growth of society. His sense of the opportunities presented by American history must have been sharpened by contrast when in 1884 he read Tolstoy's *War and Peace*. In that great novel, after vividly describing the titanic struggle between Napoleon and Alexander, Tolstoy paused to reflect on the insignificance of the deeds of these heroes, themselves mere pawns of the great underlying social forces which swept masses of men back and forth across the face of Europe with the inexorability of the tides. Perhaps it was at this time that Adams formed his notion of America and Russia as the great masses that would dominate the twentieth century. In the meanwhile, the Napoleonic struggles indicated clearly enough why European history was ill-suited to the scientific study of social change: fierce military rivalries all too frequently disrupted normal social processes. To be sure, such vivid and concrete events endowed history with its drama, and it is possible that Adams hoped to combine a romantic preoccupation with events and personalities with the new impersonal scientific historiography. But on the whole his purposes were better served by a more tranquil situation in which processes of development were unimpeded by fortuitous or extraneous factors.

The most distinguished American exemplar of the older school of romantic historians was Adams's friend, Francis Parkman, who must have puzzled over the younger man's plans for a scientific historiography. Writing to Parkman in 1884 Adams roundly declared that "democracy is the only subject for history. I am satisfied that the purely mechanical development of the human mind in society must appear in a great democracy so clearly, for want of disturbing elements, that in another generation psychology, physiology, and history will join in proving man to have as fixed and necessary development as that of a tree; and almost as unconscious." In other words, in a democratic mass society the scientifically sophisticated historian need no longer be screened off from the psychological and intellectual development of the mass of people by the pomp of royalty or the willful behavior of arbitrary rulers. With the aid of sociology and social psychology, typically democratic disciplines concerned with the behavior of masses of people, the new historian should be able to understand the laws and forces which determine that behavior. For the ordinary citizen, of course, history would doubtless remain a bewildering sequence of disconnected events; and such men would continue to thrash about, responding to the irrelevant or trivial impulses that obscured the great sociological processes operating beneath. But to the properly instructed observer-historian the history of a democracy should stand clear as naked sociological process. Here, then, was a striking contrast between history as event—the conscious acts of leaders—and history as process—the unconscious development of the mass.

The concepts that seemed most helpful in interpreting the historical development of the social mass were derived from physics—the concepts of inertia and equilibrium. These notions permitted Adams to isolate the force or power in society that produced change independently of the acts or policies of leaders. In his biography of Gallatin he remarked that there were moments in politics when "great results can be reached only by small men." The mass could stubbornly refuse to follow the dictates of its leaders, and stumbling blindly along its own path, continue to consolidate its position as a mass.[2] This insight was amplified in the *History of the Jefferson and Madison Administrations,* for which the idea that the mass moves by its own properties of inertia regardless of its formal leadership furnished the implicit framework.

In the *History,* the conception of the American population of 1800 as a mass was accentuated by the drab and uniformly mercenary qualities ascribed to it by the historian. The people were no longer animated by the exalted ideals of Puritan or Quaker, but by a sordid lust for wealth and power. "The old, well-proven, conservative crust of religion, government, family, and even common respect for age, education, and experience was rapidly melting away, and was indeed already broken into fragments, swept about by the seething mass of scum ever rising in greater quantities to the surface." [3] The image of the mass as a flowing stream of discrete individual drops led directly to the complimentary idea of equilibrium. "History is simply social development along the lines of weakest resistance." That line is ordinarily found by society as surely and unconsciously as water flows downhill, and it is followed until a state of social equilibrium is reached. Thus the direction of social inertia is determined by a kind of social gravity, resulting in social equilibrium. These metaphors represented Adams's attempt to characterize the nature of social-historical change under mass conditions.

In order to appreciate the utility of these analogies for the historian it should be noted that as Adams looked back from the vantage point of the 1880s to the first years of the nineteenth century, the intervening period formed a pattern of development to which the ideas of mass and inertia seemed peculiarly appropriate. The path was first charted during the years 1800–1816, and the stabilization of relations with Great Britain assured by the Treaty of Ghent provided the peaceful conditions under which the American mass would find its way along the line of least resistance down to the historian's own time. It was a historical course unknown to European experience, characterized by growing prosperity, social equalitarianism, democratic government, and a higher average standard of popular intelligence. As to the future, who could predict the nature of a population of hundreds of millions? Would the individuals who composed it become weak and stagnant? Such a society would require a new social science, in which individuals would be important only as types. "The steady growth of a vast population without the social distinctions that confused other histories,—without kings, nobles, or armies; without church, traditions, and prejudices,—seemed a subject for the man of science rather than for dramatists or poets." [4]

Americans themselves, to be sure, had indicated that they were not wholly content with this situation, and had made at least half-hearted attempts to transform their politicians and generals into heroes in the old-fashioned manner. The very conditions of mass and inertia that made a science of society possible also had a depressing effect. Who would prefer to live in a society in which social behavior could be studied in the same manner and spirit as one studied the structure of a crystal? Nevertheless, Adams persisted in viewing the course of American history as proceeding like a mighty Mississippi from its origin in the eccentricities of primitive individual actions through a swelling flood to a permanent equilibrium in the democratic ocean. "In a democratic ocean science could see something ultimate. Man could go no further. The atom might move, but the general equilibrium could not change." [5]

It now remained to be seen how the events of the Jefferson and Madison administrations fitted into this vast panorama. It was clear that the principal actors would merit attention not for their individual acts, however heroic, but as representatives who would illuminate the social evolution of a democratic society. The first sixteen years of the nineteenth century were of the highest significance, in Adams's judgment, because during that period the democratic character of American society was irrevocably fixed. He established that fact—to his own satisfaction—by contrasting the social conditions of the American people in 1800 with those in 1817 in the opening and closing sections of his history. At the beginning of the period, everything had been uncertain. Neither Federalists nor Jeffersonian Republicans showed much comprehension of the possibilities for the development of America. The mass of the population was sanguine and self-confident, but it had brashly discarded such traditional stabilizing institutions as an established church, an aristocracy, distinguished family leadership, and a standing army. Would the infant nation survive the fierce struggle among the European powers into which it would inevitably be drawn? All these uncertainties were resolved by 1817. The course of American development was now plainly marked. It was a course best indicated by statistical tables of demographic and economic growth rather than by the dreary succession of political administrations.

Paradoxically enough, however, it was precisely such political accounts that constituted the central bulk of Adams's *History*. The annals of Congress are unedifying at best; and when the Congress contains such grotesque figures as John Randolph of Roanoke they may be bizarre in the extreme. There was the turmoil and bitter partisanship surrounding the impeachment of Supreme Court Justice Samuel Chase. There were well-founded rumors of treason and conspiracy. There were Byzantine diplomatic maneuverings among hostile and aggressive European powers. And there was the warmongering of the jingoistic War

Hawks, culminating in the nearly disastrous War of 1812. In short, the *History* was a work rich in irony, in which the futility and ineffectuality of human purposes was held up to the scorn of the reader. It was doubly ironic in that American history, whether seen from the perspective of 1817 or of 1887, had been an indisputable success. America had grown and prospered mightily in spite of the dreary spectacle of its public life.

Adams's personal disillusionment with the politics of the Gilded Age, together with his sense of gentry displacement, sharpened his perspective on the problems of leadership in a mass society. He had complained to his British friend, Charles Milnes Gaskell, that politics always worked unsatisfactorily; but at the same time he was confessing to David A. Wells that good generally came from political confusion.[6] These ambiguities set the bounds within which his *History* was to be written, especially with respect to the possibilities and limitations of leadership.

Auguste Comte had declared that the leader can only exploit opportunities made available to him by the conditions prevailing at his own time and place. No matter how powerful or talented he might be, he would leave no trace on history if he attempted to resist the general direction of social movement. Grant Allen, a British disciple of Spencer's, carried the argument a step further by affirming that "no individual initiative has any effect in determining the course of human destiny." Adams was nevertheless reluctant to give up the ideal of a talented and influential gentry elite. After all, Francis Galton had demonstrated that there was a hereditary class of talented families, with the Adamses prominent on his list! Consequently, in his *History* Adams attempted to reconcile these divergent claims. The direction of American history was evolutionary, determined by the inertia of mass movement. But the dramatic interest was furnished by the heroes and villains acting on the stage of events. Adams had concluded that if naturalistic historiography admitted of a hero he must be, in Comte's terms, a man who sees the opportunities of the moment and exploits them. Such opportunism was hardly the stuff from which heroes were made, and it was not surprising that naturalistic historiography should have been less concerned with leadership than with social forces. Naturalistically conceived, history revealed no heroes, or very few of them. Those in positions of leadership rarely judged correctly the opportunities available to them, and their mistakes all too often exposed them as pathetic clowns rather than heroes.

Henry Adams's principal case study in anti-heroism was furnished by the presidency of Thomas Jefferson. A man of high intelligence and remarkable erudition, personally incorruptible, with exalted ideals and noble aspirations for his fellow Americans, President Jefferson nevertheless utterly failed to assess the possibilities of the moment, so that everything he projected came to nought. He nearly ruined his country economically, while bringing it to the verge of war, not knowing whether it would be war with England, France, or both. His major accomplishment, the acquisition of the Louisiana territory, was consummated reluctantly in the face of his constitutional scruples, greatness being, so to speak, thrust upon him. Having made a mess of everything and become thoroughly discouraged, he finally quit politics a beaten man.

Adams had brilliantly illuminated some of the themes and problems of history naturalistically conceived. It was all too apparent that the surface events of public life threw little light on underlying social changes. It was also clear that while in a mass society leadership might conceivably anticipate the direction of mass movements, its failures dramatically illustrated its impotence. In the narrative of events that constituted the central portion of his *History* Adams had introduced traditional historical subject matter, but whether he did so merely to demonstrate its irrelevance remains unclear. He was unable to provide an analysis of the underlying forces, nor did he succeed in indicating how public opinion ("the popular imagination") influenced public policy. The statistics of growth in population, wealth, manufactures, and transportation may have pointed clearly enough to the path America was to follow, but the data of high culture—philosophy, literature, theology, or political theory—stubbornly refused to reveal to the historian a similarly coherent pattern of development. Although Adams recognized the historic significance of the voyage of the *Clermont* as the harbinger of a technology that quickly relegated Napoleon to a class with Achilles, he failed to pursue the implications of the technological revolution which it symbolized. This was the more surprising in view of his preoccupation with historical movement as the manifestation of physical forces. Less surprising was his failure to develop an economic interpretation of history, which was repellent to him. For this reason if for no other, the mainstream of American historical thought, about to flow in the economic channel, bypassed him.

In the final analysis, Henry Adams's nine volumes of conventional historical narrative of a formative period in the nation's history was a convincing demonstration of how not to account for American success, unless the reader were to be content with the perverse conclusion that the Americans were building better than they knew. It was not surprising that Adams himself should have expressed dissatisfaction with his work even before the ninth volume was off the press, and that he should have pressed on to even more forced and exotic attempts to apply naturalistic insights to the interpretation of historical processes. He had shown persuasively that the traditional narrative of politics, diplomacy, and war did not account for "the development of the human mind in society"; but he had been unable to demonstrate how the forces of mass, inertia, and equilibrium achieved that result. Since historiography shares with nature an abhorrence of a vacuum, the void in historical interpretation left by Henry Adams was promptly filled by others who did not share his repugnance for an economic interpretation. The school of Charles A. Beard and the Marxists would soon furnish a techno-economic interpretation of American history which would attempt to show precisely how the surface events of public life were connected with the great underlying sociological processes of economic and technological change.

CHARLES ELIOT NORTON

Among the latter-day gentry the man most conscious of the deteriorating state of gentility, and consequently the most explicit in his sociological analysis of the circumstances, was Charles Eliot Norton. Andrews Norton, his father, a professor of Sacred Literature at Harvard, was known as the "Unitarian Pope," while his mother, Catherine Eliot, was the daughter of a wealthy and socially prominent Boston merchant.[7] The Eliot connection assured the Nortons' status in the overlapping group of Boston gentry and social-economic elite. Following his graduation from Harvard in 1846, Charles engaged in the overseas mercantile trade for several years, and throughout his life remained on intimate terms with the mercantile families which formed the core of the Boston economic elite.

Young Norton grew up at Shady Hill, the fifty-acre family estate in Cambridge, in an atmosphere of dignified simplicity which conformed to the most rigorous gentry expectations. He was taught a strong sense of the seriousness of life and of his high responsibilities. His biographer suggests that he never was a child, a circumstance perhaps less abnormal at that time and place than it would have been elsewhere or later.[8] At the age of seven he began to keep a diary; and at ten, during a childhood illness, he expressed the hope that he might be spared in order to edit the writings of his father.[9] The burdens suggested by these self-imposed duties undoubtedly contributed to the neurasthenia from which he was to be a life-long sufferer.

The classical training of the collegiate curriculum may not have taken with most students, but it left an indelible imprint on Norton, who acquired a comprehensive command of ancient as well as modern languages. Throughout his life he shared with his friends Longfellow and Lowell a passion for Dante, whose *Vita Nuova* he translated. His literary acquaintances included most of the gentry leaders. Frederick Law Olmsted introduced him to Godkin, with whom he formed a firm and lasting friendship. Norton enlisted the support of John Murray Forbes and other Boston capitalists for Godkin's *Nation,* and furnished frequent articles during the early years of publication. He first met George William Curtis in Paris in 1850, forming a friendship which grew in intimacy over the years. Concerning Howells, his early references reveal an appropriate condescension toward a popular novelist; but Norton was a discriminating reader, and the undeniable merit of *Silas Lapham* and *Indian Summer* prompted an increasingly respectful and appreciative regard. In the end, Howells's invincible kindliness and genius for friendship triumphed in a close relationship. The steady flow of correspondence among all these friends testifies to the firm bonds which united the last generation of gentry leaders.[10]

The obligation to serve and elevate humanity which was an integral part of the gentry tradition received early and practical expression as soon as Norton graduated from college. With the assistance of John Holmes, Francis B. Child, and Sidney Coolidge he organized a night school for working people, perhaps the first in Massachusetts.

This enterprise was followed by a more ambitious attempt to relieve slum conditions by providing decent low-cost housing for laborers on terms which would earn a reasonable return on investment. Two tenements housing forty families were built in 1854, and by 1860 Norton was convinced that their success had been so demonstrable as to attract additional capital into the field. His object was at once philanthropic and prudential. Decent housing was not only essential for the health and comfort of the "honest and self-supporting poor," but would also strengthen family life and avert the moral deterioration so evident in the urban slums. However, as the gentry themselves were becoming concentrated in the cities, a principal threat to their power came from the political machines based on the votes of immigrant masses. Norton approved the political program of the Native American or Know-Nothing Party of the 1850s, although he disapproved of the party's methods and realized that it had no political future.[11]

Norton had gone to India in 1849 on business, and had spent nearly two years there, returning by way of Western Europe. These travels were of immense importance in providing an opportunity to make observations and form opinions which would provide a framework for his thinking for the remainder of his life. In India, he discovered a small minority of Hindus who had achieved a high degree of civilized culture under English influence confronting an inert mass of common people who combined many of the vices of barbarism and civilization. This dramatic confrontation of cultured elite and barbarian mass provided Norton with a perspective from which he would always view social life.[12] On his return through Europe he established his first personal contacts with representatives of the European gentry, meeting Ruskin, Carlyle, Leslie Stephen, and the painter Edward Burne-Jones. These men remained his life-long friends, forming an international community of gentlemen who shared many convictions about the issues of the age.

Norton's first major publication, a little volume published in 1853 entitled *Considerations on Some Recent Social Theories,* was an ardent protestation of loyalty to the New England Federalist–Unitarian tradition of conservatism, which blended so conveniently with the liberal individualism of the gentry tradition. Ostensibly a critique of the ideas of Louis Blanc, Kossuth, and Mazzini, the book was in fact a first tentative statement of Norton's own theory of mass and class. Norton found that the gap between the mass and the privileged classes had become wider than ever before. While the classes were advancing with unexampled rapidity in prosperity, intellectual cultivation, and moral refinement, the mass was sinking with equal rapidity into corruption and slavery. The ignorance and helplessness of the mass rendered it easily susceptible to exploitation by demagogues. Among these were the false prophets of socialism, who flattered the people with their poisonous doctrines of mass virtue. The true friends of the mass were, of course, the gentry, "the few who have been blessed with the opportunities, and the rare genius, fitting them to lead." [13]

Depressing though the prospect for the immediate future might be, Norton did not lose hope for the ultimate progress of mankind. It would be at best a gradual process; and in the meanwhile the mass understandably cried out against injustice and oppression. Christian love and education were to be the principal means of securing advancement. Norton referred vaguely to gentry martyrdom for truth in order that ultimately the mass might be enlightened, happy, and free.[14]

The only power which could improve the condition of the mass was the power of Christian principle. This was not a matter of creed or church, but the spirit of religion in action. For the spirit of religion was the spirit of freedom, in both its social and theological senses. Liberty, the social ideal, was defined by Norton in terms reminiscent of John Winthrop's seventeenth-century definition of federal as opposed to natural liberty: liberty was the power to do the will of God. Such power might never be fully achieved, but it was certain that the savage or ignorant man had none of it. Only as men became more enlightened and virtuous would liberty be realized in increasing measure.[15]

In 1854 Norton, who was in no sense an abolitionist, became interested in the territorial aspects of the Kansas-Nebraska controversy. Although he had already voiced his antislavery principles, it was the political struggle for power rather than the institution of slavery which primarily concerned him. Because it was a moral issue, slavery poisoned and embittered politics, making settlement of the sectional conflict more difficult. In the spring of 1855, Norton made his first visit to the South and reported his first-hand observations of the slave society.

If I ever write against slavery, it shall be on the ground
not of its being bad for the blacks, but of its being
deadly to the whites. The effect on thought, on character, on aim in life, on hope, is, even in this five-days'
experience of mine, plainly as sad as anything can be,—
and among the women not less than the men.

Slavery deadened the moral feelings and obscured the intellect.[16]

Norton's view of chattel slavery was cast in the larger
framework of his conception of the social mass. Negro
slavery differed only in degree from the servitude which
was the normal condition of the mass man. The corruption of the white masters was a typical illustration of the
universal moral consequences of the exploitation of man
by man. Norton could see no solution for the problem
other than the gradual improvement which would be
wrought by the spirit of Christianity in accordance with
the general law of progress. Racial distinctions were not
important in his analysis. Although he criticized Buckle
for denying the influence of race on civilization, the word
in this context seems to have connoted the cultural traditions perpetuated by a particular nation or group rather
than a biological race.[17]

Barred by ill-health from military service during the
Civil War, Norton organized the New England Loyal
Publication Society, a propaganda organization which
prepared and distributed patriotic material to newspapers.
He always believed that it had made a useful contribution
to the Union cause. Like later American wartime propa-

gandists, he stressed the ideological issues which gave the struggle its meaning and justification. The war was a struggle for democracy, for the common rights of man against the privileged class. After it was over, he believed that the war had brought out the idealistic side of the American character, its devotion to liberty and human rights. Writing to an English friend in October 1865, he remarked that the American principle of equal rights for all brought society into harmony with the moral laws of the universe and charted a course of progress in virtue and happiness. Every effort must be made to secure to the freedman the full rights of citizenship and suffrage, and to thwart the Southern attempt to replace slavery with a system of caste subordination.[18]

But the very progress which Norton celebrated resulted, paradoxically enough, in a dull, uniform mediocrity. Especially in democratic America, where men were free to pursue their own objects, there was very little in the way of first-rate accomplishment. The creative, critical, and appreciative faculties of Americans were all mediocre, and except for some manufactured products all their work was shoddy.

> Railroads and common schools are enemies of all feeble originalities. Where education and property are universally diffused, where there is no hereditary lower class, there must be a larger proportion of intelligent mediocrities than in any other country. The average man in America is not up to an appreciation of the best things; he does not want them; but he does want better things than the average man in any other country, and he has

an appreciation of good things which is constantly becoming keener.[19]

Although he regularly reaffirmed the usual gentry faith in
education as the only certain guarantee of progress, Norton
had frequent moments of disillusionment when he realized
how superficial mass education must be. In these moments
he dismissed the invention of printing as insignificant.
"Perhaps we shall soon come to much the same state as
existed before the discovery of printing. There will be a
few profound scholars, a few deep thinkers, while the mass
of readers will be no better off than if they had no books
at all." [20]

In 1868, Norton retired from business and went to
Europe for five years. This second European visit proved
to be the pivotal experience of his life. It confirmed
valuable friendships with Carlyle and Ruskin and fixed
his scholarly interest in the history of art. Like the earlier
travels of Cooper and those of his friend Henry James, it
was indispensable in determining the point of view from
which he would thenceforth analyze social questions.

Both Europe and America were confronting the common problem of the relationship between mass and gentry
elite. Norton formed a gloomy opinion of England's prospects because of the widening gulf between rich and poor,
and the absence of a "vigorous common life" among the
various social classes. On the other hand, her prospects
were in some ways brighter than those of the United States,
owing to the greater social influence of the British gentry.
On the Continent, he found everywhere the signs of class

hatred and conflict. He admitted that to one dedicated as he was to the principle of the greatest good for the greatest number, the laboring-class arguments were unanswerable: individualism, competition, free enterprise were probably not the highest conceivable forms of social organization. But the revolutionary forces which were determined to destroy them would probably overturn civilization as well, and usher in a new dark age.[21]

In the United States, the unparalleled prosperity enjoyed by all ranks of society cast the problem in a different form. Here the mass, far from being revolutionary, reveled in its raw, uncultivated preoccupation with money-making, oblivious of its cultural shortcomings. "No serious man who knows anything of human nature and of history," Norton warned, "can cherish the optimistic fatalism that is still characteristic of the American temper, and that finds expression in the general confidence that somehow, however men may act and behave, everything will come out right in the end." He became increasingly impatient with Emerson's bland optimism, which he equated with innocence and inexperience. This dangerous doctrine tended to degenerate into a fatalistic indifference to moral considerations and personal responsibility. It lay at the root of irrational sentimentality in politics, with its assumption that all was for the best in spite of a corrupt and incompetent public leadership.[22]

Under the influence of his British friends, Norton abandoned his youthful Christian orthodoxy and became a freethinker. Like Godkin, he sought to define a rational and responsible place for criticism outside the church. But it was an exposed position for one so conservative, and when a Harvard overseer objected to a professorial appointment for Norton in 1874 on the ground that he was not religiously orthodox Norton felt that he could not complain. "It is difficult to see," he wrote to his British friend, John Simon, "what would become of a democracy if such views as you and I hold were rapidly to become prevalent." [23] The gentry indeed claimed for themselves a freedom to criticize which in less cautious and responsible hands would lead, they conceded, to confusion and anarchy.

From 1874 until his retirement in 1896 Norton was professor of fine arts at Harvard. In his teaching and writing on the history of art he followed Ruskin in considering the work of art as a cultural artifact. The fundamental moral and spiritual qualities of a community were presumed to be reflected in its art. The history of art and architecture provided "a clear and brilliant illustration of the general conditions of society, and especially of its moral and intellectual dispositions." This was a congenial conception for one whose life-long concern was with the moral foundations of social order. Civic pride and religious faith had provided the necessary conditions for the architectural achievements of the Italian renasissance. But as wealth increased and life in the Italian cities became more secular, knowledge and self-assurance replaced the earlier morality and faith. At the same time, art improved in technique while losing its imaginative power of expression. This of course implied general cultural deterioration, for "in the highest forms of human expression morality and beauty are inseparable." [24] As one of the founders of the Archaeological Institute of America and of the School of Classical Studies in Rome Norton had acted in the hope that a wider knowledge of classical culture would spread "sane thinking" among American youths. In spite of his efforts, he could only stimulate academic scholarship without stemming the tide which was running so strongly against the classical heritage of American culture.[25]

Although Norton was proud of his deep family roots in the culture of Boston, he seems to have craved further identification with the regional heritage, and he found it in the rural village of Ashfield. He discovered this western Massachusetts hill town in 1864, and established his summer home there. Aside from its pleasant surroundings, reminiscent of the English lake country, Ashfield seemed to be an ideal showcase for the regional heritage at its best. The farmers were almost wholly of old Yankee stock, and comfortably situated. Norton was charmed by their independence and sturdy good sense. He patronized the library and revivified the local Academy. The annual Academy Dinners which he inaugurated in 1879 were occasions when a succession of distinguished gentry speakers made pilgrimages to this rural shrine to pay their respects to the regional heritage.[26]

But for all his zealous attempts to perpetuate these vestiges of the past Norton knew that the drift of the times was against him. With increasing dismay he noted the social and cultural effects of democratization on both sides of the Atlantic. Democracy might "work," he informed Lowell bitterly, but it worked ignobly, ignorantly, and brutally.[27] It was in this pessimistic mood that in the last years of his life he drafted the papers on the future of democratic society which were to constitute the central item in the gentry contribution to mass theory.

The major issue of the age, he declared in 1888, was indicated by the question of whether the highest cultural achievements of the past, which had been produced by and confined to a relatively small cultural elite, could be diffused and made the foundation of a social order in which advantages would be more equally shared. Or would the establishment of a democratic mass society, with its broad distribution of material benefits, entail cultural losses that could not be made good? Norton leaned toward the latter opinion.

His characterizations of the American mass were similar to those of Godkin and Adams. Here were sixty million people living in peace, free from fear, possessed of civil liberty, enjoying an abundant prosperity and a deep sense of security. At least fifty million of them were well enough off to be kindly, good-humored, and humane. In view of the fact that most of them had arisen within two or three generations from "the servile class or the peasantry," without intellectual traditions, it was indeed surprising that they were as amicable as they were.[28] Since for them the pursuit of happiness had been such an unparalleled success, their utter disregard of historic experience was not surprising. It was the shallow materialism of mass values that was responsible for making wealth the chief form of modern power, replacing rank, honor, or learning. Even the meanest intelligence could appreciate wealth. Energies devoted exclusively to material objects were not available for the finer things of life, and it was no accident that aside from a few technological achievements America had made no distinctive contributions to intellectual life.

Norton noted the uniformity of customs and conditions which was blotting out the older distinctive regional cultures. In spite of steady immigration and a variety of ethnic stocks, the Americans were culturally the most homogeneous people in the world—excepting the Negroes and a few national enclaves in the big cities. This made for national unity, but it had serious cultural consequences. The prevailing uniformity of experience and conviction made impossible that collision of ideas essential to progress in an advanced civilization. A struggle for existence was as necessary for ideas as for biology. As life became less richly diversified the individual became less important. "In such a society public opinion exercises a tyrannical authority," stamping out independence and originality and establishing a despotism of custom. The citizen is unconscious of his own condition of mental servitude. In America more than elsewhere mediocrity dominated taste and molded the judgment of the unrefined mass.

Norton was emphatic, however, that the mass itself was not to be blamed for this sorry state of affairs. If any were at fault it was the gentry who failed to maintain standards and provide effective leadership. In spite of his growing pessimism he still clung to the traditional gentry faith in liberal education for the entire community as the only effective bulwark against an all-engulfing barbarism.[29]

In his old age Norton lost even this last refuge from

unrelieved pessimism. By 1896 he had come to think of American society as consisting of a small civilized gentry elite and a vast mass of barbarians and semibarbarians. Democracy and prosperity had endowed the mass with such a strong sense of power and complacency as to render it impervious to the lessons of experience. It confused good luck with a firm belief in its own genius. Whenever it did acknowledge any shortcoming it assumed that more education would overcome it. If Norton had formerly believed in the efficacy of liberal education under gentry auspices he had no faith whatever in popular education under public control. Schools, he now declared, can at best only instruct; they cannot educate. Home and community were the principal educational agencies: here the judgment was trained, the imagination quickened, and the moral intelligence refined and elevated. Whenever individuals were deprived of these precious advantages no amount of formal schooling could compensate for them.[30]

Before yielding to the final spasm of despair Norton made a last effort to evoke the image of the democratic gentleman. In 1893, following the death of his friends Lowell and Curtis, he eulogized them as embodying the best ideals of American culture, ideals in some respects unique to American life.

> They were gentlemen as gracious, as refined, as well-bred as any of the line of gentlemen from Sidney down to Sidney's peers in the Old World today, but with this difference, that the sentiment which inspired them was not the lingering exclusive spirit of chivalric superiority, but the larger, more generous, modern spirit of demo-

cratic society, in which each man has the opportunity and is consequently under the responsibility to make the best of himself for the service of his fellow men; and this spirit, natural to and embodied in such men as Lowell and Curtis, shows itself in character which seems to me to be, on the whole, of fairer and more promising quality than any which the world has hitherto known.

The distinctive virtues of the democratic gentleman, namely, kindness, sweetness, candor and generosity rested on a secure foundation in human nature rather than on mere convention. In the gentleman, they were doubly compelling and attractive.[31]

Thus for a brief moment Norton reverted to the largely forgotten distinction between natural and cultivated gentility. He glimpsed again, however fitfully, the promise of American life to fuse nature and convention in an ideal type under the auspices of democratic institutions. In spite of his deepening pessimism he recovered a momentary faith in the progress of man. But the mood could not be sustained.

In the end, Norton's hopes for a democratic gentleman who would articulate the generous equalitarian values of an open society flickered out. The jingoism of the late nineties revealed "a barbaric spirit of arrogance and of unreasonable self-assertion." It was only too apparent now that the rise of democracy, far from ushering in a new era of peace and civilization, had marked a reversion to barbarism. "The worst sign is the lack of seriousness in the body of the people; its triviality, and its indifference to moral principle." [32]

The triumph of the mass signalized the destruction of the gentry elite. Norton believed that he himself was one of the last survivors of his kind. In mourning the death of his friend Martin Brimmer in 1896, he wrote: "He leaves no one like him in Boston; few like him anywhere. The true gentleman is as rare as the true genius, and democracy in its present stage is not favorable to the existence of either. There are many excellent and worthy men, but very few who care for, or are capable of practicing, the social art, that finest of the dramatic arts, in which the individual nature expresses itself in modes of ideal pleasantness and refinement." [33]

The ultimate compression of gentility into the dimension of a mere "social art" squeezed out much of what had seemed most important to an earlier and more robust generation of gentlemen. Natural gentility, the spontaneous product of a democratic society, had been conceived to be the principal bond which united the gentry with the community, and Norton himself in his devotion to Ashfield had revealed his allegiance to this sentimental tradition. But he could not sustain the conviction, and in the last year of his life he dramatically repudiated the connection in commenting on the greatest of the natural gentlemen, Abraham Lincoln. Norton told his son, who had recently published an essay on the Emancipator, that Lincoln was a true child of democracy. The principle of equality had ruled his moral convictions as well as his intellectual activity. But the privations of his early life had prevented him from developing a discriminating taste for personal relations, and only his strong moral nature had rescued him from his lack of discrimination. Lincoln was not a true gentleman in the fashion of Sir Walter Scott.

> A gentleman is the result of high breeding, and it is no discredit to Lincoln that, born and bred as he was, he does not stand on the same level in this respect as Scott. I believe that as time goes on and the democracy reaches its full development, there may be just as complete gentlemen in the sense of high-bred men, as in any aristocracy with its long tradition. But a gentleman is not an immediate product of a new country, nor of a society starting on new principles like ours.[34]

Norton's ultimate loss of faith in the capacity of democratic institutions to nurture natural gentlemen can be traced to the hardening of his opinions on the mass society. The mass man had none of the redeeming qualities of the pristine democrat. It would doubtless be a mistake to regard the two types as opposed versions of the same individual, as Tocqueville seemed to see them. Rather, the mass man had gradually replaced the democratic man, and as he did so the happy association of natural gentleman, American democrat, and cultivated gentleman finally dissolved.

WILLIAM GRAHAM SUMNER

An abortive attempt to indicate more explicitly the nature of the relationship between the mass and its elite leadership was made by Norton's younger contemporary, the Yale sociologist William Graham Sumner. The son of an immigrant machinist, Sumner rose to gentry elite status through the avenue of education. A decisive event of his life occurred at the University of Göttingen, where he had gone to prepare himself for a career in the ministry. The dedicated and selfless pursuit of "the truth" which he found among the professors of Biblical studies made a profound impression on young Summer. "I have heard men elsewhere talk about the nobility of that spirit," he later recalled; "but the only *body* of men whom I have ever known who really lived by it, sacrificing wealth, political distinction, church preferment, popularity, or anything else for the truth of science, were the professors of biblical science in Germany. . . . They also taught me rigorous and pitiless methods of investigation and deduction. . . . Their method of study was nobly scientific, and was worthy to rank, both for its results and its discipline, with the best of the natural science methods." [35]

The fact that Sumner discovered the method and spirit of science among theologians, ironic though it was, may have accounted for the strong moralistic overtones that always characterized his social science. He was a latter-day Puritan animated by a powerful sense of his personal share of responsibility for the public welfare. The "science of society" to the elaboration of which he devoted a lifetime was less notable for rigor of method—his methods were in fact primitive in the extreme—than for the massive accumulation of evidence that the individual is molded by his society and swept along by forces beyond his control. It was doubly ironic that his polemical essays on the virtues of competition should have established his reputation as a "social Darwinist" when in fact the total drift of his thought was in quite another direction.

At the heart of Sumner's social theory was a perennial tension between cooperation and competition. Social evolution consisted of a dialectical development in which technological innovations released new sources of energy and required more elaborate institutional forms of organization. When social institutions expanded to the point where they became unwieldy and inefficient they broke down into component units, and competition among them replaced the previous institutional cooperation. Because of the importance of technological innovation as the ultimate cause of social change, Sumner assigned the highest place in the pantheon of cultural heroes to the inventor. The gifted man whose innovations enabled his fellows to extend their dominion over nature was the most valuable citizen, and Sumner organized his social theory around this assumption.

In the age of Darwin and Spencer it was not surprising that Sumner should have emphasized the themes of competition and cooperation. Darwin's theory of natural selection assumed a universal competition among dissimilar organisms. Spencer had emphasized the analogy of society to a biological organism, and thus set the bounds within which competition and cooperation were to be reconciled. The mass society with its democratic values and social mobility emancipated the individual, who, mass man though he was, could now be isolated and measured with respect to socially significant characteristics. The age of quantification was under way. The measurement of individual features, whether the IQ of school children, the height of military conscripts, the weight and complexion of automobile drivers, or the measurements of beauty queens, now became standard practice. Sophisticated statistical techniques were rapidly developed to permit precise expression of these differences. Darwin's cousin, Francis Galton, drew upon the Belgian statistician Quetelet's pioneer work in probabilities to establish numerical scales representing the distribution of "genius" in the population. He incidentally discovered and measured the relative concentration of "genius" in family lines. The German sociologist, Otto Ammon, developed a diagrammatic scale tying all of these factors together, which Summer took over and incorporated in his book on the folkways.[36]

In view of the rapid growth of the population and the increasing sense of isolation and insecurity among the gentry at the end of the nineteenth century, it was inevitable that social critics like Sumner should inquire into the worth of each individual's contribution to the great cooperative enterprise that was human society. Otto Ammon's diagrammatic representation of the mass society was organized on a scale of "societal value." Each individual was to be located on a vertical scale according to the value of his contribution to the ongoing work of society. The component elements of societal value were specified by Sumner as mental ability, common sense, good health, and luck. Societal value would be found to conform in a general way to such practical criteria as relative "success," income, status, competence, and energy. When each individual was located on the vertical scale of societal value, the top indicating the greatest value, and the bottom the least, the distribution would form a bell-shaped curve of probable error. Located at the top of the scale would be the small number of geniuses, followed by a larger number of talented people. At the other end were the comparably small number whose contributions to society were less than nil: the defectives, dependents, and delinquents. Above them were a class of marginally employables designated as proletarians; and above them, a somewhat larger group of unskilled and illiterate workers. The vast bulk of the population clustering about the middle of the scale constituted the mass. Thus in terms of the relative value of their contribution to society the mass occupied the middle position between the flanking classes of leaders and dependents. To what degree the scale of societal value conformed to a functional scale was left unclear.

In Western Europe and especially in new countries like the United States, there was much upward social mobility within the mass, stimulated by abundant economic opportunities and universal education. Social and economic differences within the mass were reflected in the formation of distinct social strata, such as lower professionals, merchants, and laboring men. Sumner was emphatic, however, that few individuals from the mass were capable of rising into the talented class, and few of the latter lapsed back into the mass. Talent, after all, was an innate possession, and Francis Galton had demonstrated that it was very largely hereditary.

In spite of the mobility found in modern society, Sumner regarded the mass as a stabilizing influence. It was the conservative core of society. Its members lived a life of tradition and habit governed by instinct, "just like animals." Such instinctive conservatism reflected an innate inertia, and was not to be confused with the self-conscious conservatism of the privileged elements of society. Mass conservatism reflected the fact that the mass was the bearer of the mores of the society, those basic values and convictions which gave to every society its distinctive tone and character. Social change occurred to the extent that the mass adopted the new attitudes and ways of behavior introduced by the talented classes. The assimilation of new ideas was always a slow process of accommodation and adaptation of the new to the old. Sumner was certain in any event that it was a fallacy to assume with the Marxists that the mass was the possessor of mystical wisdom or virtue. The answers to life's problems, if there were any, must come from the classes and not from the masses. In point of fact, mass and class much cooperate; neither had an exclusive right to rule society.

Sumner made no attempt to develop a political theory out of his concept of mass society. The implications appeared to be elitist, but he never challenged the democratic ideology explicitly. He was content to observe that democracy was a product of the momentarily favorable man-land ratio in the United States. He did insist, however, that masses of men substantially equal to one another could never be anything more than hopeless savages if deprived of their talented class leadership. Such a primitive horde would quickly be either exterminated or enslaved. The dependence of the mass upon class leadership (i.e., of the less gifted upon the abler) was the reason why the mass would always be subject to exploitation. It consisted of workers who would always labor for others, of taxpayers who would fill the treasury for others to spend, of conscripts for the armed forces, and of voters for demagogues to manipulate. In various ways, the mass would always be organized, led, and exploited. Sumner was willing to concede that thanks to modern prosperity the rigors of this exploitation had momentarily been mitigated, and institutions of civil liberty had brought a measure of independence to individuals within the mass. These salutary innovations had been the accomplishment of the leaders, not the mass. But Sumner had nothing but contempt for sentimental believers in inevitable progress. In phrases reminiscent of Hobbes he declared that the historical process was still full or error, folly, selfishness, violence, and craft.

Although his discussion of mass in the context of mores and folkways suggests that Sumner regarded mass as a universal phenomenon, he was concerned primarily with the distortions resulting from the democratization of the American mass society. Beneath the complacent local prejudices lay harsh universal realities. No doubt men everywhere were wont to congratulate themselves on their superior wisdom and virtue, but Americans had proven themselves particularly adept at this form of self-deception. The institutions of democracy were all designed to flatter the common man. Press, pulpit, politicians, and commercial advertisers all conspired to flatter and feed his ego. All were constantly reminding him that he was the master of his destiny, whereas in fact, as Summer well knew, the mass never possessed the power of self-determination. It was always neutral with respect to social policy. It could only respond to proposals originating in the talented classes, framing its judgments in terms of the prevailing mores. These responses were necessarily primitive, centering on personalities rather than issues. Sumner died too soon to witness the twentieth-century obsession with subversive disloyalty, which would have illustrated very well his conception of mass emotionalism. To complete his characterization of the mass: it was not brutal, producing few criminals; but was shallow, narrow-minded, and prejudiced.

Sumner noted that whatever the circumstances of its origin, the mass society at the end of the nineteenth century had become urbanized. The flight from farm to city had occurred most spectacularly in New England, where abandoned farms were everywhere reverting to nature while the cities grew apace. Cities were no longer consumers of population, thanks to improved social and health services. Opportunities to achieve comfort and even luxury had never before been available to so large a portion of society. Under the urban influence mass mores were becoming increasingly secular, realistic, materialistic, and commercial. In the economic struggle for existence the mass man was turning more frequently to politics rather than to religion for support. The eighteenth-century doctrine of natural rights was now generally understood to guarantee the welfare of the mass. Rights, justice, liberty, equality were now watchwords, rather than faith, heaven, and hell. "The amount of superstition," Sumner pointed out, "is not much changed, but it now attaches to politics, not to religion." [37]

Although he did not develop a detailed analysis of the communications media Sumner recognized their central role in disseminating urban mores. It was the media which were primarily responsible for the volatile nervousness that expressed itself in a constant search for amusement and excitement. The media were also responsible for the creation of the potentially tyrannical public opinion which was the democratic counterpart of the older forms of political tyranny. Democratic government by will of the majority merely substituted one ruling power for another in the perennial struggle over the distribution of the national income. In typical Mugwump fashion Sumner would have preferred to accomplish this distribution "by free contract under the play of natural laws." [38]

Nevertheless, the relative measure of economic security and abundance provided by the industrialized mass society had important psychological consequences, in view of the privation and scarcity which normally confronted mankind. Sumner concluded that "if I were called upon to say what I think is the greatest effect of modern power over nature on human nature, I should say that it is the infusion into the great mass of mankind of a way of looking at life from in front, not from behind. Modern men are led by hopes, not pushed by experience." But because their ideals and hopes were rarely realized in more than slight measure, the prevailing mood of the mass society was one of discontentment and frustration.[39]

Sumner had no confidence in mass education, which he regarded as a contradiction in terms. Education implied that there was something to be learned and students who wanted to learn it. But the mass man neither needed nor wanted to learn anything. He took the world as he found it. The brief formal schooling available to him was insignificant; it merely provided him with the literacy necessary for access to the media. Education was for the talented classes, not for the masses.

Nevertheless, it was of the highest importance to the welfare of the whole society that the upper stratum of the mass be composed of comfortably prosperous, industrious, God-fearing people of exemplary morals and manners who maintained good home life and supported worthy causes. Under such circumstances the mores of the community would be wholesome and rational. On the other hand, if control of the mass were centered in a lower stratum, violence and social convulsions could result. Should the mass be divided by the hostile confrontation of labor and employers, political parties would soon come to reflect the conflict, and the mores would express passion and discord. It was apparent, then, that the capacity of the classes to initiate and lead was severely limited by the character of the mass and by its power to dispose.

At what point on the scale of societal value did Sumner locate himself and the gentlemen with whom he so closely identified? It is impossible to tell with certainty. His stance of detached, scholarly observer itself speaks eloquently of the displacement of the gentry which was already far advanced in Sumner's time. He had noted how the German scholars had sacrificed status and influence for the pursuit of truth, and it may be that he took it for granted that this must be the lot of any scholar in his day and age. The model of the scientist as dispassionate investigator, when adopted by the student of society, necessarily implied a degree of detachment which weakened his sense of identification with a particular place on the social scale. Sumner did not emphasize the distinction between primitive and civilized cultures commonly drawn by the evolutionary anthropologists. He brought his anthropology into his sociology, and looked at the modern mass man with the same cool eye with which he would have looked at a Bushman, expecting in truth to find little difference. His personal sympathies, so far as he permitted himself to reveal them, were with "the forgotten man," the sober and industrious citizen of the upper stratum of the mass to whom the nineteenth-century gentry had always looked for support.

It was not surprising in view of his detached and aloof stance that the scientist of society should have become convinced that he alone understood the nature of the historical process. He thought of himself as a scientific pioneer making his way in a wasteland of ignorance and complacent misconceptions. He had discovered that technological developments and economic processes were the underlying causes of historical change. But because few men understood this, the properly instructed observer noted the glaring discrepancy between what men thought they could do and what he could see was bound to happen. In Sumner's eyes, history provided a continuing demonstration of the foolish and futile efforts of rulers and policy-makers to control social forces they did not understand.

The decisive event of modern history had been the discovery and settlement of the New World. In North America, the favorable man-land ratio had resulted in civilized amenities which the settlers and their descendants liked to think were peculiarly American. The overseas expansion of Europe provided Sumner with a dramatic illustration of his dialectical pattern of "growth, reaction, destruction, new development, and higher integration." But it was also apparent that

> the judgments of statesmen and philosophers about this process from its beginning have been a series of errors, and that the policies by which they have sought to control and direct it have only crippled it and interrupted it by war, revolt and dissension. . . . The fact is, as the history clearly shows, that the extension of the higher civilization over the globe is a natural process in which we are all swept along in spite of our ethical judgments.[40]

Thus for Sumner, as for Henry Adams, the course of historical development was determined by forces which fixed the direction of mass movement. The attempts of leaders to control the process merely produced a mindless chaos. History did indeed reveal progress in the sense that civilization was admittedly an advance over savagery and barbarism, but it was a progress the causes of which men had not understood; and in their misguided efforts to control it they had only compounded their problems.

A BRIEF HISTORY OF MASS THEORY

Modern mass theory developed in the context of gentry displacement, and inevitably reflected that fact in the detached and increasingly critical stance of mass theorists. During the nineteenth century, the American gentry elite, overlapping as they did with the social-economic and political elites, had identified sympathetically with the major thrust of democratic development. Adams and Sumner were more sensitive than many of their fellow intellectuals in realizing the subtle changes which would eventually obliterate gentility as a cultural influence. In the meanwhile, however, the American contributions to the early statements of mass theory were generally more complacent in their assessment of mass potentialities than were the European writings on which they drew.

Two traditions—judgmental and analytic—blend together in modern mass theory. The former has sometimes been considered aristocratic because of its doubts about the competence of the mass. The principal figures in this tradition are Tocqueville, Matthew Arnold, Gustave LeBon, José Ortega y Gasset, Emil Lederer, and Hannah Arendt. The analytic tradition is more neutral and descriptive, and is represented chiefly by Americans: Edward A. Ross, Robert E. Park, Herbert Blumer, Philip Selznick, and Kurt and Gladys Lang. It attempts to analyze the distinctive kinds of situation that produce mass phenomena.

Both traditions presuppose democratization in the broad sense that the mass is presumed to possess power and influence, and is aware of and responsive to the environment of ideas in which it lives. Indeed, they take it for granted that the mass plays a crucial role in the social process, that it is the decisive factor in the big decisions, and that its values are generally acknowledged to be the highest social values. The mass is presumed to consist of large numbers of people occupying an extensive territory, with industrial development and effective political organization. In all these respects mass society may be said to be a post-democratic development.

From Tocqueville's time down through the nineteenth century, the judgmental tradition was in effect a critical commentary on the social transformation stemming from the French Revolution. Although at first glance it might seem reactionary, it was not in fact the usual aristocratic type of reaction. It was rather the response of a newly detached group, the intellectuals, whose peculiar loyalties and perspective were revealed by Sir Francis Galton and Matthew Arnold. To whom but an intellectual like Galton would it have occurred to classify men according to ability? Or to proceed in the same spirit, as Arnold did, to distinguish between aristocratic "barbarians," bourgeois "philistines," and lower-class "populace"? While the drift of this theory was at least cautiously critical of democratization it should be borne in mind that democracy in Europe remained controversial long after it had become the universally accepted ideology in America. In applying mass concepts to local circumstances American theorists, even though they were themselves experiencing the uncomfortable transformation of gentlemen into professionals, tended to neutralize the normative connotations of the theory. An illustration of the difference was provided by the "sea change" which occurred to the concepts of French social psychologist Gustave LeBon when applied to American circumstances by Josiah Royce.

Mass theory assumed a recognizably modern form in the nineties with the work of LeBon.[41] Under certain circumstances, according to LeBon, a collective mind formed in a group of people who constituted a mass. Without necessarily being in personal contact with one another they became a single being in which the conscious personality of individuals vanished. Men were said to think, feel, and act differently as members of the mass than they would in isolation. In the mass, their common qualities were elements of character rather than of intellect. Transmitted by contagious suggestibility, emotions and convictions would run through the mass, transforming its individual members into barbarians, who would display the typical violence, heroism, and ferocity of primitives.[42]

As a cultural evolutionist, LeBon regarded mass formation as a reversion to an earlier, precivilized condition. The coming age of the mass posed a threat to civilized society with its discipline and rationality hated and feared by the mass. Unable to sustain the objective detachment of a social psychologist, LeBon confused massification, a process to which all men are susceptible, with a social stratum that was distinct from middle or upper classes. His conservative prejudices led him to associate mass with the tradition of violent revolution stemming from the French Revolution. Civilization was now seen to have been the product of an intellectual aristocracy which the anarchistic mass was determined to replace with primitive communism.[43]

Mass leaders had always been morbidly deranged individuals with the hypnotic gift for arousing intense enthusiasm among their followers. Such leaders as Buddha, Jesus, Muhammad, Joan of Arc, and Napoleon had all wielded despotic authority. LeBon shared Sumner's view as to the manner in which ideas influence the course of historical development. Ideas originate in the highest social class, where they have little or no social consequences. But if they are taken up by mass leaders they are reworked and distorted for agitational purposes and propagated among the mass. Eventually they returned to influence the behavior of the upper class. "In the long run," LeBon concluded, "it is intelligence that shapes the destiny of the world, but very indirectly." [44]

The Frenchman also shared Sumner's ambiguity as to the role of the mass in social change. Both agreed that historical changes were preceded by changes in thought. But the mass does not think, strictly speaking; its mental processes consist of a series of disconnected images called up by various exciting causes. Its instincts are conservative; it fears novelty, and is respectful of tradition. Its presumed revolutionary role is only superficial.[45] Nevertheless, at certain moments in history, when great changes are impending, the mass does play a decisive role. It may lack the capacity to initiate constructive changes, but its destructive power is overwhelming. These revolutionary movements occur when the traditional assumptions of society—the mores—have lost their persuasive power. "The beginning of a revolution is in reality the end of a belief." [46] LeBon thus wavered between the conception of mass as a form of collectivity peculiar to modern social conditions, which was his true contribution, and the more conventional notion of mass as a submerged class with revolutionary potential, derived no doubt from Marxian socialism.[47]

The Harvard philosopher Josiah Royce had no difficulty in distinguishing between LeBon's fruitful insights and his lapses into prejudice. In an essay on American provincialism published in 1908, Royce incorporated LeBon's theory of mass in his own critique of American society. He defined mass as "a company of people who, by reason of their sympathies, have for the time being resigned their individual judgment." [48] He agreed with LeBon that the leading ideas of the mass were atavistic, and that highly trained individuals were liable to resign their critical faculties when caught up in a mass. But by substituting "sympathies" for LeBon's suggestibility Royce significantly softened the harshness of the Frenchman's criticism, while at the same time emphasizing a distinctive quality of modern American society which opened up useful avenues of investigation. It would prove to be far more revealing to be able to identify the sources of the sentiment of sympathy in the mass than merely to deplore the mass man's vulnerability to charismatic leaders.

Normally a commendable trait in the individual, sympathy as the psychological basis of mass behavior produced what Royce considered some of the more dubious

features of modern civilization. Never before had men
been so eager to sympathize with the lot of any portion of
mankind. The leveling tendency produced by the communications media, popular education, and business consolidation subjected everyone to the same ideas and social
forces. Individuality was discouraged, while all approached
"a dead level of harassed mediocrity." Under these circumstances, the mass was repeatedly swept by waves of emotional enthusiasm as various worthy causes aroused its sympathies. The number of exotic religious faiths which
flourished even among sophisticated Americans testified to
the excessive spiritual plasticity of those who constantly
searched for novelty. The ugly scars of exploitation in
the countryside and the hideous jerry-built cities failed to
inhibit sentimental dreams, which remained unrealized.
The nation itself had become an incomprehensible mon-
ster in which the individual had lost his rights, his self-
consciousness, and his dignity. The greatest national
danger at that moment came from idealistic but imprac-
tical, ill-conceived reform proposals such as Henry
George's single-tax movement, Bellamy's utopian commu-
nitarianism, and Bryan's free silver, each of which entailed
consequences that could not be foreseen. These mass movements displayed an emotional fervor and recklessness characteristic of a people who, as Sumner observed, were led
by hopes rather than pushed by experience.[49]

Nevertheless, in spite of the ominous susceptibility of
modern civilization to these mass tendencies, Royce believed that the American tradition of regional cultural
autonomy provided an effective antidote. While individ-

uals in the mass resigned their critical faculties, in a "rightly constituted" social group the critical faculties of participants were enhanced. Each member of such a group felt his own responsibility for his part in the social enterprise, and the clash of ideas resulted in a collective or group wisdom greater than that of the individuals who constituted the group. Language, Roman law, and the British constitution were examples of such collective wisdom. "Keep the province awake, that the nation may be saved from the disastrous hypnotic slumber so characteristic of excited masses of mankind." [50] Royce's theory of the healthy autonomy of regional culture was at once one of the last of the gentry celebrations of ethnic-cultural regionalism and an anticipation of the modern mass theorist's concern over the loss of insulation of nonelites. The mass is susceptible to manipulation by its own demagogic leadership because of the breakdown of mediating institutions.[51] Royce was hopeful that regional loyalties springing from attachment to the primary institutions of the locality would sustain critical faculties in the face of mass pressures.

The same year in which Royce published his essay witnessed the appearance of E. A. Ross's *Social Psychology,* which its ebullient author believed to be the first systematic treatise on that subject in any language. Ross also leaned heavily on LeBon's analysis of the mass, but he further refined the concepts by taking up Gabriel Tarde's distinction between crowd and public. The public differed from Tarde's more conventional definition of the crowd in that its members were not in personal contact with one another. Publics were unified by the communications media, with as many publics as there were organs of opinion. Ross believed that crowds were declining in significance; the twentieth century was to be the era of publics.[52]

If the formation of publics seemed to promise a more rational and civilized order than crowd culture Ross was not aware of the fact. A dynamic society undergoing constant change inevitably lost its respect for custom and tradition. It became a habit to break habits. "It is a delusion," Ross concluded, "to suppose that one who has broken the yoke of custom is emancipated. The lanes of custom are narrow . . . but there is as much freedom and self-direction in him [sic] who trudges along the lane as in the 'emancipated' person, who finds himself in the open country free to pick a course of his own, but who, nevertheless, stampedes aimlessly with the herd. A dynamic society may, therefore, foster individuality no more than a static society. But it *does* progress, and that, perhaps, ought to reconcile us to the mental epidemics that afflict us." It was a curious kind of progress whose symptoms included religious revivalistic frenzy, financial booms and busts, political tidal waves producing dangerous rhythms in public affairs, a fickle foreign policy, and war fevers.

As an antidote to the diseases of a mass society Ross could only assert that gentry social values would continue to be relevant and would promote the growth of individuality. A type of education which would combine classical wisdom with modern sociology and psychology would provide a bulwark against the corrupting influence of the media. Property ownership, family solidarity, healthful country living, devotion to sports, and participation in voluntary associations all contributed to the development of intellectual, moral, and religious qualities best calculated to resist mass pressures.[53] Such values became a common bond between Ross and Theodore Roosevelt, one of the last of the gentlemen to occupy the White House.

The "Chicago school" of sociology founded by Robert E. Park at the turn of the century was to become a principal center for the academic versions of mass theory. A student of Royce's at Harvard, Park had gone to Germany for doctoral training in sociology and had written a dissertation on *Masse und Publicum* (1904).[54] His association with Booker T. Washington led to the study of race relations in the urban context, and to the development of a theory of the formation of communities as a result of group conflict and accommodation. He also insisted strongly on distinguishing between descriptive and normative approaches to the study of society. Going behind the conventional concepts of crowd and public, Park specified collective behavior—that is, the behavior of individuals under the influence of a common impulse—as the basic social phenomenon. Its most elementary form was social unrest, representing a challenge to established routines and a preparation for collective action. Park believed social unrest to be distinctive of populous modern societies in which emancipation from primary social controls freed individuals for participation in collective behavior. These concepts related closely to the typically modern preoccupation with social change, reform, and revolution.[55]

Park's successor at Chicago, Herbert Blumer, provided in 1939 the most specific formulation of mass theory yet to appear. Mass was defined as a spontaneous collective grouping composed of people aroused by a public event, such as a war or a murder trial, or who participate in some such form of behavior as a land rush or a large migration. Blumer specified the following features of a mass: (1) its members come from all walks of life; (2) they are not in personal contact and cannot identify one another prior to the precipitating event; (3) there is little interaction among them, since they are physically separated; and (4) they are loosely organized and unable to act with the concertedness of a crowd. The distinctively modern character of the mass phenomenon lies in the responsiveness of individuals to remote and abstract objects focused by the mass media. These objects lie outside local groups and cultures, and are not comprehended by the rules and understandings of the local situation. In this respect the mass is composed of detached and alienated individuals confronting objects not readily understood. Therefore, the mass is confused and uncertain, its members being unable to communicate with one another effectively.

Clearly, then, the mass does not reveal the characteristics of a society or a community. It has no social organization, no customs or traditions, no established rules or rituals, no organized sentiments, no structure of status roles, and no established leadership. In short, the mass is simply a haphazard collectivity which materializes on occasions when a precipitating stimulus draws individuals out of their normal group associations. The mass man retains his self-awareness—unlike the member of a crowd—and he responds as an individual to the object that stimulates him. But where large numbers are involved these responses may converge, in which case the total effect can be tremendous.

Today, under modern urban industrial conditions, mass behavior is of increasing magnitude and importance. A variety of forces, including education, the various mass communications media, and population mobility, detach people from their local groups and cultures and precipitate them into a larger world where for the most part they are unaided in selecting among the varied options available to them. Under such circumstances mass behavior often resembles crowd behavior.[56]

Nevertheless, the accidental or coincidental nature of mass behavior as Blumer conceived it should be noted. Each person seeks to satisfy his own needs, and acts as a self-aware individual. Mass behavior, paradoxically, does not arise from concerted action, and in this respect Blumer's notion of the mass was very different from Le-Bon's. It is only when the lines of individual action happen to converge, whether accidentally or in response to some common object, that mass behavior may have momentous significance. Mass behavior is not so much a durable condition as it is a potentiality to which modern society is susceptible. When it materializes it has a disintegrating effect upon social institutions. Thus, "a political party may be disorganized or a commercial institution wrecked by . . . shifts in interest or taste." [57] Mass behavior is an antisocial phenomenon, a tendency of modern society toward disintegration, checked only by the surviving social structures which continue to give order and stability to life.

Blumer acknowledged that when mass behavior becomes organized in a mass movement there is a sense in which it ceases to be mass behavior, for it now acquires structure, program, and a defining culture, and thus becomes societal in nature. Attention to the circumstances under which uncoordinated mass behavior becomes a deliberately organized mass movement introduced an important new phase in the history of mass theory. Just as the French Revolution and the rise of democracy had prompted the first formulation of mass concepts, so the totalitarian fascist movements of the twentieth century were to be interpreted in terms of the deliberate exploitation of mass conditions by demogogic political elites determined to fashion new tyrannies out of carefully manipulated mass movements.

Mass theory subsequent to 1939 was in an important sense a critical diagnosis of the sociological factors which had made possible the totalitarian fascist revolutions. Several of the most prominent mass theorists were Jewish refugees from Nazi persecution who fled to England or the United States, and whose analyses included anguished warnings that "it should not happen here." Some of them were also former Marxists who had renounced the faith because of the scandalously faulty Marxist diagnosis of fascism as simply the mature stage of capitalist development. It was essential to them to distinguish between the Marxists' mystical veneration for the proletarian masses and their own critical diagnosis of the role of the mass in the tragic rise of totalitarianism. Mass theory enabled them to show how the tactics of the emerging dictatorships were the overt consequences of tendencies at work for some time —even in the Germany of the Weimar Republic, where they had been undermining liberal and progressive policies. It would no longer serve to attribute the rise of Nazism simply to the vindictive terms of the Versailles Treaty.[58]

One of these refugees was Emil Lederer, whose book, *State of the Masses,* appeared in 1940. His principal purpose was to explain totalitarian dictatorship as the appropriate if not inevitable form of government of the amorphous mass. As a former Marxist, Lederer had been forced to reconsider the conventional Marxist ideal of the classless society as well as the role of the proletarian masses in the realization of such a society. The failure of the Marxists to understand modern dictatorship led Lederer to rediscover the value of social classes as barriers to "massification." [59]

The fascist dictatorships were at once the culmination of mass tendencies and the catalytic agents that swept aside all remaining obstacles to complete massification. The dictator was both the child of the mass and its captor. His object upon seizing power was to sweep away all remaining class or institutional pockets of resistance in the name of the mass. In a sense, he gave stability and durability to mass conditions by institutionalizing terror through the secret police and armed forces. The loyal support of the mass was secured by fervent appeals to patriotism and to hatred of foreigners. The mass was now emotionally unified through deliberate manipulation of the mass media, focused upon the charismatic figure of the leader. Lederer spoke of the "mass state" as the institutionalized expression of total politicization. The term "mass society" now became for him a contradiction in terms. A new order of existence had come into being which negated all former conceptions of social value.[60]

The stage was now set for the mature statements of mass theory which have appeared during the two decades 1950–1970. Philip Selznick's concise formulation of 1951 [61] incorporated both the institutional analyses of earlier theorists and the more recent preoccupation with the symbolic content of social behavior. "Mass," as Selznick defined it, was not a term of designation of any particular society, but rather a state of social pathology which might afflict any population. This disorder can be identified by a number of symptoms. (1) Creative or culture-sustaining elites become debilitated. (2) Values are stereotyped and only superficially adhered to. This is seen in a weak attachment to major cultural symbols, or in an attachment to the symbol itself rather than to its meaning. When values become stereotyped, the symbol and its meaning are divorced, so that the symbolic content is easily manipulated. Acts taken in the name of official values may in fact violate them. Public responses to patriotic symbols and their ideological content furnish abundant illustration of this mass characteristic. (3) Mass behavior is associated with activist interpretations of democracy, and with increasing reliance on force to resolve social conflict. Selznick attached great importance to the distinction between symbolic content that is mediated by the values of primary associations and content perceived directly by the mass without such mediation. Since mass behavior involves the withdrawal of deference for established institutions, the traditional values associated with such institutions no longer interact with mass objectives to cushion the impact of change. Thus the use of obscenities by protest groups is a generalized repudiation of traditional usages, since respectability is felt to be a barrier to change. (4) In a durable society, the web of social institutions expresses shared social values which furnish the individual with his self-image. Mass behavior, on the other hand, devalues social institutions and subverts their character-defining functions. The mass man becomes in some fundamental sense dehumanized.

The mass movements which arise out of these conditions also reveal distinctive characteristics. Contrary to the opinion of LeBon and the social psychologists who stressed the total commitment of the mass man to a movement, Selznick emphasized "segmental participation," the partial or limited commitment typical of mass involvement. Individuals interact not as whole personalities but only in terms of the roles they play in a given situation. In fact, a fully developed mass organization seeks to prevent primary face-to-face relationships, which elicit their own loyalties and hence resist the manipulation of the mass by its leadership. Here the theorist drew upon the older distinction between primary and secondary institutions, as well as upon more recent experience with totalitarian dictatorships.

Alienation from primary community relationships is thus a necessary precondition for the mobilization of the population into a mass movement. That the high degree of involvement displayed by members of a mass movement should arise out of weakened primary relationships is certainly paradoxical, and Selznick sought to explain it as the consequence of deliberate symbolic and organizational manipulation carried out by the elite leadership. Mass symbols brought to bear directly upon alienated individuals may elicit extreme behavior through unsatisfied emotional craving. Thus the mass will express strong emotional allegiance to patriotic stereotypes at the expense of traditional values, whereas in a well-structured community patriotism expresses itself indirectly, without irrational aggression against deviants.

The principal remaining task of the mass theorists was now to formulate a theory of leadership and to indicate the nature of its relationship to the mass. Leadership is provided by an indefinite number of elites, each social function which society considers important having its own elite leadership. The leaders achieve their status either through exceptional skill or through monopolistic control of the function, however achieved. Thus there are economic, political, professional, religious, and entertainment elites, to mention only a few, sometimes with overlapping personnel. It is important to note that the elites are distinguished by their functions, and that the individuals who constitute them lack status apart from function. Because functional leadership is not a durable basis for social status the elites are relatively vulnerable to mass pressures, and their members are often insecure. In this respect there is a sense in which the mass society is a classless society, which may account for the somewhat euphoric tone of certain mass theorists.[62] Perhaps the most spectacular illustration of mass control of its elites was its disposition of gentility. Other elites may be relatively less vulnerable; but even the economic elite by mid-twentieth century had been driven into personal anonymity and deprived of much of its power by mass pressure exerted through political and social agencies.

The vulnerability of elites can be most vividly appreciated by contrast with the measure of stability and security enjoyed by leadership in a class-structured society. Neither the mass nor its elites constitute classes in the traditional sense. Traditional ruling classes always controlled elite functions, either exercising them directly or acting as patrons of the creative and professional people. By virtue of their power and hereditary privileges they exercised these functions through successive generations as prerogatives taken for granted. Apart from the inheritance of wealth, elite status in the mass society must be won through personal effort and competence, while the measure of prestige is determined by mass preferences. Even where the same occupational preference is apparent in families through successive generations, as in the medical families of Boston or Philadelphia, elite status is still dependent on individual skill. Elite personnel is for the most part recruited from the mass. Sumner's notion that elites are self-generating by virtue of superior hereditary aptitudes is a quaint historical curiosity.

The authoritarian control exercised over the mass by the totalitarian fascist regimes would appear to be a paradox requiring explanation. If masses produce their own elites, how do those elites acquire autocratic power? Part of the explanation may have been provided by Everett Cherrington Hughes's account of the way in which social movements acquire institutional structure.[63] The ongoing "unfinished business" of a social movement inevitably creates institutions which call for manipulation and management, and thus a leadership emerges. In the few cases where that leadership succeeded in capturing all power the environing circumstances had to be propitious.

Mass characteristics are themselves antithetical to some of the commonest properties of social class. Unlike the members of a social class, who relate to each other and to outsiders in distinctive ways which establish their identity as a class, mass men are relatively isolated and unrelated to each other. This is a principal reason why mass action, when and if it occurs, tends to be direct action, outside institutionalized channels of behavior. Thus William Kornhauser has defined mass as a "large number of people who are not integrated into any broad social groupings, including classes." [64] Although mass theory would appear at first glance to lack the dynamic quality of Marxist class theory it does in fact offer its own interpretation of social change, which is diametrically opposed to that of Marxism.

Whereas Marxism regards a classless society as the ideal goal toward which history should proceed, mass theory concentrates on the social-pathological symptoms attending the breaking down of social structures into the mass— or classless—condition.

MASSIFICATION AND CULTURE

While the sociologists and social psychologists were analyzing the social structure of the mass society, literary critics were looking with increasing apprehension at the cultural life generated by mass conditions. As early as 1915, Van Wyck Brooks noted the widening gulf between "highbrow" and "lowbrow," the immaculate but dessicated gentry culture on the one hand and the breezy, vulgar opportunism of the popular culture on the other. "Between university ethics and business ethics, between American culture and American humor, between Good Government and Tammany, between academic pedantry and pavement slang, there is no community, no genial middle ground." Brooks's sense of the gap between the two cultures conveyed effectively enough the feeling of defensive isolation on the part of the highbrows, but it failed to indicate a dynamic relationship between the cultures. American life merely drifted chaotically between genteel culture and stark utility.[65]

By 1930, however, Brooks's notion of a bifurcated culture was yielding to a realization of the all-encompassing power of mass culture. When Matthew Josephson undertook his historical survey of the arts in America he found that a mechanized, unfeeling mass society was stifling the expression of individualistic, creative impulses. The routine of machines to which the mass was subjected served to stamp out the "natural emotions." What was to become of the artist, the man of sensibility and taste, in a mass society? Expatriation and primitivism both suggested his approaching obliteration. The dilemma of the artist was recognized by Josephson as a special case of the broader predicament of the gentry as a whole. "Under mechanism, the eternal drama for the artist becomes resistance to *the milieu,* as if the highest prerogative were the preservation of the individual type, the defense of the human self from dissolution in the horde." [66] Such a defensive posture, inevitable and necessary though it may have been, threatened to absorb all the energies of the artist, tempting him into the idiosyncratic and the obscure and diverting him from a positive and public affirmation of his genius.

As mediators between the artist or writer and his audience, the critics were particularly sensitive to the breakdown of communication which affected all the arts in the twentieth century. W. H. Auden traced the breakdown to the substitution of mass for community. In terms reminiscent of Royce he contrasted the intimate interplay of community life with the sterile isolation of the mass man. In the mass or "open" society the individual is emancipated from traditional institutional bonds and attains consciousness of self. He must now be either consciously active or consciously passive. All too often the latter choice is made, and the individual is ready to be drugged with large doses of mass culture.[67]

The fragmentation of cultural elites following the disintegration of gentility after World War I was an event of major consequence in American intellectual life. In the absence of a common social bond, writers, artists, and scholars went their separate ways and no longer reaped the advantages of a recognized common identity. Professionalization provided a refuge of sorts for scholars, but no such haven was available to creative people before mid-century, when places were found for many of them in teaching institutions. Occupational and social mobility no longer coincided for creative people and scholars, for many of whom a new designation—"intellectual"—came into vogue, signifying a detached and isolated status in relation to the sources of power. In fact, the loyalties and affiliations of those who would formerly have subscribed to gentility were now distributed across the entire spectrum of social and ideological possibilities. Successful writers and professors now often identified with labor or farm protest movements, or were professed revolutionaries. Such fragmentation of the intellectuals left high culture more vulnerable to the assaults of mass culture.[68]

Although the cultural life of a mass society might be said to distribute itself along a continuum reaching from the most coarse and commercialized mass culture to the refined subtleties of high culture it is common to divide the scale into three parts, designated superior, mediocre, and brutal cultures (Edward Shils), or high culture, midcult, and masscult (Dwight Macdonald). Such divisions serve the purpose of underscoring the ongoing conflict of cultures which in mass theory replaces the older social class conflict as the central object of attention.[69] All observers are impressed with the complacent contempt of the mass for high culture, and with the aggressive thrust of mass culture into the educated class formerly considered the proper province of high culture.

Dwight Macdonald, literary critic and political writer, published an extended analysis of these problems in his book *Against the American Grain* (1962). He pressed to its limits the distinction between mass and community. Men in the mass are unable to express their human qualities because they cannot relate to each other, either as individuals or as members of a community. As an "aggregate mass," to use the Langs' terminology, men are related only through impersonal and abstract agencies such as political parties, TV programs, or the system of industrial production. Hence the paradoxical fact that whereas a true community produces individuality and exhibits a constant tension between individual and group, the mass destroys individuality. Appreciating this outcome, the architects of totalitarian regimes had deliberately sought to create mass conditions by systematically destroying community institutions and activities. Mass man is non-man, a theoretical construct toward which all are being pushed.

As a former Marxist, Macdonald had had to purge himself of the Marxist dogma of the wisdom of the masses. When he did so he discovered that the vast majority of the community, regardless of income or educational levels, stubbornly preferred a vulgar and meretricious "masscult" to the rigorous demands of high culture. It would no longer suffice to attribute this preference to cynical ex-

ploitation of the mass by the "Lords of Kitsch." Macdonald abandoned hope that the mass could be brought to
appreciate the glory of high culture; he reconciled himself
to the prospect of a crude and commercialized masscult for
the majority and a refined high culture for the few capable
of appreciating and supporting it.[70]

But such a prospect, viable though it might be in principle, overlooked the full complexity of the cultural situation. While in theory one might willingly settle for a high
culture for the cognoscenti and a masscult for the ig-
noscenti, in fact no clear line separating the two cultures
could be drawn. Between them flourished a bland midcult, a middle-brow compromise that threatened to absorb
both its parents. Midcult had the essential characteristics
of mass-cult: the formula, the built-in reaction, and the
lack of any standard except popularity. It pretended to
respect high culture while in fact diluting and vulgarizing
it. Several of the more popular contemporary writers were
contemptuously assigned by Macdonald to the role of
purveyors of midcult. Such people affirmed their loyalty
to high culture by belatedly championing the avant-garde
of a previous generation without concerning themselves
about the lack of worthy successors. It was Macdonald's
fear that midcult would become the norm for cultural
values, and that high culture would cease to exist as a
living tradition.

It was fitting that the critic and poet Richard P. Blackmur, who had made a close study of the work of Henry
Adams, should formulate a decisive critique of contemporary mass culture. Blackmur located the principal chal-

lenge to high culture in the literate mass society.[71] A "new illiteracy"—a mass population possessed of the ability to read but lacking the skill or will to read the things that ought to be read—had created a unique cultural situation in which the survival of civilization itself seemed to be in jeopardy. The new illiteracy was nourished by a press almost as illiterate as its clientele. Public opinion had displaced knowledge, opening the door to demagoguery. All of this had occurred in the context of new and immense physical energies which swept society along, as Henry Adams had predicted long before, "at a rate and with consequences beyond our intellectual power to grasp." Blackmur believed that the tempo of affairs would remain out of control so long as the new illiteracy remained the source of political power.

Although every country which had experienced massification desperately needed a stronger cultural elite, Blackmur was driven to the conclusion that higher education in these countries no longer cultivated serious literacy. In the United States, the rapid growth of the country during the nineteenth century had prevented the necessary concentration of intellectual and creative energies, which had remained dispersed and unorganized. Thanks to the inertia of the mass, America had kept ahead of her problems, but her cultural and educational institutions had operated at a very low level. Consequently, her talented people had all too frequently formed sterile cliques, become eccentric, sought refuge in expatriation, or fallen silent. In the absence of influential and authoritative cultural institutions the gentry had lacked the power or influence to sustain a high aesthetic standard. Talented men like Mark Twain or Melville, who sensed the hollowness of gentry culture and turned against it, could not sustain or cultivate their gifts in isolation.[72]

Mass education, far from realizing the dream of an enlightened society, had merely succeeded in producing a new intellectual proletariat composed of formally trained people who found themselves with no use for their training and were consequently alienated because they were superfluous. In America, the intellectual was now the only proletarian.

> The double apparition of mass society and universal education is producing a larger and larger class of intellectually trained men and women the world over who cannot make a living in terms of their training and who cannot, because of their training, make a living otherwise with any satisfaction. The American distrust of the intellect, and the painful shrinkage of the confidence of the intellect in itself turns out to be a natural phenomenon of mass society and universal education.[73]

Aside from its capacity to produce technically trained people, the educational system had lamentably failed to produce a class of true intellectuals. Blackmur was persuaded that true literacy would flourish only so long as society believed that the dignity of man inhered in his intelligence and reason. But since dignity was a product of action, and not of education, education alone could not dignify. There must be useful roles for the educated man to play. Unfortunately, a mutual distrust prevailed between the educated person and the public. The latter

quite properly distrusted the former because of his inadequate training and lack of independence. He in turn,
sensing this, hesitated to speak the truth in a forthright
manner, finding it prudent to say what the public wanted
to hear. Thus from both sides circumstances conspired to
produce the banalities of midcult. "The old safety—the
immemorial hard straw pillow—of undifferentiated ignorance in the masses is being replaced (as we see everywhere in the world at different velocities and intensities)
by the differentiated and energized ignorance which results from low level universal education." [74] Blackmur's
analysis of magazine circulation during the past hundred
years showed how inferior journals had taken over the
readership which earlier would have been served by magazines of higher quality. In the struggle for readers, which
was an essential aspect of culture conflict, midcult was
clearly encroaching on the ground formerly held by high
culture.

· VIII ·

THE DECLINE
OF GENTILITY

THE OUTWARD PERFECTION of the gentleman as a type her-
alded his demise. In the later decades of the nineteenth
century the tradition of gentility reached full development
in the genteel. In perfection of dress and manner, but
even more in refinement of taste and delicacy of sentiment, the gentleman achieved the final realization of the
form. By doing so he widened the gulf separating himself
from the rough, vigorous industrial society of which he
was, incongruously, a member.

Although historians have accurately equated the genteel
with decadence, it should be said that moral decadence, at

least, was no part of the gentleman's problem. On the contrary, his prudery was notorious. He approved Howells's admonition to fix the attention on the "more smiling aspects" of life, and he shared Lowell's indignation at the unchastity of mind which the critic found, for instance, in certain of the poems of Swinburne. It was Lowell who voiced the gentry sentiment when he wrote: *"Virginibus puerisque?* To be sure! Let no man write a line that he would not have his daughter read." The editors of *Scribner's, Harper's, Atlantic Monthly,* and the *Century* regularly censored or rejected material likely to distress gentry readers. *Harper's,* for instance, complained of a story of George Washington Cable that "the disagreeable aspects of human nature are made prominent, and the story leaves an unpleasant impression on the mind of the reader." [1] The literary rebellion about to occur was to concern itself as much with the restoration of artistic over moral and social priorities as with the more widely publicized naturalistic preoccupation with the disagreeable aspects of life.

Ineffectuality was the central symptom of decay, and the gentry were generally well aware of it. Fresh from his study of the robust Elizabethan literature Barrett Wendell complained of the "self-analytic inaction" of his own generation. Introspection and fastidious withdrawal were paradoxical in the age of the robber barons. "Over-refinement is the curse of the century," Wendell pontificated. [2] A mood of pessimism prompted nostalgic recollections of better times. In the national centennial year, Lowell harked back half a century to the Fourth of July in 1826, when he had perched in a cherry tree at Elmwood to watch his father walk out from town bearing the news of the death of John Adams. "I wish I could feel, as I did then," he mourned, "that we were a chosen people, with a still valid claim to divine interpositions. It is from an opposite quarter that most of our providences seem to come now." [3]

The sentimentalism which had first manifested itself earlier in the century in the new mass literature of fiction and the magazines now thoroughly infected the gentry. Sentimentalism came to be especially associated, at least in the popular mind, with the genteel lady, who unquestionably played a larger role in genteel culture. Henry James protested, through one of his fictional characters, that "the whole generation is womanized; the masculine tone is passing out of the world; it's a feminine, a nervous, hysterical, chattering, canting age, an age of hollow phrases and false delicacy and exaggerated solicitudes and coddled sensibilities, which, if we don't look out, will usher in the reign of mediocrity, of the feeblest, and flattest and the most pretentious that has ever been seen." [4] The Boston feminists were not the only ones to be scandalized by such outspoken antifeminism; for the most part the gentlemen observed with condescension or even with pride the continuing success of the ladies in activities formerly reserved to men. It was the ultimate irony that a tradition that had always prided itself upon its masculinity should come to find itself best represented by its women.

THE NEW RICH AND THE
DECAY OF MANNERS

Prior to the Civil War, the gentry had played an aggressive and independent role in American life, while the social-economic elite had been on the defensive. The rich could then best serve their cultural ambitions by emancipating themselves from the narrow and parochial world of the business elite and establishing contact with the gentry. An overlapping group consisted of members of the economic elite who had successfully negotiated the gulf, together with the gentry with whom they associated. After his return from Europe in 1833, Cooper urged both groups to enlarge and strengthen the overlapping sector, since this offered the best solution to the American social problem. It would be a mistake to regard the overlapping relationship as one of simple patronage by the rich. Money undoubtedly had its uses, but before he was accepted the rich man had to demonstrate his genuine involvement in gentry interests. Once established in the overlapping group, individuals and their descendants were often able to migrate in either direction. In Philadelphia, descendants of economic elite families at the beginning of the nineteenth century were sometimes found in gentry ranks at the end of the century.[5] In general, however, in the years before the Civil War the best of the social-economic elite were drawn into the overlapping group.

After the war, this was no longer the case. The two groups drew apart, and in the separation the gentry were

the principal sufferers. The economic elite itself was rapidly changing in character. The older commercial families
of the seaboard cities were thrust into the background by
new industrial, financial, and utilities magnates, many of
them from cities of the interior, who did not share the
cultural interests of the older mercantile elite. From the
perspective of her older elite connections Edith Wharton
had observed the change, beginning in the 1880s with the
invasion of New York by the newly rich from Pittsburgh
and the West. By the time of the First World War, the
older traditions and usages of New York society had been
destroyed. "What had seemed unalterable rules of conduct became of a sudden observances as quaintly arbitrary
as the domestic rites of the Pharaohs." [6] New money as
seen from the vantage point of the older elites did not have
the effect commonly attributed to it of widening the gulf
between social classes. On the contrary, money was the
great leveler. It destroyed the social distinctions which had
formerly prevailed, substituting for them a common mercenary standard. Differences were no longer of kind, but
only of degree. In place of the former stability of a society
divided into relatively firm social classes there now
emerged the restless universal flux of the mass society.

The economic elite, who had been timid and peripheral
in the 1830s, now in the later decades of the century
dominated the American social landscape. They continued
to caricature the overt features of gentility, often going to
grotesque extremes of ostentatious living. The gentry
were now eclipsed and isolated from the centers of power
as they had never been previously. As the two groups drew

apart, the overlapping sector disintegrated in spite of oc-
cational efforts to perpetuate it. In her Boston home Julia
Ward Howe attempted to hold them together, inviting society friends to hear papers by such gentry luminaries as
Louis Agassiz, Edwin P. Whipple, and James Freeman
Clarke. In later years she conducted a more ambitious
campaign in Newport, where the overlapping group organized the Town and Country Club. Its object was to
check the growth of a "fast world" of shallow pleasures by
providing a diet of scholarly lectures and intellectual conversation. The members heard talks on science by William B. Rogers of MIT, by Alexander Agassiz, Dr. S.
Wier Mitchell, and the Vassar astronomer Maria Mitchell.
Thomas Davidson lectured on Aristotle, and the historian
George E. Ellis talked about the Indians of Rhode Island
and about the philosopher Bishop Berkeley, an earlier
resident of Newport. Although the club lasted for more
than thirty years, Mrs. Howe was obliged to admit that
fashionable Newport finally killed it. By the end of the
century, the old resort where gentry and social elite had
mixed in an "exquisite social atmosphere, half rustic, half
cosmopolitan, and wholly free," was gone forever. The new
rich with their seaside chateaux and uniformed lackeys had
forced the gentry families of "moderate fortunes" to take
their vacations elsewhere.[7] If it came to the attention of
the social-economic elite that they were expected to patron-
ize high culture they did so through agents, without becoming personally involved.

Manners had always been so basic to gentility that the
deterioration of gentry manners furnished an accurate

measure of decline. The fate of gentility was sealed by a subtle process of diffusion, expropriation, and dilution which eventuated in a general uniformity of manners. There was a sense in which the gentry themselves initiated their own expropriation. Throughout the nineteenth century their educational program was intended to disseminate gentry manners and values and thus transform their whole society into gentlemen. What they did not anticipate was the subtle perversion of gentility which inevitably accompanied the process of dissemination.

Expropriation of gentle manners by the business community was an important part of the process. Charles Butler had observed in 1836 that business did not have a higher place in public esteem because of its reputation for being grasping and devious. It seemed to him that in a country like the United States where it played so large a role it would be "good policy" for business to create for itself a more favorable public image. Franklin had already charted the way for the businessman as gentleman with his doctrine that an ingratiating manner paid practical dividends. Rationalization of business methods, one of the more important trends in the later nineteenth century, involved among other things a carefully calculated theory and practice of customer relations. Starting with Chesterfield's maxim that gentility was the art of pleasing, it followed readily enough that the salesman who made a favorable personal impression on the potential customer enjoyed an initial advantage not to be lightly disregarded. Hence the universal attention paid by latter-day salesmen to the dress and manners of the gentleman. By the turn of

the century, a genial demimonde of glad-handing commercialism had emerged. As early as 1889 Lucy Larcom
was complaining that the word "lady" had already lost its
original meaning of a giver of sympathy and service. In
America, where one person was presumed to be as good
as another, every woman had become a lady. With unin-
tended irony this erstwhile mill worker protested against
the common practice of speaking of "sales ladies" and
even of "chamber ladies." [8]

The overshadowing of the gentry by the business elite
had a direct bearing on the expropriation of manners. Earlier in the century it had been the gentry who were the
objects of emulation. Now, however, the prestige and
grand manner of the social-economic elite made them the
center of attention. Etiquette books now described in
precise detail the elaborate and meticulous usages of the
rich in dress, table manners, and social intercourse. The
consumption of such books greatly exceeded the volume
of sales in the earlier period, with several new publications
appearing each year between 1870 and 1917.[9] Needless to
say, few of the readers of etiquette books would ever be
privileged to polish their manners in elite circles, but the
popularity of the genre suggests the readiness with which
readers identified themselves vicariously with the rich.

In commenting on these tendencies Charles Eliot Norton attributed the deterioration of manners to their detachment from a hereditary class of gentlemen. Looking backward nostalgically to the old eighteenth-century gentry,
which he assumed to have been an hereditary class, Norton
reiterated the familiar maxim that "it took three genera-

tions to make a gentleman." Manners and good breeding had meant the same thing. In the 1880s, however, manners and breeding had become wholly divorced from each other. More people were paying attention to polite behavior than ever before, and the assumption prevailed that with a little effort anyone could acquire good manners. But the divorce of manners from class introduced insidious seeds of corruption.

> The resentment which the vulgar man feels against the refined man leads him, in a free society like ours, to do what he can to spread and foster vulgarity, just as his enemy does refinement, and this may serve to explain the phenomenon, certainly noticeable in our day, of a constantly increasing refinement of manners generally, contrasted with and accompanied by a rapid progress in vulgarity.[10]

One of the last discussions of gentility as a social ideal was published in the columns of the *Century* magazine, beginning in 1909. The *Century*'s editor, Robert Underwood Johnson, had followed the decay of good manners with increasing dismay. He chided the gentry for no longer insisting upon good manners even in their own children and servants. Johnson clung to the older notion of gentility as the code of a class, and he realized that if the class succumbed the code would die with it. "There can be no society without deference, and the quality of the society is indicated by the proper direction and gradation of this deference." In their struggle for equality Americans were jeopardizing both their liberty and their Christianity. If the distinctive qualities of gentility were to survive there must be "simple ceremonies of deference." [11] Johnson's contribution to this final campaign consisted of a series of editorials on the social dimensions of the problem, together with solicited contributions by prominent authors and educators.

Thomas Nelson Page agreed with Johnson in fixing primary responsibility for the decay of manners upon the social-economic elite. "After all things are considered, the chief cause of the decadence of manners is the lack of manners on the part of the upper class, from which the lower class take their cue and tone." In the mad pursuit of wealth the refinements of life were being swept away. To revive manners it would be necessary to set aside wealth as the chief foundation of respect and restore gentry values in its place. Page was especially indignant at the lack of respect for age and merit in fashionable circles. The final and most recently acquired ingredient of gentility, kindliness, was lost upon those wholly absorbed in the gratification of selfish desires. There were still, to be sure, certain sheltered circles of breeding and refinement where the arts and sciences were nourished. But the gentry had virtually been driven out of the cities, where civility had traditionally flourished. Urbanity had been reduced to suburbanity.[12]

Page and Johnson agreed that although rudeness of manners in a democracy had often been noted, the fault lay with the elites rather than the mass. Johnson had observed that the respectful demeanor and speech of recently arrived immigrants were quickly destroyed by the false notions of equality that prevailed here. The responsibility for this sorry state of affairs was laid to the failure of the privileged to maintain standards of excellence. Johnson cited a recent report of Dean Keppel of Columbia on the deterioration of manners among college students. On the campuses, it seemed, no one wanted to be accused of politer-than-thou behavior. It was particularly depressing that students from families socially prominent for several generations and presumably well bred were frequently the worst-mannered. If responsibility were to be located more precisely within the family it would have to be charged to the women, since women had been chiefly responsible for the inculcation of good manners among all civilized peoples. Perhaps the greatest tragedy of the gentry lay in the failure of the lady to maintain good manners in the marital relationship and in the training of children.[13]

President Eliot had a deeper awareness of the impact of democracy on manners than did his journalistic colleagues. He knew that manners should be more homogeneous in a democracy than in a class-structured society, and that the family would share its influence with school, church, and the agencies of government. He felt strongly that the success of democracy depended upon a high average degree of civility. As an educator, Eliot was particularly conscious of the socializing function of the schools. He was disturbed to discover from a survey of 1,400 school systems that in only 155 was there regular systematic instruction in manners. Wherever it was offered, such instruction invariably touched upon morals, thus underscoring the close connection between the two. Since the success of democratic society depended upon mutual good will, kindliness, and cooperation Eliot stressed the fundamental importance of the function of the schools in teaching manners and morals.[14]

During the course of the nineteenth century, the social context of manners had changed significantly. In Cooper's time the qualities of independence and individuality seemed of supreme importance, and the standards of gentility were accommodated to them. The natural gentleman was one whose environment happily nourished these qualities. By the end of the century, however, social conditions no longer assigned a central place to these values. Social equality and the mutual rights and duties of citizenship were now central, and the manners which facilitated social intercourse among all kinds of men seemed most appropriate to the democratic gentleman. As Eliot observed, with unconscious reference to Cooper, savages might often exhibit the highest measure of composure, dignity, and decorum, but their social manners were none the less deplorable—uncleanliness, slovenly eating, lack of consideration for the weak, and emotional abandon.

It was the crowning paradox of the history of the gentry that the perfecting of the social type in the genteel should coincide with the rapid diffusion of gentlemanly qualities throughout the population. This "dispersion of civility" is recognized as a characteristic of mass society, and it inevitably involved the screening out and distortion of certain values.[15] Most notable was the elimination of the ideal of individuality, the quality which made the archetypal gentleman the complete individual, standing whole and entire. The dispersion of civility had the opposite effect of making individuals more accessible to each other, breaking down independence of character, and making a virtue of camaraderie and good fellowship on a level that effectively weakened individuality. The pedagogical theory of John Dewey and the social analysis of David Riesman depicted in detail the characteristics of the new democratic type.

The best that could be said for gentility in a democratic society was said by Samuel McChord Crothers, in 1903. In an age of democratic equality, observed Crothers, the gentlemanly ideal is freed from its class connotations and becomes a universal ideal.

> An ideal democracy is a society in which good manners are universal. There is no arrogance and no cringing, but social intercourse is based on mutual respect. This ideal democracy has not been perfected, but the type of men who are creating it has already been evolved. Among all the crude and sordid elements of modern life, we see the stirring of a new chivalry. It is based on a recognition of the worth and dignity of the common man.[16]

NERVOUSNESS

One of the symptoms of decline was the prevalence among the gentry of more or less incapacitating nervous illness. The list of sufferers included the names of such prominent gentry leaders as Horace Bushnell, William Graham Sumner, William James, Octavius Brooks Frothingham, Charles Eliot Norton, and Edmund C. Stedman. George William Curtis complained periodically of a "pudding head" and nervous prostration. The younger John Quincy Adams, brother of Henry and Brooks, broke down under the stress of financial losses in the panic of '93. The frequent references to ill health and to travel "in search of health" encountered in the records of the era must often indicate incapacitating nervous illness.

The traditional gentry emphasis on obligation and personal responsibility, on what Theodore Roosevelt called "manliness," undoubtedly accentuated other tendencies to nervousness. Max Weber was probably right when he observed that the social ethic of Puritanism survived its theology, although he chose a poor illustration in the hedonist Ben Franklin. More apt illustrations might have been found among the gentry, with their strain of idealism resulting in the internalized discipline that Irving Babbitt was later to call "the inner check." One such example would have been William Graham Sumner, who worked himself to the verge of physical breakdown, and who knew full well what he was doing to himself when he coined the grim maxim that man is born to labor and that it is work that kills.

An even better example would have been the young William James, who fancied himself a thoroughbred sniffing the smoke of battle with distended nostril and agonizing over the paralyzing nervousness that kept him immobilized. This analogy was an appropriate one. Gentlemen had always applied the concept of good breeding both to themselves and to their animals. The history of the thoroughbred was roughly coterminous with gentility. Man and animal were intelligent, refined, spirited, trained to accept life as a challenge—and nervous. When the touring car replaced the matched pair, a revealing symbol of gentility had vanished.

The pioneer analysis of gentry nervousness was made by the New York neurologist and physician George Miller Beard. Dr. Beard enjoyed a brief notoriety in 1882 as a result of his vigorous criticism of the execution of President Garfield's assassin, whom he believed to have been insane. But Beard was soon forgotten, leaving to posterity little besides a new word, neurasthenia. Beard noted that in the thirty years between 1850 and 1880 there had been a great increase in the various symptoms of extreme nervousness: insomnia, dyspepsia, vertigo, headache, depression, heart palpitations, etc. Nervousness was for all practical purposes a new disease. The Greeks had no word for it; and as recently as the eighteenth century the term had signified simply irritability. Beard's concept of nervousness was strictly functional and materialistic. The organism possessed only so much nerve force, and when this force was drawn upon to excess the symptoms of nervousness appeared.[17]

A frequent European traveler and correspondent with European physicians, Dr. Beard noted that although nervousness was beginning to appear in the countries of Northwestern Europe, it was nevertheless a distinctively American disease. Those prone to be afflicted constituted a definite physiological type: small in size, with a frail, fine constitution, frequently of superior intellect and a strong emotional nature. They formed the cultivated social circles of the cities where the distinction between mental and manual labor was most sharply drawn. The nervous type of constitution was more commonly found among women than among men. It was apparent that Dr. Beard had identified a disease especially prevalent among the gentry, although his mechanistic assumptions inhibited detailed consideration of the social and psychological aspects of nervousness.

At the same time that the gentry were becoming more fastidious and refined in their tastes and manners, the physician noted certain physiological changes. There was, for instance, a marked recent increase in sensitiveness to stimulants and narcotics. Prior to mid-century, everyone had had a tremendous capacity for both, and Europeans still did; but among the American gentry drinking had now become a lost art.[18] Half the doctor's nervous patients had voluntarily given up alcoholic beverages before consulting him; the women almost entirely so. The same was true with respect to the use of tobacco. Simultaneously, the effects of narcotics were undergoing radical changes. A dose of opium that formerly would have put a patient to sleep now kept him awake. From these generalizations Dr. Beard specifically exempted recent German and Irish immigrants.

Intolerance of stimulants was in one sense fortunate, because the nervous type tended toward compulsive drinking. The United States was the first country to require institutions for the care of inebriates. By way of contrast, along the northern shores of the Mediterranean, where drinking was habitually heavy, one rarely encountered inebriety or alcoholism. Similar problems were found with respect to diet. The characteristic digestive disorders of the nervous person contributed directly to nervous exhaustion, with a corresponding effect upon food habits. Pork had formerly been the principal meat in the American diet, but it was so no longer because the nervous person could not digest it. "The pig, like the Indian, flees before civilization."

The physician noted parenthetically certain cultural manifestations of nervousness. The distinctive American brand of humor was found to have a deep foundation in nervousness. Humor was an inevitable reaction to excessive strain. The peculiarly American humor of exaggeration, the grotesque, and the absurd had been developed not by the coarse, vulgar type of person, but by the gentry type. The humorous lecture of the later nineteenth century had replaced the educational or edifying lyceum-type lecture of an earlier day because of a deeply felt need for laughter. Laughing aloud had formerly been considered vulgar; but nervous people were now increasingly resorting to laughter because they had discovered its therapeutic value. The American language similarly showed the influence of nervousness in the course of its divergence from the mother tongue. Clipped words, compressed idioms, indistinct articulation, greater rapidity of speech, the high and monotonous sameness of pitch, all testified to the same cause. Even the musical instruments in the United States were said to be pitched higher than in Europe.

In casting about for the causes of nervousness Beard commenced with modern civilization itself. The Greeks had been civilized and they were not nervous. But if one took civilization in general and stirred in the special ingredients of steam power, the periodical press, the telegraph, science, and the mental activity of women the result would be nervousness. Specialization of function, unless offset by other activities, was particularly exhaustive of nerve force. So was the time-keeping imposed by precision of routine. Beard knew nervous men who could not look at their watches without sending up the pulse rate. Telegraphic communication brought all the woes of the world to each man's doorstep with the morning paper.

Adaptation to rapidly successive changes in modern living was undoubtedly a great drain on nervous energy. The readjustment of ideas required by the dynamic tempo of intellectual life was an even greater drain, and one which bore primary on those who took intellectual issues seriously. Beard knew of a young man whose hair had turned white in a single day as a consequence of the mental anguish of confronting the conflicting claims of science and religion. (Edmund Gosse's vivid account of his father's struggle with the same problem at about the same time furnishes corroborating evidence.) Beard believed that the civilized man's exposure to suffering was much greater than that of the savage. Love and jealousy could both be nerve-wracking emotions. Modern philanthropy rested on sympathy, which in turn derived from vicarious participation in the suffering of others. Religion and politics in their American forms were more exhausting than elsewhere because of the greater measure of personal involvement. (Beard noted that no Catholic country was very nervous.) The libertarian individualism of the United

States and the relative absence of class barriers were prime causes of nervousness.

But modern civilization was not confined to the United States, and it was still necessary to explain why the Americans were the most nervous of civilized peoples. Another causal factor peculiar to the United States must also be present, and Dr. Beard identified it as climate. He knew that the physician could stimulate the body with alternating applications of ice and hot water. Used briefly, such treatment strengthened; but if protracted, it weakened the body. This therapeutic technique suggested the importance of the fact that in the northeastern and north central regions of the United States the inhabitants were subjected to more sudden and frequent alternations of extreme heat and cold than was experienced in any other civilized country. Half a year they roasted and the other half they froze. These repeated alternations produced energy, restlessness, and nervousness. They also increased sensitivity to heat and cold. Beard observed that an earlier generation had been comfortable with an indoor temperature of sixty degrees; now people required seventy to seventy-five degrees for comfort. The American climate was also drier than the European, and dryness produced headache, neuralgia, and nervousness, due to more rapid metabolism.

On a map of the United States the nervous belt was a broad band extending westward from southern New England and the Middle Atlantic states along the southern shores of the Great Lakes to southern Minnesota and Iowa and back eastward through the Ohio Valley. North of the nervous belt, in Canada, and south of it, in the

southern states, nervousness was much less frequently encountered. The causes of nervousness were the pressures of
modern civilized living encountered by frail types under
the least favorable environmental conditions.

One may assume that most of Dr. Beard's patients were
gentry, and that it was the gentry who suffered extensively
from the ravages of the new disease. The nineteenth-
century gentry were not a leisure class. They bore a heavy
burden of cultural responsibility at the same time that
they attempted to perpetuate the elborate usages of
gentility. Consequently, traditional refinements, such as
dressing for dinner, had to be abandoned. The gentlemanly style of life had developed when the tempo of living
was slow and considerable leisure time was available. At
the end of the century, the men of Judge Grant's generation, burdened with "that dreadful, nervous, hurried feeling," looked back enviously to the delightful condition of
equipoise their ancestors were believed to have enjoyed.
For some, the burden was well-nigh intolerable. Barrett
Wendell doubted that anyone ever reached the age of
thirty-five in New England without wanting to kill himself.[19]

ETHNIC CHANGES AND
REGIONAL DECLINE

The deepening sense of frustration and pessimism that
gripped the gentry in the later years of the nineteenth
century determined the perspective from which ethnic
changes in the composition of the population were viewed.
New England experienced spectacular population changes

during the nineteenth century, and it was doubtless inevitable that gentry spokesmen should see in the displacement of the old Yankee stock the causes of the disintegration of the ethnic-regional heritage. The Massachusetts physician and demographer Nathan Allen pointed out in 1883 that emigration from the region had begun after the Revolution and had gone on steadily throughout the following century. The emigrants were presumably the younger and more vigorous elements, whose departure robbed the region of its most valuable citizens. At the same time, internal migration within the region witnessed a steady flow of population from the rural areas of Maine, New Hampshire, and Vermont to the new manufacturing towns of Massachusetts. By 1880 the urban residents of New England outnumbered the rural four to one.

Another significant change was occupational. In the single decade 1870–1880 the number of persons classified as professional had more than doubled. Whatever might be said of the civic virtues of the professional class, Allen had no doubt that they tended to degenerate physically.

A third major change was the massive influx of foreigners which had begun about 1830. By 1880 there were 793,122 foreign-born residents in New England. The census reports did not distinguish second-generation descendants of immigrants during that period, but Allen estimated them to number 1,200,000 in 1880. More ominous still was the fact that the birthrate of the foreign elements was twice that of the natives. Taken together, these statistics seemed to make it clear that the region would no longer serve as a nursery for natural gentlemen.[20]

Implicit in Dr. Allen's analysis was the assumption—

shared by his fellow physician John Ellis, who also investigated the changing demographic situation [21]—that gentility contained the seeds of its own destruction. Both observers noted the steady decline in the birthrate of the old Yankee population, rural as well as urban, a fact that could not be explained by migration or ethnic displacement. The regional heritage itself, with all the complex forces that produced the natural gentleman and launched him upon the course culminating in the cultivated gentleman, contained its own irreversible cycle. As physical labor gave way to sedentary occupations, muscle tissue was replaced by nerve fiber, digestive powers were impaired, and vitality diminished. The lady was the central figure in this transformation. New England women, and especially the girls, had traditionally done their own housework, greatly to their physical advantage. Now the girls went to school, while their mothers aspired to transfer the household chores to servants. The result was the notoriously sickly female, marrying late if at all, bearing few children, and suffering from the assorted nervous disorders diagnosed by Dr. Beard.

A final appreciation of the cultural significance of regionalism was penned by the Philadelphia historian Sydney G. Fisher, in 1894. Fisher proposed an explanation of why it was that America's leading men of letters had all been born between 1780 and 1825, most of them in Massachusetts. The answer could not be found in wealth, educational opportunities, or leisure, all of which were more abundantly available after the period of flowering had passed. The only explanation satisfactory to Fisher was the stability and homogeneity of the population prior. to the 1820s. Massachusetts had had no appreciable immigration after 1640, a fact only somewhat less true of the other English colonies. For a century and a half these closely knit peoples had slowly developed the sense of sympathy and rapport which were essential preconditions of creative cultural achievement. Thus it had been with the Greeks and the Jews, and thus it was with the Yankees. "Literature of genius is not the expression of the man who writes it. It is the expression of the deep, united feeling of his people." America's great literary figures had all passed their impressionable years before the tide of European immigration had set in. After 1825, the conditions which had nurtured great cultural achievement no longer existed.[22]

The waning vitality of regional cultures, coinciding as it did with population changes, led the gentry to embrace racist doctrines. No other fact of intellectual history indicates so clearly the course of genteel decline. In his *Law of Civilization and Decay* (1893) Brooks Adams affirmed the view that mental characteristics were strongly hereditary. Families famous in one century sank into obscurity in the next not because they had degenerated but because the field of activity in which the ancestors had won their laurels was later closed to their descendants.[23] No doubt Adams had his own family in mind, although the generalization applied to the gentry as a whole. The particular environmental change which, in the opinion of both Brooks and his brother Henry, was fatal to gentry interests was the rise of the great financiers whose control of credit and markets destroyed gentry financial autonomy.

The symbol of the status revolution for many of the gentry was the Jew. A homeless wanderer, but with influential connections in many lands, the Jew represented an alien threat to the regional stability of gentry culture.[24] He also symbolized the overwhelming threat of newly made money to gentry values. Lowell's complex guilt feelings expressed themselves in the conviction that he himself possessed Jewish blood, derived from unknown sources. Light was perhaps thrown upon this strange obsession by Barrett Wendell, who reported a theory current in Boston that Norfolk and Lincolnshire had been centers of English Jewry before the Reformation, and that under persecution many Jews had renounced their religion and had been absorbed into the local population. Many of the New England Puritans from those regions thus presumably had had Jewish blood in their veins.[25] By identifying themselves with a group they despised, these two gentlemen gave eloquent testimonial to their own sense of alienation.

In the end, the last defense of the gentry was the bare fact of priority—their ancestors had been here first. As historians they turned with loving care to the chronicling of the early years of settlement, always with the implied or explicit assumption that the original institutions and ideals transplanted from the European homeland were the clues to American greatness. There was of course no reason to assume that only the first comers should contribute to the American Way, and it was inevitable that someone would claim for each successive generation of immigrants a share of the glory. When Barrett Wendell asserted that it took three generations to Americanize an immigrant's de-

scendants Mary Antin retorted that she was more American
than Wendell himself, precisely because she was a newcomer; in a land made by immigrants let the descendants
of earlier settlers accommodate themselves if they could.
Wendell acknowledged that she had had the last word
when he moaned: "The racial agony in which we are
being strangled by invading aliens, who shall inherit the
spirit of us, grows heavier with me, as the end of me—and
of ours—comes nearer." [26]

With the disintegration of the gentry at the beginning
of the twentieth century the remaining elements were
widely scattered, coming to rest in a number of different
social locations. A sizable fragment exchanged gentry
status for professionalism. Doctors, lawyers, and teachers
now thought of themselves in terms of the ideals and expectations of their own professional groups. Although
there was nothing in professional life as such that was
incompatible with gentility, the grinding, sustained, and
specialized skills of the twentieth-century professions nevertheless tended to narrow the interests of their practitioners.
Thus Barrett Wendell complained that those who proposed to do serious literary work appeared to be mere
amateurs, and suffered the loss of public esteem.[27]

Another of the precipitates from the dissolution of
gentility was what has come to be called the intellectual.
Richard Hofstadter defined the intellectual as one dedicated in a central way to the life of the mind. But he was
obliged to distinguish intellect from mere intelligence, and
he was unable to identify the intellectual with any occupational or social group, unless it be the writers in the "little

magazines." The fact is that modern intellectuals lack a distinct social status of their own; hence their vulnerability. They are scattered among various occupational and social groups none of which they can control, and upon whose patronage they cannot entirely depend. F. Scott Fitzgerald recognized this when he remarked: "My generation of radicals and breakersdown never found anything to take the place of the old virtues of work and courage and the old graces of courtesy and politeness." [28]

A small but vocal group of "New Humanist" followers of Irving Babbitt and Paul Elmer More deplored the passing of gentry leadership, which they attributed to the deficiencies of democratic mass society. Babbitt had been a student and disciple of Charles Eliot Norton, from whom he may well have derived his conception of democracy as a "huge mass of standardized mediocrity." His critique of the mass society emphasized its hedonistic absorption in the pursuit of happiness, and the "full-blown commercial insolence" with which it expressed its preferences in cultural matters. Whatever the theory of democracy might be, in practice it was standardized and commercialized melodrama. With his stress on the spiritual indolence and philistinism of the mass man Babbitt anticipated a central theme of Ortega y Gasset.[29]

A weakness of democracy which especially concerned the New Humanists was its evasion of the problem of leadership. Babbitt deplored the Progressive drift toward the direct democracy of initiative, referendum, and direct primary election. He emphatically repudiated the suggestion that such techniques of self-government afforded a substitute for leadership. "No movement, indeed, illustrates more clearly than the supposedly democratic movement the way in which the will of highly organized and resolute minorities may prevail over the will of the inert and unorganized mass." Democracy, like any other form of society, required leadership; the only question was whether the leaders would discipline and educate the mass or demagogically exploit it. The qualities with which Babbitt endowed his ideal leaders showed that he envisioned a revivified gentry. "The hope of civilization lies not in the divine average but in the saving remnant." [30]

The principal contribution of the New Humanists to the emerging theory of mass society was to insist upon the vital role of the cultural elite in sustaining the ethical standards which supported high culture. Paul Elmer More realized that this had been the chief function of the nineteenth-century gentry. More knew that in order to revive the gentry it would be necessary to distinguish this "natural aristocracy" from the plutocracy. While the object of the gentry would be the establishment of true democracy, this democracy was to be defined as the selection and promotion of the best men, not as a higher standard of living for the masses. More bitterly resented the misplaced humanitarianism which professed a greater concern for the wages of the bricklayer or trainman than for those of the artist or teacher. Hearing so much about the class consciousness of the proletariat, he pointed out that the remnants of the gentry had lost all sense of class identity, and were condemned to "sterile seclusion," a condition his jeremiad did little to alleviate.[31]

It was particularly galling to men like Babbitt and More to observe how frequently those whose tastes and standards would formerly have identified them with gentry interests now not only lacked a sense of their proper affiliations but even took up causes directly opposed to their own true interests. The young teachers, lawyers, journalists, and writers who threw themselves into the Progressive reform movements of the turn of the century conceived of public issues in terms of economic class conflict, and were oblivious to the humanist warning that they were acting contrary to their own interests. The appeal of socialism to the more idealistic among these young radicals was notorious. Whether in the form of Marxism or of the more attenuated types of naturalistic social theory, the doctrine of economic class conflict furnished the universal frame of reference for the younger generation, and in this context there was no place for the gentry unless they were to be identified with the social-economic elite, which was often the case. Nor was the theory of class conflict congenial to the nascent conception of a mass society taking shape in the minds of the older generation of gentry.

During the first half of the twentieth century, analysis of social issues in terms of social-economic classes blotted out the approach to these issues in terms of the sociology of mass society. It was only after World War II that the theory of mass society was revived and applied to current problems. But the intellectual continuity had been broken. The inspiration now came from European theorists, and the earlier American explorations of the meaning of the mass society were forgotten.

Final respects were paid to the gentry by Henry Dwight Sedgwick, in 1935.[32] By that date it was possible to see that the First World War had climaxed a series of changes in manners and opinion that spelled the demise of gentility. It was now apparent to Sedgwick that the gentleman had been a social type whose function was to fuse intellectual, social, and moral qualities in an ideal man who was to serve as a standard for all to emulate. But the distinctions of quality which the gentleman proposed to perpetuate had proven unacceptable to the democratic mass. The gentry themselves had been unable to achieve a successful fusion of gentility with democratic sentiments, and their position had become increasingly equivocal. The energy which they had devoted to good causes and public service in the earlier part of the nineteenth century was increasingly transferred to private purposes, while the dwindling number of those who retained a sense of their gentry heritage were unable to sustain the positive and optimistic attitude of earlier times. The last days of the gentry were days of futility and despair.

LIBERALISM

The life span of gentility in the mass society virtually coincided with the rise and fall of liberal individualism. The latter-day gentleman was in fact the perfect embodiment of the ethical aspect of liberalism, even as the entrepreneur represented its economic side. A fundamental assumption of liberalism—as often taken for granted as explicitly affirmed—concerned the power of ideas and ideals. Freedom of speech and press meant little apart from the belief that the power of persuasion had potentially important consequences. The liberal world was one of sensitivity to ideas, one in which men were presumably governed by the mind. Education would provide the individual both with the practical skills to assure success in a socially mobile society and with the body of knowledge and interests that would provide the educated class with a common outlook.

Liberalism was an international philosophy, especially influential in England and America, where it provided the foundation of the cultural cosmopolitanism of the gentry on both sides of the Atlantic. Liberalism meant just and rational sentiments, emancipation from prejudice and provincialism. In this respect liberalism and gentility were one, since gentlemanliness was a Western and almost a worldwide code, uniting its devotees in a great international brotherhood. Cooper felt especially strongly about the cosmopolitanism of the gentry, making this the central theme of his didactic novels *Homeward Bound* and *Home as Found*. His principal characters, the Effingham family, represented American gentility at its cosmopolitan finest, moving with equal poise and assurance on either side of the Atlantic. Homeward bound on a transatlantic packet, the Effinghams encountered a British gentry family with whom they quickly established pleasant relations based on their common manners and liberal sentiments. By way of contrast, the vessel also carried nongentry citizens of the two countries. But the Cockney bounder and the Western ring-tailed roarer, each imprisoned in his own provincial prejudices, could only clash discordantly.

In the earlier years of the century, when the mood of the gentry was predominantly optimistic, two facets of liberalism received especial emphasis. One was the idealization of labor broadly conceived as the creative exercise of all the faculties and powers. This ideal, so appropriate to a liberal democracy, replaced the older aristocratic ideal of leisure in which labor was despised as menial. The celebration of labor was one of the bonds linking the gentry to the yeomanry, and separating it from fashionable society. Although historians have often traced the idealization of labor to Puritan and Protestant sources, its exemplification during the nineteenth century in Thoreau, Howells, the Marxists, Sumner, Veblen, and Dewey would seem to trace more immediately to gentry than to religious sources. As Harriet Martineau put it, the hero of the new society was neither soldier nor king, but the artisan, inspired and led by poets and martyrs. The new morality rested on the conviction that complete toil of body and spirit enriched with a truth that could not otherwise be obtained.[33]

A second emphasis was upon the cultural potentialities of popular government. Unlike a monarchy, where political power was concentrated and cultural life consequently centered in a metropolis, a republic displayed local autonomy of cultural life and recruited its talent from the farthest bounds. Edward Everett spoke of the American states as "schools of character and nurseries of mind," each providing through its educational system the stimulus and opportunity for the development of talent. Political organization had had to come first, but now that republican institutions were firmly established a cultural flowering would shortly follow. This was the more certain because native talents were distributed at random throughout the population, and not confined to a privileged class. Free institutions would provide for the release and nurturing of these talents wherever they might appear.

Everett anticipated the emergence of new cultural and literary forms appropriate to the distinctive character of American society. Language and literature would come to reflect in their vigor and intensity the social spontaneity of a free society. The immense size and diversity of the United States promised a "nationality at once liberal and great." [34]

But after a promising start, the hopeful expectations of the American gentry that they would lead the new democratic society to a great cultural flowering dissipated in painful frustrations. As the contours of the mass society gradually took shape it became increasingly apparent that gentry leadership was ill-suited to the new social realities. The gentry individualists who had operated effectively in the relatively stable institutional context of the earlier nineteenth century became increasingly vulnerable after the Civil War as older institutional patterns crumbled and varied forms of "collective" behavior reflected new conditions in which the gentry rapidly became obsolete. The development of mass theory revealed the growing awareness that their liberal expectation of the emancipation of the mass mind from ignorance and provincialism was to remain unrealized.

NOTES

·I·

DEMOCRACY AND GENTILITY

1. Harriet Martineau, *Society in America* (3 vols. in 2, 2d ed., London, Saunders, 1837), III, 92–96; and *Retrospect of Western Travel* (2 vols., New York, Harper, 1838), I, 64.

2. James Fenimore Cooper, *Notions of the Americans* (2 vols., London, Colburn, 1828), II, 416–21.

3. Ralph Waldo Emerson, "Manners," in *Essays, Second Series;* "Behavior," *The Conduct of Life; Works* (4 vols. in 1, New York, Tudor, n.d.), I, 316, 318; III, 110–30.

4. Jackson Turner Main, *The Social Structure of Revolutionary America* (Princeton, Princeton, 1965); Robert E. and B. Katherine Brown, *Virginia, 1705–1786: Democracy or Aristocracy* (East Lansing, Michigan State, 1964); Robert E. Brown, *Middle-Class Democracy and the Revolution in Masaschusetts, 1691–1780* (Ithaca, Cornell, 1955).

Democracy and Gentility (continued)

5. Michael Chevalier, *Society, Manners, and Politics in the United States* (Garden City, Doubleday Anchor, 1961), p. 291; Martineau, *Society in America*, I, 16–17.

6. Alexis de Tocqueville, *Democracy in America* (2 vols., New York, Colonial Press, 1899), II, 27, 255–56, 238, 104–106.

7. Cooper, *Home as Found* ([1838, Leatherstocking Edition] New York, Putnam, n.d.), p. 414.

8. See the studies of success literature by Irvin G. Wyllie, *The Self-Made Man in America* (New Brunswick, Rutgers, 1954); John G. Cawelti, *Apostles of 'the Self-Made Man* (Chicago, University of Chicago, 1965); Richard M. Huber, *The American Dream of Success* (New York, McGraw-Hill, 1971). Stephen Thernstrom, *Poverty and Progress. Social Mobility in a Nineteenth Century City* (Cambridge, Harvard, 1964), esp. pp. 158–65.

9. Quoted in Wyllie, *The Self-Made Man*, p. 14.

10. R. G. Albion, *The Rise of New York Port* (New York, Scribner, 1939), pp. 241–51. Wyllie, *The Self-Made Man*, 26–30; John G. Cawelti, *Apostles of the Self-Made Man* (Chicago, U. of Chicago, 1965), pp. 54, 105.

11. Tocqueville, *Democracy in America*, I, 269–71; Frances Trollope, *Domestic Manners of the Americans* ([1832] D. Smalley, ed., New York, Knopf, 1949), pp. 308–10; David Ludlum, *Social Ferment in Vermont, 1791–1850* (New York, Columbia, 1939), p. 97.

12. *Democracy in America*, II, 100, 90–93.

13. The literature of mass theory is voluminous, deriving in a general way from Tocqueville himself. Among the classics are José Ortega y Gasset, *The Revolt of the Masses* ([1930] New York, Norton, 1932), Emil Lederer, *The State of the Masses* ([1939] New York, Fertig, 1967), and Hannah Arendt, *The Origins of Totalitarianism* ([1951] New York, Meridian, 1958). Especially suggestive for historians are the essays of Leo Lowenthal, *Literature, Popular Culture, and Society* (Englewood Cliffs, N.J., Prentice-Hall, 1961).

14. George W. Pierson, *Tocqueville and Beaumont in America* (New York, Oxford, 1938), pp. 549–51.

15. Francis Grund, *Aristocracy in America* (New York, Harper, 1959), p. 84; *American Quarterly Review*, XXII (1837), 427.

16. Martineau, *Society in America*, III, 14–15, 36; I, 19–21; III,

28–32. Van Wyck Brooks, *The World of Washington Irving* (New York, Dutton, 1944), p. 427. Chevalier, *Society*, pp. 418–19. Grund, *Aristocracy, passim.* Pierson, *Tocqueville*, p. 413.

17. *Diary of George Templeton Strong* (4 vols., New York, Macmillan, 1952), II, 92; Tocqueville, *Democracy in America*, II, 256, 168–71.

18. Pierson, *Tocqueville and Beaumont*, provides a meticulous account of the tour, identifying their numerous informants. Tocqueville's own notes of his conversations are printed in J. P. Mayer, ed., *Alexis de Tocqueville, Journey to America* (trans. by George Lawrence, London, Faber and Faber, 1959).

19. Mayer, *Journey*, pp. 271, 196, 235, 179.

20. *Ibid.*, pp. 214–16; Tocqueville, *Democracy in America*, II, 274, 119–22.

21. Tocqueville, *Democracy in America*, I, 184–88.

22. Pierson, *Tocqueville and Beaumont*, pp. 69–70; Mayer, *Journey*, pp. 67–68, 19–20, 15–16.

23. Mayer, *Journey*, pp. 68–69.   24. *Ibid.*, pp. 87, 257–58.

25. *Ibid.*, p. 70.

26. Tocqueville, *Democracy in America*, II, 100.

27. *Ibid.*, II, 90–93.

28. Mayer, *Journey*, pp. 69–70, 182–83, 56–57.

29. Tocqueville, *Democracy in America*, II, 27, 238, 255–56, 130–31.

30. Mayer, *Journey*, pp. 15, 51–52.

31. Tocqueville, *Democracy in America*, II, 104–106.

32. Mayer, *Journey*, pp. 19–20, 17, 86–87.

33. *Ibid.*, pp. 61–62, 217–19.

34. Pierson, *Tocqueville and Beaumont*, pp. 549–51.

35. Tocqueville, *Democracy in America*, II, 202–207.

36. *Ibid.*, II, 4.

37. Mayer, *Journey*, p. 76; Tocqueville, *Democracy in America*, II, 172–73, 182, 239.

38. Pierson, *Tocqueville and Beaumont*, p. 510.

39. Mayer, *Journey*, pp. 70, 92–93, 98, 48, 53, 21, 236–37.

40. *Ibid.*, pp. 258–61; Tocqueville, *Democracy in America*, II, 168–71, 40.

41. Tocqueville, *Democracy in America*, I, 330–31.

·II·

AN AMERICAN THEORY OF MANNERS

1. Esmé Wingfield-Stratford, *The Making of a Gentleman* (London, Williams and Norgate, 1938), pp. 19–39.

2. Louis B. Wright, *First Gentlemen of Virginia* (San Marino, Huntington Library, 1940).

3. Wingfield-Stratford, *Making of a Gentleman,* pp. 207–10.

4. A. M. Schlesinger, *Learning How To Behave* (New York, Macmillan, 1946), p. 5.

5. Esther Singleton, *Social New York Under the Georges, 1714–1776* (New York, Appleton, 1902), pp. 373–85.

6. Moncure D. Conway, *George Washington's Rules of Civility* (London, Chatto and Windus, 1890), pp. 7–36.

7. Conway, *Rules of Civility,* pp. 37, 102.

8. C. M. Sedgwick, *Morals of Manners* (New York, Putnam, 1846), pp. 4–5; *Means and Ends* (3d ed., Boston, Marsh, 1839), p. 142.

9. Ralph Waldo Emerson, "Behavior," *Works* (4 vols. in 1, New York, Tudor, n.d.), III, 111.

10. Charles Butler, *The American Gentleman* (Philadelphia, Hogan and Thompson, 1836), pp. 134–42.

11. *North American Review,* XIX (July 1824), 95–98; Richard Hildreth, *Theory of Morals* (Boston, Little & Brown, 1844), pp. 81, 17–21, 99; Butler, *American Gentleman,* p. 150.

12. Theodore Sedgwick, *Hints to My Countrymen* (New York, Seymour, 1826), p. 46.

13. Caroline Kirkland, *Evening Book* (New York, Scribner, 1853), pp. x, 107, 110; N. P. Willis, *Hurry-Graphs,* quoted in Schlesinger, *Learning How To Behave,* p. 21.

14. Sedgwick, *Means and Ends,* pp. 149–50.

15. Sedgwick, *Means and Ends,* pp. 142–65. See also Sarah J. Hale, *Manners* (new ed., Boston, Lee and Shepard, 1889), pp. 18, 87.

16. Catharine Beecher, *A Treatise on Domestic Economy* ([1842] rev. ed., New York, Harper, 1855), pp. 25–38; C. Beecher and

Harriet B. Stowe, *American Woman's Home* (New York, Ford, 1869), pp. 198–99.

17. Butler, *The American Gentleman*, pp. 171–79.

18. Emerson, "Manners," *Works*, I, 334.

19. N. P. Willis, *Hurry-Graphs; or, Sketches of Scenery, Celebrities, and Society, Taken from Life* (2d ed., New York, Scribner, 1851), pp. 263–67. Cf. Mary E. W. Sherwood, *Manners and Social Uses* ([1884] New York, Harper, 1918), pp. 165–66.

20. Edith Wharton, *A Backward Glance* (New York, Appleton, 1934), pp. 68–69, 93–95.

21. Julia Ward Howe, *Reminiscences, 1819–1899* (Boston, Houghton Mifflin, 1900), pp. 145–46, 152–53.

22. Historians often distort Holmes's meaning of the term by identifying the "Brahmins" with the rich.

23. J. T. Morse, *Life and Letters of Oliver Wendell Holmes* (2 vols., Boston, Houghton Mifflin, 1897), I, 18; O. W. Holmes, *Elsie Venner* ([1861] New York, Signet, 1961), pp. 15–25.

24. Russell B. Nye, *George Bancroft* (New York, Washington Square Press, 1964), pp. 1–12; Daniel Boorstin, *The Americans: The National Experience* (New York, Random House, 1965), pp. 369–70.

25. Anna L. Dawes, *Charles Sumner* (New York, Dodd Mead, 1898), pp. 38–62; David Donald, *Charles Sumner* (New York, Knopf, 1960), pp. 39–44, 71–74, 103–32.

26. G. W. Curtis, *The Potiphar Papers* (New York, Harper, 1856).

27. Mary E. Dewey, *Life and Letters of Catharine M. Sedgwick* (New York, Harper, 1872), pp. 113–14.

·III·

THE NATURAL GENTLEMAN

1. See chapter VII on the history of mass theory.

2. Leo Lowenthal, *Literature, Popular Culture, and Society* (Englewood Cliffs, N.J., Prentice-Hall, 1961), pp. 52–108; Trevor Colbourn, *The Lamp of Experience* (Chapel Hill, U. of North Carolina, 1965), pp. 20, 17–18, 14–15; Daniel Boorstin, *The Americans: The Colonial Experience* (New York, Random House, 1958), pp. 319–40; James D. Hart, *The Popular Book, a History of America's Literary*

The Natural Gentleman (continued)

Taste (New York, Oxford, 1950), p. 15. Bernard Bailyn, ed., *Pamphlets of the American Revolution* (Cambridge, Harvard, 1965), I, 3–19; A. M. Schlesinger, *Prelude to Independence; the Newspaper War on Britain, 1764–1776* (New York, Knopf, 1958), pp. 296 ff.; F. L. Mott, *American Journalism* (New York, Macmillan, 1941), pp. 113–62, 167–68; W. G. Bleyer, *Main Currents in the History of American Journalism* (Boston and New York, Houghton Mifflin, 1927), pp. 154–65; A. M. Lee, *The Daily Newspaper in America* (New York, Macmillan, 1937), pp. 711–19 (tables).

3. Alexis de Tocqueville, *Democracy in America* (2 vols., New York, Colonial Press, 1899), II, 40–41.

4. Michael Katz, *The Irony of Early School Reform* (Cambridge, Harvard, 1968).

5. Harriet Martineau, *Society in America* (3 vols. in 2, London, Saunders, 1837), III, 7–8.

6. Tocqueville, *Democracy in America,* I, 184–88.

7. Frances Trollope, *Domestic Manners of the Americans* ([1832] D. Smalley, ed., New York, Knopf, 1949), pp. 92–94, 311, 322; James Fenimore Cooper, *Homeward Bound, Home as Found* ([1838, Leatherstocking Edition] New York, Putnam, n.d.), *passim.*

8. Martineau, *Society in America,* III, 27.

9. R. W. Emerson, "Manners," *Essays, Second Series,* in *Works* (4 vols. in 1, New York, Tudor, n.d.), I, 316–18.

10. *American Quarterly Review,* XXII (Dec. 1837), 421–26.

11. William Tudor, *Letters on the Eastern States* (New York, Kirk and Mercein, 1820), p. 170.

12. Cooper, *Home as Found,* p. 45.

13. *The Works of William Ellery Channing, D.D.* (6 vols., 22d. ed., Boston, American Unitarian Association, 1872), I, 243–50.

14. Cooper, *The Redskins* (Leatherstocking Edition), p. 443. The principal source for Cooper's views on the sociological cycle of frontier development is found in *The Pioneers,* the first of the Leatherstocking novels.

15. Josiah Quincy, *Figures of the Past, from the Leaves of Old Journals* (Boston, Little, Brown, 1926), p. 296.

16. William Cooper Howells, "Self-Made Men" (unpublished

manuscript), pp. 6–8. Quoted with permission of Professor VanDerck Frechette. I am indebted to Andrew Franklin for bringing this essay to my attention.

17. Odell Shepard, ed., *The Journals of Bronson Alcott* (Boston, Little, Brown, 1938), p. 238.

18. See Thomas Bailey Aldrich, *An Old Town by the Sea* (Boston and New York, Houghton Mifflin, 1893), pp. 82–123.

19. *Alcott Journals,* pp. 89, 24–25.   20. *Ibid.,* pp. 130–31.

21. *Ibid.,* pp. 135–36, 317–18.

22. Theodore Sedgwick, *Hints to My Countrymen, by an American* (New York, Seymour, 1826), pp. 16–18, 27–33.

23. Edward Everett, *North American Review,* XIX (July 1824), 95.

24. *Harper's Monthly Magazine,* XIX (1859), 411–13.

25. Edward Everett, *Orations and Speeches on Various Occasions* (4 vols., 7th ed., Boston, Little, Brown, 1865), I, 17; M. A. DeWolfe Howe, *Barrett Wendell and His Letters* (Boston, Atlantic Monthly, 1924), p. 256.

26. G. F. Hoar, *Autobiography of Seventy Years* (New York, Scribner, 1903), pp. 40–41.

27. Lucy Larcom, *A New England Girlhood* (Boston and New York, Houghton Mifflin, 1889), pp. 19, 91–92, 118–20, 126–36.

28. Cooper, *Satanstoe, passim;* R. U. Johnson, *Remembered Yesterdays* (Boston, Little, Brown, 1923), pp. 25–48; *Alcott Journals,* p. 133.

·IV·

THE GENTRY AND AMERICAN SOCIETY

1. Caroline Kirkland, *The Evening Book* (New York, Scribner, 1853), pp. 18, 20. Mary E. W. Sherwood, *Manners and Social Usages* ([1884] New York, Harper, 1918), pp. 155–56.

2. Catharine Sedgwick, *Means and Ends* (3d ed., Boston, Marsh, 1839), p. 163.

3. Sarah J. Hale, *Manners* (New ed., Boston, Lee and Shepard, 1889), pp. 308–309.

4. Ferris Greenslet, *The Life of Thomas Bailey Aldrich* (Cam-

The Gentry and American Society (continued)

bridge, Riverside, 1908), pp. 87–88. Longfellow later used the idea in his poem, "The Hanging of the Crane."

5. Horace Bushnell, *Christian Nurture* ([1847] New York, Scribner, 1903)..

6. Bernard Wishy, *The Child and the Republic. The Dawn of Modern American Child Nurture* (Philadelphia, University of Pennsylvania, 1968), p. 55.

7. Kirkland, *Evening Book,* pp. 18–20.

8. Esmé Wingfield-Stratford, *The Making of a Gentleman* (London, Williams and Norgate, 1938), pp. 114–15.

9. Quoted in Catharine E. Beecher, *A Treatise on Domestic Economy for the Use of Young Ladies at Home* ([1842] rev. ed., New York, Harper, 1855), pp. 28–29.

10. Josiah Quincy, *Figures of the Past, from the Leaves of Old Journals* (Boston, Little, Brown, 1926), p. 221.

11. "American Women and American Character," in John A. Hague, ed., *American Character and American Culture* (DeLand, Fla., Everett Edwards, 1964), pp. 65–84.

12. Catharine E. Beecher, *Woman Suffrage and Woman's Profession* (Hartford, Brown and Gross, 1871), pp. 43–44.

13. Mrs. A. J. Graves, *Woman in America; Being an Examination into the Moral and Intellectual Condition of American Female Society* (New York, Harper, 1843), pp. 162–63.

14. Graves, *Woman,* pp. 155–59.

15. N. P. Willis, *Hurry-Graphs; or, Sketches of Scenery, Celebrities, and Society, Taken from Life* (2d ed., New York, Scribner, 1851), pp. 268–71. Frances Trollope made similar observations, expressed in less charitable language; Frances Trollope, *Domestic Manners of the Americans* ([1832] D. Smalley, ed., New York, Knopf, 1949), pp. 156–57.

16. Graves, *Woman,* pp. 28–33; Beecher, *Woman Suffrage,* pp. 21–34.

17. Sedgwick, *Means and Ends,* pp. 267–71.

18. Graves, *Woman,* p. 66.

19. Barbara Cross, ed., *The Educated Woman in America* (New York, Teachers College Press, 1965), pp. 1–2.

20. Andrew Sinclair, *The Better Half; the Emancipation of the*

American Woman (New York, Harper and Row, 1965), pp. 118–19.

21. John Randolph, *Letters of John Randolph to a Young Relative* (Philadelphia, Carey, 1834), pp. 209–10.

22. Sinclair, *Better Half*, p. 11.

23. Catharine E. Beecher, *The Evils Suffered by American Women and American Children; the Causes and the Remedy* (New York, Harper, 1846), pp. 3–11; Beecher, *Woman Suffrage*, pp. 43–60.

24. S. E. Morison, *The Life and Letters of Harrison Gray Otis, Federalist, 1765–1848* (2 vols., Boston, Houghton Mifflin, 1913), I, 12.

25. Quincy, *Figures of the Past*, p. 280.

26. James D. Hart, *The Popular Book, A History of America's Literary Taste* (New York, Oxford, 1950), pp. 28, 57. Hart estimates that more than a third of American fiction published prior to 1820 was written by women.

27. Among the more notable representatives of this genre were Susan Warner's *The Wide, Wide World* (1850), and Catharine M. Sedgwick's *A New England Tale* (1822).

28. Julia Ward Howe, *Reminiscences, 1819–1899* (Boston, Houghton Mifflin, 1900), pp. 304–306.

29. Sinclair, *Better Half*, pp. 107–109.

30. Hart, *Popular Book*, p. 86.

31. Catharine E. Beecher and Harriet Beecher Stowe, *The American Woman's Home* (New York, Ford, 1869), p. 13; Howe, *Reminiscences*, pp. 215–17.

32. Beecher, *Woman Suffrage*, pp. 18–19.

33. Robert Grant, *Fourscore* (Boston, Houghton Mifflin, 1934), pp. 228, 220.

34. Robert Grant, *Law and the Family* (New York, Scribner, 1919), pp. 165–97, 113–62.

35. *Daedalus* (Spring 1960), pp. 291–93; Dwight Macdonald, *Against the American Grain* (New York, Random House, 1962), pp. 3–75. See also chapter VII.

36. E. L. Godkin, *Reflections and Comments, 1865–1895* (New York, Scribner, 1895), pp. 201–205.

37. Richard Hofstadter, *The Age of Reform* (New York, Knopf, 1955), pp. 131–63.

38. Grant, *Fourscore*, p. 166; "The Art of Living," *Scribner's Magazine*, XVII (1895), 3–15, 615–27, 760.

39. Willis, *Hurry-Graphs*, pp. 283–89; Robert Underwood John-

The Gentry and American Society (continued)

son, *Remembered Yesterdays* (Boston, Little, Brown, 1923), pp. 90–93; *The Life and Letters of George Ticknor* (2 vols., London, Sampson and Low, 1876), I, 48; M. A. DeWolfe Howe, *Memories of a Hostess* (Boston, Atlantic Monthly, 1922), pp. 6–16.

40. Edward Waldo Emerson, *The Early Years of the Saturday Club, 1855–1870* (Boston and New York, Houghton Mifflin, 1918), pp. 4–13.

41. Kenneth W. Cameron, "Emerson, Thoreau, and the Town and Country Club," *Emerson Society Quarterly*, No. 8 (1957), pp. 2–17.

42. Emerson, *Saturday Club*, pp. 4–13.   43. *Ibid.*, pp. 14–38.

44. Virginia Harlow, *Thomas Sergeant Perry: A Biography* (Durham, Duke, 1950), pp. 46–47; M. A. DeWolfe Howe, *Portrait of an Independent, Moorfield Storey, 1845–1929* (Boston, Houghton Mifflin, 1932), pp. 241–42; Ernest Samuels, *The Young Henry Adams* (Cambridge, Harvard, 1965), p. 217. For other comments on Boston club life see Martin Duberman, *James Russell Lowell* (Boston, Houghton Mifflin, 1966), pp. 441–42; Helen Howe, *The Gentle Americans, 1864–1960* (New York, Harper and Row, 1965), pp. 45–46; Frederic J. Stimson, *My United States* (New York, Scribner, 1931), pp. 110–11; Grant, *Fourscore*, pp. 125, 258–59.

45. Grant, *Fourscore*, p. 199; Sara Norton and M. A. DeWolfe Howe, *Letters of Charles Eliot Norton with Biographical Content* (2 vols., Boston, Houghton Mifflin, 1913), II, 196–98.

46. Francis G. Fairchild, *The Clubs of New York* (New York, Hinton, 1873), pp. 29–56; Perry Miller, *The Raven and the Whale* (New York, Harcourt, Brace, 1956), p. 16; Henry Holt, *Garrulties of an Octogenarian Editor* (Boston, Houghton Mifflin, 1923), pp. 109–12.

47. Thomas M. Spaulding, *The Cosmos Club on Lafayette Square* (Washington, privately printed, 1929), pp. 1–29;. *The Twenty-fifth Anniversary of the Founding of the Cosmos Club of Washington, D.C.* (Washington, Cosmos Club, 1904), pp. 25–41; Ernest Samuels, *Henry Adams, the Middle Years* (Cambridge, Harvard, 1958), pp. 36–37.

48. *The Works of Charles Sumner* (15 vols., Boston, Lee and Shepard, 1875), IX, 51–54; E. L. Pierce, *Memoir and Letters of*

Charles Sumner (Boston, Roberts, 1877–93), IV, 192. For earlier discussions of the desirability of academies see William Charvat, *The Origins of American Critical Thought, 1810–1835* (Philadelphia, U. of Pennsylvania, 1936), pp. 3–6; A. W. Read, "Membership in Proposed American Academies," *American Literature*, VII (1935), 145 ff.

49. Ralph L. Rusk, ed., *The Letters of Ralph Waldo Emerson* (6 vols., New York, Columbia, 1939), V, 392–97.

50. *The Nation*, VI (June 18, 1868), 486–88.

51. Johnson, *Remembered Yesterdays*, pp. 439–52.

52. William Dean Howells, *Criticism and Fiction* (New York, Harper, 1891), p. 104.

53. Howells, *Criticism and Fiction*, p. 139.

54. Howe, *Gentle Americans*, p. 48.

55. Henry Steele Commager, *The American Mind* (New Haven, Yale, 1950), p. 58.

56. Howells, *A Hazard of New Fortunes* (New York, Bantam, 1960), p. 190.

57. Howells, *The Minister's Charge* (Boston, Ticknor, 1887), p. 458.

·V·

GENTRY POLITICS

1. Richard Hofstadter, *Anti-Intellectualism in American Life* (New York, Knopf, 1963), p. 165.

2. Sidney H. Aaronson, *Status and Kinship in the Higher Civil Service* (Cambridge, Harvard, 1964), pp. 61, 67–74, 104–105, 116–17, 124, 90–91, 102, 119. Aaronson's categories include father's occupation, social eminence, occupation, ethnic origin, education, and kinship.

3. Henry Adams, *The Education of Henry Adams* (Boston, Houghton Mifflin, 1918), chapter XVII.

4. S. E. Morison, *Life and Letters of Harrison Gray Otis, Federalist, 1765–1848* (2 vols., Boston, Houghton Mifflin, 1913), I, 227, 307.

5. *The Nation*, V (Aug. 22, 1867), 153–54.

Gentry Politics (continued)

6. David Donald, *Charles Sumner and the Coming of the Civil War* (New York, Knopf, 1960), pp. 112–13, 169–77.

7. G. F. Hoar, *Autobiography of Seventy Years* (New York, Scribner, 1903), pp. 30, 132, 152–54.

8. Rollo Ogden, *Life and Letters of Edwin Lawrence Godkin* (2 vols., New York, Macmillan, 1907), I, 11–12.

9. Frederick Law Olmsted, *A Journey in the Seaboard Slave States* (New York, Dix and Edwards, 1856).

10. Ernest Samuels, *Young Henry Adams* (Cambridge, Harvard, 1948), pp. 137–38.

11. Ogden, *Godkin*, I, 221.   12. Ogden, *Godkin*, II, 45–50.

13. E. L. Godkin, *Problems of Modern Democracy* (Cambridge, Harvard, 1966). pp. 200–202.

14. Godkin, *Problems*, p. 85.   15. Ogden, *Godkin*, II, 46.

16. E. L. Godkin, *Reflections and Comments* (New York, Scribner, 1895), pp. 155–63.

17. *The Nation*, VI (March 12, 1868), 206–208.

18. Godkin, *Reflections*, pp. 202–203.

19. *North American Review*, CX (1870), 398–404.

20. *Ibid.*, pp. 416–17.   21. *Ibid.*, p. 419.

22. Ann Leger, "Moorfield Storey, an Intellectual Biography" (unpublished Ph.D. dissertation, U. of Iowa, 1968), p. 18. For gentry politics of the post-Appomattox years, see John G. Sproat, *"The Best Men." Liberal Reformers in the Gilded Age* (New York, Oxford, 1968).

23. R. U. Johnson, *Remembered Yesterdays* (Boston, Little Brown, 1923), pp. 121–22; C. E. Norton, ed., *Letters of James Russell Lowell* (2 vols., New York, Harper, 1894), II, 173–75; Thomas Nelson Page, *Meh Lady; A Story of the War* (New York, Scribner, 1893).

24. Quoted in Abigail Adams Homans, *Education by Uncles* (Boston, Houghton Mifflin, 1966), pp. 31–32.

25. C. F. Adams, *Richard Henry Dana* (2 vols., Boston, Houghton Mifflin, 1890), II, 341–49; Benjamin F. Butler, *Butler's Book. Autobiography and Personal Reminiscences* (Boston, Thayer, 1892), p. 921; R. H. Dana, ed., *Speeches in Stirring Times* (Boston, Houghton Mifflin, 1890), p. 510.

26. *Lowell Letters,* II, 266–67.

27. Frederic Bancroft, ed., *Speeches, Correspondence, and Political Papers of Carl Schurz* (6 vols., New York, Putnam, 1913), II, 255; *Lowell Letters,* II, 77; Earle D. Ross, *The Liberal Republican Movement* (New York, Holt, 1919); M. A. DeWolfe Howe, *Portrait of an Independent, Moorfield Storey, 1845–1929* (Boston, Houghton Mifflin, 1932), pp. 141–42.

28. M. T. Downey, in *Journal of American History,* LIII (March 1967), 736.

29. *Schurz Papers,* II, 359.

30. As late as 1903, Senator George Frisbie Hoar remarked that no Massachusetts gentleman would for a moment stoop to make a personal solicitation for political support. He himself had never lifted a finger nor spoken a word to any man in his own behalf. Hoar, *Autobiography,* p. 3.

31. *Schurz Papers,* II, 378–84.

32. *Journal of American History,* LIII, 748–50.

33. *Schurz Papers,* III, 240–58; Samuels, *Young Henry Adams,* pp. 280–84; Howe, *Storey,* p. 146; *Lowell Letters,* II, 173–75.

34. F. J. Stimson, *My United States* (New York, Scribner, 1931), pp. 118–23; Geoffrey Blodgett, *Gentle Reformers: Massachusetts Democrats in the Cleveland Era* (Cambridge, Harvard, 1966), pp. 9–10; Howe, *Storey,* p. 149.

35. C. E. Norton, ed., *Orations and Addresses of George William Curtis* (2 vols., New York, Harper, 1894), II, 145; Howe, *Storey,* pp. 144–54; Blodgett, *Gentle Reformers,* pp. 1–30.

36. Blodgett, *Gentle Reformers,* pp. 208–33.

37. *Curtis Orations,* I, 331–35, 317–21, 349–51.

38. *Ibid.,* pp. 15, 263–66; II, 485–88; Gordon Milne, *George William Curtis and the Genteel Tradition* (Bloomington, Indiana, 1961), pp. 140–44.

39. *Curtis Orations,* II, 37.

40. *Ibid.,* p. 30; Ari Hoogenboom, *Outlawing the Spoils* (Urbana, University of Illinois, 1961).

41. *Curtis Orations,* II, p. 502.   42. *Ibid.,* p. 9.

43. *Ibid.,* pp. 20–21, 49–50.

44. *Ibid.,* pp. 123–25.   45. *Ibid.,* pp. 133–40.

46. *Curtis Orations,* I, 272–80; Henry Adams, *Democracy. An American Novel* (New York, Signet, 1961), pp. 180–81. In the cli-

Gentry Politics (continued)

mactic passage of the novel Senator Ratcliffe admitted that he had changed his vote on a measure in order to obtain the funds to prevent an electoral victory that would have put the government "into the bloodstained hands of rebels," i.e., the Democrats.

47. *Curtis Orations*, II, 145–54.

48. *Ibid.*, pp. 487–90, 160–66, 156.

49. Moorfield Storey, *Politics as a Duty*, pp. 11–14, quoted in Leger, "Moorfield Storey: An Intellectual Biography," p. 94.

50. George M. Frederickson, *The Inner Civil War* (New York, Harper & Row, 1965), p. 202.

51. Moorfield Storey, *Problems of Today* (Boston, Houghton Mifflin, 1920), p. 45; Howe, *Storey*, p. 172; Henry Holt, *Garrulities of an Octogenarian Editor* (Boston, Houghton Mifflin, 1923), pp. 166–67.

52. William Howard Taft, *Four Aspects of Civic Duty* (New York, Scribner, 1906), pp. 27–30, 7–8.

53. Alfred B. Rollins, *Roosevelt and Howe* (New York, Knopf, 1962), p. 20.

·VI·

ANCIENTS AND MODERNS:

AN EDUCATION CONTROVERSY

1. Charles Francis Adams, *A College Fetich. An Address Delivered before the Harvard Chapter of the Fraternity of the Phi Beta Kappa,* June 28, 1883 (3d ed., Boston, Lee and Shepard, 1884), pp. 3–5.

2. Adams, *Fetich,* pp. 10–37.

3. Cleveland Amory, *The Proper Bostonians* (New York, Dutton, 1947), p. 294.

4. Sidney H. Aaronson, *Status and Kinship in the Higher Civil Service* (Cambridge, Harvard, 1964), p. 126.

5. Ernest Samuels, *The Young Henry Adams* (Cambridge, Harvard, 1948), p. 290.

6. Henry Holt, *Garrulities of an Octogenarian Editor* (Boston, Houghton Mifflin, 1923), p. 290.

7. George Wilson Pierson, *Yale College, an Educational History, 1871–1921* (New Haven, Yale, 1952), pp. 6–8.

8. Pierson, *Yale*, pp. 57–65.

9. William Allen Neilson, ed., *Charles W. Eliot, the Man and His Beliefs* (2 vols., New York, Harper, 1926), I, 38–70.

10. Neilson, *Eliot,* I, 1–37.   11. *Ibid.*

12. *Ibid.,* pp. 38–70.

13. *Princeton Review,* Series 4, Vol. 14 (1884), 195–218.

14. *Princeton Review,* Series 4, Vol. 13 (1884), 111–26.

15. *Ibid.,* pp. 127–40.

16. Thorstein Veblen, *The Higher Learning in America* (New York, Huebsch, 1918).

17. *Cosmopolitan,* XXIII (July 1897), 263–71.

18. Neilson, *Eliot,* I, xxiii; II, 335–49.

19. Edward A. Krug, ed., *Charles W. Eliot and Popular Education* (New York, Teachers College, Columbia University, 1961), p. 107.

20. See John Dewey, *The School and Society* ([1899] Chicago, Phoenix, n.d.), *passim.*

21. Krug, ed., *Charles W. Eliot and Popular Education,* pp. 103–16.

22. Neilson, *Eliot,* II, 634–48.

23. Neilson, *Eliot,* I, 189–204, 539–43.

24. *Atlantic Monthly,* LXXXV (1900), 773–78.

25. Frederic J. Stimson, *My United States* (New York, Scribner, 1931), pp. 191–93.

·VII·

THE HERITAGE OF TOCQUEVILLE

1. Ernest Samuels, *The Young Henry Adams* (Cambridge, Harvard, 1948), pp. 136–40.

2. Henry Adams, *The Life of Albert Gallatin* (Philadelphia, Lippincott, 1880), p. 432, quoted in Ernest Samuels, *Henry Adams, the Middle Years* (Cambridge, Harvard, 1958), p. 53.

3. Henry Adams, *History of the United States of America During the Administrations of Thomas Jefferson and James Madison* (9 vols., New York, Scribner, 1889–1890), I, 177–78, quoted in A. N.

The Heritage of Toqueville (continued)

Kaul, *American Vision. Actual and Ideal Society in Nineteenth-Century Fiction* (New Haven, Yale, 1963), pp. 29–30.

4. Adams, *History*, IX, 224.   5. Adams, *History*, IX, 225.

6. Samuels, *Young Henry Adams*, pp. 293–94.

7. Sara Norton and M. A. DeWolfe Howe, eds., *Letters of Charles Eliot Norton* (2 vols., Boston, Houghton Mifflin, 1913), I, 13; Kermit Vanderbilt, *Charles Eliot Norton, Apostle of Culture in a Democracy* (Cambridge, Harvard, 1959), p. 22.

8. Vanderbilt, *Norton*, p. 22.

9. *Norton Letters*, I, 82–83. The editorial desire was gratified in due course.

10. *Norton Letters*, I, 153–54, 283, 296, 67–68, 226; II, 33, 172, 322, 410–11.

11. *Norton Letters*, I, 26–27, 204–206, 116–17.

12. *Ibid.*, p. 57.

13. Charles Eliot Norton, *Considerations on Some Recent Social Theories* (Boston, Little, Brown, 1853), pp. 145–47, 19–20.

14. Norton, *Recent Social Theories*, pp. 126, 138, 20–22.

15. *Ibid.*, pp. 152–54, 24–31.

16. *Norton Letters*, I, 105–109, 122, 125–27.

17. *Ibid.*, pp. 193–94.   18. *Ibid.*, pp. 269, 285–87.

19. *The Nation*, I (July 13, 1865), 43–44.

20. *Norton Letters*, I, 208.

21. *Ibid.*, pp. 314, 320, 329, 298–99, 371–72; *North American Review*, CIX (1869), 149–54.

22. *Norton Letters*, II, 22, 25–26; I, 485, 503–507.

23. *Norton Letters*, I, 475; II, 54–55.

24. Charles Eliot Norton, *Historical Studies of Church Building in the Middle Ages. Venice, Siena, Florence* (New York, Harper, 1880), pp. 10–13, 156–57, 285–86, 29; *Norton Letters*, II, 53.

25. *Norton Letters*, II, 97–100, 111–12.

26. *Norton Letters*, I, 269–74; II, 87–90.

27. *Norton Letters*, II, 155–57, 166.   28. *Ibid.*, pp. 219–20.

29. *New Princeton Review*, VI (1888), 312–24.

30. *Forum*, XX (February 1896), 641–51.

31. *Harper's New Monthly Magazine,* LXXXVI (May 1893), 846–47.

32. *Norton Letters,* II, 236–37.

33. *Ibid.,* pp. 242–43.   34. *Ibid.,* pp. 398–99.

35. W. G. Sumner, *The Challenge of Facts and Other Essays* (New Haven, Yale, 1914), p. 6.

36. W. G. Sumner, *Folkways* ([1906] Boston, Ginn, 1934), p. 40.

37. W. G. Sumner, *War and Other Essays* (New Haven, Yale, 1911), pp. 158–59.

38. *Ibid.,* pp. 222–23.

39. W. G. Sumner, unpublished manuscript copy, courtesy of Professor Bruce Curtis.

40. W. G. Sumner, *War and Other Essays,* pp. 272–73.

41. Gustave LeBon, *La Psychologie des Foules* (Paris, 1895), translated as *The Crowd. A Study of the Popular Mind* (London, Fisher Unwin, 1895 and subseq. eds.). American sociologists and social psychologists have attached other meanings to the word *crowd.* A better translation would have been *mass.*

42. LeBon, *The Crowd,* pp. 26–36.   43. *Ibid.,* pp. 13–19.

44. *Ibid.,* pp. 133–51.   45. *Ibid.,* pp. 62–77, 81–122.

46. *Ibid.,* p. 162.

47. Jean Stoetzel has observed that it was LeBon's fate to be remembered principally for his mistakes. *International Encyclopedia of the Social Sciences* (17 vols., New York, Macmillan, 1968), IX, 82–84.

48. Josiah Royce, *Race Questions, Provincialism and Other American Problems* (New York, Macmillan, 1908), pp. 85–87.

49. Royce, *Race Questions,* pp. 87–88, 92–95, 74–76, 118–21, 129–36, 115–18.

50. *Ibid.,* p. 96.

51. Philip Selznick, "Institutional Vulnerability in Mass Society," *American Journal of Sociology,* LVI (January 1951), 320–31.

52. Edward A. Ross, *Social Psychology* ([1908] New York, Macmillan, 1918), pp. 63–65.

53. Ross, *Social Psychology,* pp. 79–92.

54. Robert E. Park, *Masse und publicum: eine methodologische und sociologische untersuchung* (Bern, Lach und Grunau, 1904).

The Heritage of Toqueville (continued)

55. R. E. Park and E. W. Burgess, *Introduction to the Science of Sociology* (2d ed., Chicago, U. of Chicago, 1924), pp. 792–94, 868–909.

56. Herbert Blumer, in A. M. Lee, ed., *New Outline of the Principles of Sociology* ([1939] New York, Barnes and Noble, 1946), pp. 185–89.

57. Blumer, in *New Outline* (1939 edition), p. 243.

58. The most notable of these works was Hannah Arendt's *The Origins of Totalitarianism* ([1951] 2d, enlarged ed., New York, Meridian, 1958).

59. Emil Lederer, *State of the Masses. The Threat of the Classless Society* ([1940] New York, Fertig, 1967), pp. 9–16.

60. Lederer, *State of the Masses,* pp. 17–151.

61. Selznick, "Institutional Vulnerability," pp. 320–31.

62. Edward Shils, in *Daedalus* (Spring 1960), pp. 288–90.

63. Cited in R. E. Park, *Collected Papers,* Vol. III (3 vols., Glencoe, Free Press, 1955), p. 25.

64. William Kornhauser, *The Politics of Mass Society* (Glencoe, Free Press, 1959), p. 14.

65. Van Wyck Brooks, *America's Coming of Age* (New York, Huebsch, 1915), pp. 7, 14.

66. Matthew Josephson, *Portrait of the Artist as American* (New York, Harcourt Brace, 1930), p. xiii.

67. Donald A. Stauffer, ed., *The Intent of the Critic* (Princeton, Princeton U. Press, 1941), pp. 134–35.

68. See Stuart Hughes, in *Daedalus* (Spring 1960), pp. 388–93.

69. Edward Shils, in *Daedalus* (Spring 1960), pp. 291–93; Dwight Macdonald, *Against the American Grain* (New York, Random House, 1962), pp. 3–75.

70. Macdonald, *Against the American Grain,* pp. 234–36.

71. R. P. Blackmur, *The Lion and the Honeycomb* (New York, Harcourt Brace, 1955), pp. 4–7.

72. *Ibid.,* pp. 52–55.   73. *Ibid.,* pp. 7–8.

74. *Ibid.,* pp. 8–9, 16–19.

·VIII·

THE DECLINE OF GENTILITY

1. C. E. Norton, ed., *Letters of James Russell Lowell* (2 vols., New York, Harper, 1894), I, 377; Edmund Wilson, *Patriotic Gore* ([1962] New York, Oxford, 1966), pp. 556–91.

2. M. A. DeWolfe Howe, *Barrett Wendell and His Letters* (Boston, Atlantic Monthly, 1924), pp. 68–70.

3. *Lowell Letters,* II, 173.

4. Henry James, *The Bostonians* ([1886] New York, Modern Library, n.d.), p. 343.

5. E. Digby Baltzell, *Philadelphia Gentlemen. The Making of a National Upper Class* (Glencoe, Free Press, 1958).

6. Edith Wharton, *A Backward Glance* (New York, Appleton, 1934), pp. 5–7.

7. Julia Ward Howe, *Reminiscences, 1819–1899* (Boston and New York, Houghton Mifflin, 1900), pp. 306, 400–408.

8. Charles Butler, *The American Gentleman* (Philadelphia, Hogan and Thompson, 1836), p. 31; Lucy Larcom, *A New England Girlhood* (Boston and New York, Houghton Mifflin, 1899), pp. 199–201.

9. A. M. Schlesinger, *Learning How to Behave* (New York, Macmillan, 1946), p. 34.

10. *Nation,* XXVI (June 28, 1883), 546–47.

11. *Century,* LXXIX (December 1909), 310–12.

12. *Century,* LXXXI (April 1911), 881–87.

13. *Century,* LXXIX (February 1910), 639; LXXXIII (December 1911), 310–12.

14. *Century,* LXXXIII (December 1911), 173–78.

15. Edward Shils, in *Daedalus* (Spring 1960), p. 289.

16. Samuel McChord Crothers, *The Gentle Reader* (Boston, Houghton Mifflin, 1903), pp. 225–26.

17. George Miller Beard, *American Nervousness, Its Causes and Consequences* (New York, Putnam, 1881).

18. Cf. the observation of Judge Robert Grant that the "two bottle men" of Webster's generation had wholly disappeared from

The Decline of Gentility (continued)

gentry circles by the end of the century. Robert Grant, *Fourscore* (Boston, Houghton Mifflin, 1934), pp. 42–43.

19. Robert Grant, "The Art of Living," *Scribners,* XVII (May 1895), 753; Howe, *Wendell,* p. 42.

20. Nathan Allen, "Changes in New England Population," *Popular Science Monthly,* XXIII (August 1883), 433–44.

21. John Ellis, *Deterioration of the Puritan Stock and its Causes* (New York, privately printed, 1884), pp. 1–23.

22. Sydney G. Fisher, in *Forum,* XVI (January 1894), 562–67.

23. Brooks Adams, *The Law of Civilization and Decay* (New York, Knopf, 1943), pp. 58–59.

24. Barbara Solomon, *Ancestors and Immigrants, A Changing New England Tradition* (Cambridge, Harvard, 1956); Edward Everett Hale, *James Russell Lowell and His Friends* (Boston, Houghton Mifflin, 1899), p. 276; *Lowell Letters,* I, 415–16.

25. Howe, *Wendell,* pp. 104–105. 26. *Ibid.,* pp. 254, 281–82, 162. 27. *Ibid.,* p. 47.

28. *The Letters of F. Scott Fitzgerald,* quoted in *The New Republic* (November 16, 1963), p. 24.

29. Irving Babbitt, *Democracy and Leadership* (Boston, Houghton Mifflin, 1924), pp. 240–41, 275–76; J. Ortega y Gasset, *The Revolt of the Masses* ([1930] New York, Mentor, 1950).

30. Babbitt, *Democracy and Leadership,* pp. 264, 309–10, 278.

31. Paul Elmer More, *Shelburne Essays, Ninth Series* (Boston, Houghton Mifflin, 1915), pp. 3–38.

32. Henry Dwight Sedgwick, *In Praise of Gentlemen* (Boston, Little, Brown, 1935).

33. Harriet Martineau, *Society in America* (3 vols. in 2, London, Saunders, 1837), II, 293–312.

34. Edward Everett, *Orations and Speeches on Various Occasions* (4 vols., 7th ed., Boston, Little, Brown, 1865), I, 9–44.

BIBLIOGRAPHICAL NOTE

THE SOURCES FOR THE STUDY of gentility are so voluminous and scattered that a comprehensive bibliography would be impracticable. The notes accompanying the text indicate the sources I have used, which are only a small sample of the relevant material available. Among secondary works, the best general history of gentility in Western culture is Esmé Wingfield-Stratford, *The Making of a Gentleman* (London, Williams and Norgate, 1938), Chapters 12 and 13 of which deal with the Victorian middle class in England, to whom the power of the old landed gentry had passed by the middle of the nineteenth century. His account of the difficulties of aping the gentry within the context of a class-structured society, however moribund, contrasts vividly with the American situation in which gentry values were freely available to all. For witty and perceptive comments on the differences between British and American gentility in recent times, see Harold Nicolson, *Good*

Behavior. Being a Study of Certain Types of Civility (Garden City, Doubleday, 1956).

The only general history of gentility in America is by Edwin Cady, *The Gentleman in America; A Literary Study in American Culture* (Syracuse, Syracuse University Press, 1949), a work by a literary scholar from which I have profited. A volume of essays by Samuel McChord Crothers, *The Gentle Reader* (Boston, Houghton Mifflin, 1903) contains a chapter (pp. 201–26) on the historical evolution of the gentleman. One of the earliest of the surveys of the historical variants of gentility is George H. Calvert, *The Gentleman* (Boston, Ticknor and Fields, 1863). Henry Dwight Sedgwick, himself the scion of one of the great gentry families of America, has written *In Praise of Gentlemen* (Boston, Little, Brown, 1935), in which is found an analysis of the "forces of destruction," specified as science, democracy, business, and occupational specialization.

Topical studies often contain useful information or insights into gentry problems. Readers curious or sceptical about my distinction between the old colonial gentry class and the new nineteenth-century gentry may wish to consult Parts IV and V of Gordon S. Wood's *The Creation of the American Republic, 1776–1787* (Chapel Hill, University of North Carolina Press, 1969), where the political implications of the transition from the one type to the other are made explicit. The older type of gentility is well illustrated in the *Letters of John Randolph to a Young Relative* (Philadelphia, Carey, Lea, and Blanchard, 1834), which reflects the influence of Chesterfield. Marvin Meyers, *The Jacksonian Persuasion: Politics and Belief* (New York, Vintage Books, 1960) contains an excellent chapter (pp. 57–100) on James Fenimore Cooper's gentry outlook. The transitional character of Cooper's gentility is readily apparent in his *American Democrat* edited by H. L. Mencken (New York, Knopf, 1931). A revealing account of the daily life of a mid-nineteenth-century gentleman may be found in the classic *Diary of George Templeton Strong,* edited by Allan Nevins and Milton Halsey Thomas (4 vols., New York, Macmillan, 1952).

Gentility became more self-aware in the later nineteenth century, a fact which has doubtless guided students to the later period in greater numbers than to the earlier period and which has resulted in a richer biographical and topical literature. For gentility in the Gilded Age see John Tomsich, *A Genteel Endeavor: American Culture and Politics in the Gilded Age* (Stanford, Stanford University Press, 1971). More specialized studies include Gordon Milne, *George William Curtis and the Genteel Tradition* (Bloomington, University of Indiana Press, 1961) and Kermit Vanderbilt, *Charles Eliot Norton, Apostle of Culture in a Democracy* (Cambridge, Harvard University Press, 1959). On gentry politics see John G. Sproat, *"The Best Men." Liberal Reformers in the Gilded Age* (New York, Oxford, 1968), and Geoffrey Blodgett, *Gentle Reformers. Massachusetts Democrats in the Cleveland Era* (Cambridge, Harvard, 1966). Howard Mumford Jones, *The Age of Energy. Varieties of American Experience, 1865–1915* (New York, Viking, 1971), appeared after my manuscript was completed. Jones's reading of the gentry mind of the late nineteenth century is considerably more positive than my own.

The lady as a historical type has received relatively little attention, doubtless because of her subordinate relationship to the gentleman. Emily James Putnam, *The Lady. Studies of Certain Significant Phases of Her History* ([1910] London and New York, Putnam, 1917) is a useful older work. Andrew Sinclair, *The Better-Half: The Emancipation of the American Woman* (New York, Harper and Row, 1965) distinguishes the various types of women involved in the women's rights movement, including the lady. For the impact of the ideal of gentility on popular culture see R. Gordon Kelly, "Mother Was a Lady: Strategy and Order in Selected American Children's Periodicals, 1865–1890" (unpublished Ph.D. dissertation, University of Iowa, 1970), especially Chapter III.

Because the distinction between gentility and fashion is not often made by scholars, many of the histories of fashionable society are of tangential concern to the present work. One of the most readable of these is Dixon Wecter, *The Saga of American Society* (New York, Scribner, 1937). *The History of American Life,* a series of volumes by various authors edited by A. M. Schlesinger and D. R. Fox (13 vols., New York Macmillan, 1927–1944), contains chapters on the social life of the social-economic elite. Histories of social usages and manners deal with an important aspect of gentility. See especially Arthur M. Schlesinger, *Learning How to Behave. A*

Historical Study of American Etiquette Books (New York, Macmillan, 1946), and Gerald Carson, *The Polite Americans. A Wide-Angle View of Our More or Less Good Manners Over 300 Years* (New York, Morrow, 1966).

A sociologist's account of the history of mass theory may be found in Leon Bramson, *The Political Context of Sociology* (Princeton, Princeton University Press, 1961). Bramson's materials are primarily sociological, and are viewed within an implicit social class context. Daniel Bell's chapter, "America as a Mass Society: A Critique," in his *The End of Ideology. On the Exhaustion of Political Ideas in the Fifties* (Glencoe, Free Press, 1960) provides a briefer account. The characteristics of modern society to which mass theory is relevant are indicated in Karl Mannheim, *Man and Society in an Age of Reconstruction* (London, Kegan Paul, Trench, and Trubner, 1940). The spring 1960 issue of *Daedalus* was devoted to articles by various authors on "Mass Culture and Mass Media." The central place of cultural issues in the mass context is indicated by Leo Lowenthal, *Literature, Popular Culture, and Society* (Englewood Cliffs, Prentice-Hall, 1961). For an analysis of American political prospects in terms of mass concepts see William Kornhauser, *The Politics of Mass Society* (Glencoe, Free Press, 1959). Philip Selznick, *The Organizational Weapon. A Study of Bolshevik Strategy and Tactics* (Glencoe, Free Press, 1960) contains a chapter (pp. 275–314) on the vulnerability of elites in the mass context.

A systematic and comprehensive exposition of mass theory may be found in Kurt Lang and Gladys Lang, *Collective Dynamics* (New York, Crowell, 1961). Mass behavior is here analyzed as a form of collective as distinct from group behavior, and a mass society may be designated as one in which collective behavior plays a large role in human affairs. A perception of the shifting balance between the two types of behavior runs back through nineteenth-century American thought to Tocqueville, and furnishes the theme around which the history of mass theory has been reconstructed in this book.

INDEX